With HAWKS and ANGELS

Episodes from a Southern Life

Joel Lafayette Fletcher III

Foreword by Ann Brewster Dobie

University Press of Mississippi / Jackson

Willie Morris Books in Memoir and Biography

The University Press of Mississippi is the scholarly publishing agency of the Mississippi Institutions of Higher Learning: Alcorn State University, Delta State University, Jackson State University, Mississippi State University, Mississippi University for Women, Mississippi Valley State University, University of Mississippi, and University of Southern Mississippi.

www.upress.state.ms.us

The University Press of Mississippi is a member of the Association of University Presses.

Copyright © 2023 by University Press of Mississippi
All rights reserved
Manufactured in the United States of America

First printing 2023
∞

All photographs are from the author's collection unless otherwise noted.

Library of Congress Cataloging-in-Publication Data

Names: Fletcher, Joel Lafayette, III, author. | Dobie, Ann B., writer of foreword.
Title: With hawks and angels : episodes from a Southern life / Joel Lafayette Fletcher III ; foreword by Ann Brewster Dobie.
Other titles: Willie Morris books in memoir and biography.
Description: Jackson : University Press of Mississippi, [2023] | Series: Willie Morris books in memoir and biography
Identifiers: LCCN 2022056863 (print) | LCCN 2022056864 (ebook) | ISBN 9781496844699 (hardback) | ISBN 9781496844705 (epub) | ISBN 9781496844712 (epub) | ISBN 9781496844729 (pdf) | ISBN 9781496844736 (pdf)
Subjects: LCSH: Fletcher, Joel Lafayette, III. | Gay men—Louisiana—Biography.
Classification: LCC HQ75.8.F59 A3 2023 (print) | LCC HQ75.8.F59 (ebook) | DDC 306.76/62092 [B]—dc23/eng/20230111
LC record available at https://lccn.loc.gov/2022056863
LC ebook record available at https://lccn.loc.gov/2022056864

British Library Cataloging-in-Publication Data available

For J. A. C.

> Angels take turns around you,
> some at night and some by day.
> —*From a collection of prophetic traditions
> written down by Muslim scholars*

> We must wait until evening to see
> how splendid the day has been.
> —*Sophocles*

CONTENTS

Foreword by Ann Brewster Dobie ~ xi
Acknowledgments ~ xiii
Introduction ~ 3
1. Easter Weekend, 1873 ~ 7
2. Home ~ 17
3. Uncle Will ~ 27
4. Fannie's Gin Soup ~ 29
5. The New Coach's Wife ~ 31
6. Black Lives That Mattered ~ 32
7. Fricassee, Gumbo, and Other Beasts ~ 41
8. My Decisive Moment? ~ 45
9. The Camellia Pageant ~ 47
10. My Father Is Kissed by a Frenchman While the Bishop Watches, and I Become a Francophile ~ 48
11. Growing Up Nervous ~ 52
12. Aunt Bill's Biscuits ~ 57
13. The Long and Short Life of Guinevere ~ 63
14. Robert Rauschenberg and the Sweet Potato Queen ~ 64
15. The Republican Party Comes to Louisiana ~ 67
16. Louisiana Live Oak Society ~ 69
17. Les Vaches de M. Mouton ~ 71
18. The Pink Dress ~ 74
19. My Beautiful Sister ~ 81
20. Hullabaloo ~ 85
21. Information from the Other Side ~ 93

22. Learn the English of Today! — 106
23. Riso — 116
24. Da Nello — 123
25. Loretta — 127
26. Mr. Ambassador — 130
27. Count Francesco — 135
28. The Second Act of Parsifal? — 141
29. Paris, Finally — 143
30. Thérèse Bonney and the Repudiation of Chic — 154
31. M. de Lafayette Chez Les Lafayettes — 159
32. Eating Paris — 163
33. The Other Ms. Guggenheim — 170
34. Lunch at the Hôtel du Parc Royal — 175
35. The Emira — 177
36. Stealing Angels — 181
37. 9 Lower Mall — 186
38. Ein Wanderjahr — 196
39. The Return of the Prodigal Son — 207
    Epilogue — 219

FOREWORD

Joel Fletcher has had an interesting life. He grew up as a Protestant Anglo in a colorful, French Catholic community in Louisiana, then went on to travel the world and rub elbows with stimulating, well-known people. He has lived surrounded by art and music and books, and, not to be slighted, good friends. *With Hawks and Angels: Episodes from a Southern Life* tells the stories of the people he met, the places he visited, and the experiences he had. Some of them are humorous; some are bittersweet. All of them ring true.

With Hawks and Angels does more than simply tell the story of the Fletcher family and the adventures of one of its sons. It recounts poignant, often humorous tales of his southern boyhood, his education, and his life as a young naval officer with a secret. It recounts his adventures as an expatriate, first running a language school in Florence, then beginning a promising career in the field of international education in Paris and London, all the while taking advantage of the cultural riches offered by Europe in the mid-twentieth century. He describes his realization of the need to create a life in which he could be himself and how it led to a very different career as an international art dealer.

Fletcher's memoir describes the difficult decisions facing a young, talented gay man living in a largely homophobic society, the stresses of satisfying a desire to live an expanded life when expected to "settle down," and the ultimate satisfaction of finding one's soul mate. It is an account of how one man dealt with such problems with grace and dignity and humor. His experiences are not unique. They are situations encountered in many lives and thereby transcend the simply personal or regional.

In addition to being the story of Fletcher's life, *With Hawks and Angels* presents a rich interplay of characters, incisive commentary on social change, and depiction of places at mid-twentieth century as they moved towards the new millennium. The anecdotes and profiles he provides give the reader sometimes unusual and almost always new insights into growing up in the South, living in Europe in the last century, and the lives of other fascinating, creative people. Because it is more than the story of a single life, it matters to those who want to remember those times and to those too young to have known them.

This is a charming and thoughtful narrative that pleases with its honesty and humor. For those of us old enough to remember the era in which it is set it brings back poignant memories. For all readers it charts the course of a life marked by the desire to live fully and deeply.

—Dr. Ann Brewster Dobie

ACKNOWLEDGMENTS

I wish to thank my friends and relatives who over the years have supplied me with the information, suggestions, corrections, and encouragement that made this book possible. I hope that I have not forgotten anyone.

Earlye and Cathy Barron
Jackie Brenner
Guy Bordelon
Gene Broussard
James Lee Burke
Patricia Chadwick
Dr. Ann Dobie
The late Kathleen Bordelon Duplantier
Dr. Stephen Duplantier
Pamela Friedman
Philip Gould
Joe Howard
Joe Lewis
Michael Llewellen
Dr. Stephen Stuart Lottridge
Cory MacLauchlin
Franklin Mouton
Paul Nevels
James Nolan
Edwin Patout
Peter Patout
Carl Selph
Dr. Vaughan Simpson
Dr. Michael Wade
Dr. George Wickes

I also wish to thank the people at the University Press of Mississippi who encouraged and helped me, including Director Craig Gill; Lisa McMurtray, my always supportive editor; Todd Lape, who did an inspired job of designing the book; Valerie Jones, Joey Brown, and Peter Halverson. I am also grateful to my copyeditor, Bridget Manzella, who was meticulous in eliminating typos and other embarrassments.

And above all, I must thank John Alden Copenhaver Jr., who, for the last thirty years, has made the improbable possible.

INTRODUCTION

I

I am grateful and somewhat amazed that I am a still active, still lucid octogenarian, looking forward to each new day. I was impressed when I was a young man by a quotation attributed to the ancient Greek historian Herodotus (though some say Sophocles): "Call no man happy until he dies"; I have always taken it to heart, but how can I not be thankful for the good fortune that has got me this far, no matter what lies ahead, as I near the end of a long and privileged life.

I sometimes wonder if it was luck alone. The older I become, the easier it is for a skeptic like myself to believe something might have been watching over me. Could I have a guardian angel, or perhaps more than one? "There are more things in heaven and Earth, Horatio, / Than are dreamt of in your philosophy."

When I was younger, feckless, and fortunate, such an idea would never have entered my mind. I was first nudged toward disbelief in the divine when I was five. My beloved Boston bull terrier, Mr. Potter, went missing, and I prayed for his return fervently and optimistically to the Presbyterian God who, I had been told, would answer prayers. But He didn't.

My youthful agnosticism was reinforced by the Presbyterian ministers who were responsible for nurturing my spirituality. The first was a mild-mannered, no doubt well-meaning, but Caspar Milquetoast kind of man whose sermons were much less interesting than the imaginative daydreams I indulged in while he was preaching. The second was a bigot from Alabama, dedicated to preserving the southern status quo. He was also something of a drama queen who spewed unconvincing visions of fire and brimstone. By the time I graduated from high school, my twig was bent away from beliefs that some of my generation firmly held.

But that was long ago, and perhaps I was wrong. I believe I once may have had a glimpse of a guardian angel, in a kind of waking dream.

It was Christmas Eve in a farmhouse in southwestern Virginia. John, who was already my partner, but not yet my spouse, and I were in the back bedroom on the second floor of the house in which John and his brothers had grown up, and where his mother still lived. We were sleeping in a bed in which several generations of

Copenhavers had been born and died. On the walls were large tinted photographic portraits in gold frames of some of John's more recent ancestors.

We had gone to bed early and, just before midnight, I woke with John's head heavily asleep on my arm. When I opened my eyes, a winged figure with blond hair and a long blond beard, wearing a royal blue robe, glided over my head and through the wall behind the bed. He looked a lot like one of the portraits that hung on the wall. The vision, if that is what it was, lasted only a few seconds, but it was long enough for the figure to communicate to me that his name was Fred and that he was welcoming me and watching over me.

I tried to wake John before Fred disappeared, but he was sleeping too soundly, and I could not rouse him. The next morning, I told him what I had seen. The portrait that the angel resembled was his maternal grandfather, Fred Andes.

II

In graduate school, John wrote a paper on the symbolism of birds, and the idea of a hawk as a symbol of good fortune remained with him.

On our many road trips across the United States, driving a van filled with artwork from Nantucket to Houston and many places in between, while on our way to or from the charity antiques shows at which we exhibited for more than a quarter of a century, John always looked for hawks—perched on fences, in trees or bushes, on telephone poles or wires—as omens of good luck. He became very expert at spotting them and would count them up out loud: "That makes five," he would say, or six or ten or twelve. Several times he saw more than twenty.

There did not seem to be an exact correlation between how many hawks John saw en route and how many pictures we sold at the show we were on our way to, but we did have years of financial success, good times, and made great friends while hawks and angels perhaps were watching over us.

III

I was born in Lafayette, Louisiana, and lived there and in New Orleans until I graduated from Tulane at twenty. I then lived in a number of places, including California, Italy, France, and England, for the next twenty years. On my fortieth birthday, I returned to Lafayette and remained there until I was fifty. For most of the subsequent thirty years plus, I have lived in Virginia. Until recently, I still considered myself very much a Louisianan and only felt really at home when I was back on a visit. But that Louisiana no longer exists, and while I will never be a Virginian in spite of all my years here, Louisiana is no longer my home.

There are things I miss about it. A close friend, a distinguished art historian who was born in Ohio, has been with me on several occasions when I have run into someone from Louisiana and has always been amazed when I am suddenly engaged in a long conversation with a person I have never laid eyes on before. "I don't understand it," he told me. "When I run into people from Ohio, I never have anything to say to them." The best I could offer by way of explanation is that since he is not from Louisiana he could never hope to understand. Most Louisianans who meet away from home immediately begin to talk to each other about their state. Louisiana is, after all, one of the most interesting places in the United States, and there is much to talk about: people, places, events, and always food.

I was lucky while growing up to have sufficient experience of the three very different and distinct parts of Louisiana: the French-Acadian southwest where I was born, the highly Protestant north of red clay hills and pine woods where most of my relatives lived, and New Orleans where I was taken frequently by my parents and later lived while attending Tulane.

New Orleans was and still is, of course, the most exciting and exotic of the three Louisianas. My first vivid memory of New Orleans, from when I was a child, was tasting horseradish sauce at the restaurant Galatoire's, a sensation somewhere between pleasant and unpleasant that made my eyes water and cleared my sinuses.

My memories of New Orleans also include glimpses of some of the most remarkable people who lived there or were passing through. In 1949, when I was fourteen, I went to New Orleans with an older sister for Mardi Gras and saw Louis Armstrong as King of Zulu pitching silver-painted coconuts from his float. I was a little older when, while having breakfast with my parents at the Monteleone Hotel coffee shop, we spotted Tennessee Williams and his elderly and frail Episcopalian grandfather a few tables away. Many years later when my parents came down for my graduation from Tulane, they stayed, as they always did, at the Monteleone, and we celebrated by going to see Dorothy Lamour who had been discovered when she was an elevator girl at the hotel and returned every year for an engagement in the Monteleone's Swan Room. That night her performance was interrupted by her loud and drunken sister who still lived in New Orleans and had not become a famous movie star.

My most memorable and fortunate link to New Orleans came from my friendships with John Kennedy Toole, author of what many consider the best novel ever written about New Orleans: *A Confederacy of Dunces*, and with Bob Byrne, the monumental eccentric who was the inspiration for the antihero of the novel: Ignatius J. Reilly. On one long and entertaining evening, I sat with them at the Napoleon House in the French Quarter and listened to their detailed dissection of their uptown New Orleans neighborhood, the place and the people who later were to be transformed into Toole's masterpiece. I remember being slightly miffed because I had expected them to be fascinated by my tales of Europe, from which

I had recently returned, but all my efforts to bring Paris, Rome, Florence, and London into the conversation were defeated by their total absorption in the few square blocks around St. Charles Avenue.

What follows here includes some of the tales I never got to tell Ken and Bobby, and many more, from years that were past and years that were yet to come.

1

EASTER WEEKEND, 1873

HOLY SATURDAY, APRIL 12

On the evening of April 12, 1873, Holy Saturday, my maternal grandfather, James Andrew McLees, in his second year at Davidson College, wrote a letter to his "dearest Cousin Mamie." The letter, which in a postscript he asked her to destroy, somehow survived and made its way to the Davidson College Library. There is no record of how it got there.

James Andrew was twenty-five years old when he wrote this letter, and though he did not then know it, his life was half over. He was the sixth of the eight children of Thomas Jefferson McLees and had grown up on the family farm at Sadler's Creek, South Carolina. His brother, Julius Augustus, seven years older, had enlisted in the Fourth South Carolina Infantry at the Anderson County Courthouse on April 14, 1862, and was killed one year and half a month later at the Battle of Seven Pines, Virginia, aged twenty.

Andrew McLees, Sr., James Andrew's great-grandfather, had arrived in Charleston on January 1, 1787, on a ship named the *Irish Volunteer*.

Although his family was originally Scottish, Andrew Sr. had grown up in Antrim County, Ireland, and brought with him from Ireland his wife, Margaret, and their children, James, Jeanette, Robert, and Martha. They first went to Newberry County and settled on land that had originally belonged to a Revolutionary War soldier named Crosby. Andrew Jr., my grandfather's grandfather, was born there in 1788, the first of his family to be born in America.

In 1805, the family moved to a farm in Anderson County, near the Savannah River, now under the waters of Lake Hartwell, where James Andrew was born and raised.

His grandfather, Andrew Jr., lived there until his ninetieth year. On his eightieth birthday, a local newspaper, the *Anderson Intelligencer*, published an account of the celebration that took place on the farm. His large family and many friends, about forty people in all, attended "and spent the day in pleasant social intercourse, and partook of a sumptuous dinner prepared for this occasion."

The article continued:

> Mr. McLees has been a worthy citizen of this district for sixty-three years. He and his aged consort have been married for fifty-nine years. They were industrious and economical and hence were in comfortable circumstances, although they owned no slaves.
>
> They brought up their children to the same industrious habits, which proves a peculiar benefit in these days of adversity and want. Mr. McLees has ever led a quiet and orderly life. He never had any quarrels with his neighbors nor any law-suits in Court. He says that he has now the same stock of horses that he had when he moved into the District and plants the same kind of corn.

The McLees family had been for generations devout Presbyterians. Two of Andrew Jr.'s sons, John and Hugh, became Presbyterian ministers and other relatives became ruling elders in the church. Thomas Jefferson McLees, James Andrew's father, was an elder in the Roberts Presbyterian Church, near Anderson, for thirty years. So, it is not surprising that my grandfather decided to study for the ministry.

James Andrew enrolled in Davidson College in 1872, graduated in 1876, then went to study at the Columbia Theological Seminary from which he graduated in 1880.

Shortly after his graduation, he married Jennie McBryde, a year older than he, from Anderson County, South Carolina. She was the daughter of a Presbyterian minister and had been born four years after her parents returned from missionary work in China. Before her marriage at age thirty-four, she had lived at home, given piano lessons, and was never in the best of health.

Shortly after their marriage they left on a long journey, stopping in Atlanta and Bolton, Mississippi, on their way to northern Louisiana where Reverend McLees had been sent to replace the recently deceased Dr. J. E. C. Doremus, pastor of the Red River Presbytery.

On her wedding day, May 12, 1881, Jeannie began to keep a diary tersely recording the events of her life: the sermons, the prayer meetings, the visits, sewing, practicing the piano, giving a few piano lessons, learning how to cook ("Cooked candied potatoes for dinner—nothing else."—"Made my first biscuits for breakfast—won't say with what success."), writing letters home, feeling homesick. One October day during her first year in northern Louisiana, she went "with Mrs. Simmons and a troop of children to gather persimmons." But too often she wrote "Sick all day," "Sick all night," "Not well," "Sick again," "Too sick to get breakfast."

James Andrew and Jeannie had been married not quite two years and had no children when she died in Ruston in April 1883.

Her diary is now in the library of Louisiana Tech University in Ruston, and I have a small photograph of her that shows a pretty young woman with a wistful gaze.

During Jeannie's final illness, she was treated by Dr. William Samuel Kendall, a graduate of Tulane, living in Ruston. At the time, one of his wife's young cousins, Mary Ellen McMurray, was living with the doctor and his wife. Mary Ellen had been sent to live with the Kendalls because her father had been killed in the Battle of Mansfield, considered a Confederate victory even though a thousand Confederate soldiers lost their lives or went missing in action.

Mary Ellen and Jeannie seem to have become friends and she is mentioned in Jeannie's diary: "*Saturday, July 16, 1881*—Miss Ellen McMurray & myself drove to church. Mr. McLees going ahead on horseback. Mr. M. lost his way and did not reach the church for some time after Miss E. & I made some pleasant acquaintances."

A year after Jeannie died, Reverend McLees married Mary Ellen McMurray. They had one son and four daughters, the youngest being my mother, who was only a year old when James Andrew died.

Reverend McLees died a few days short of his fifty-first birthday, probably of a stroke or heart attack. A fellow Presbyterian minister, a close friend, shortly thereafter wrote of him: "Brother McLees was an ideal pastor. Just a few hours before his death he sat ministering to a sick railroad man, wiping the perspiration from his aching temples, smoothing the pillows with the gentle and deft fingers of a woman, and directing the needy soul to the Lamb of God who taketh away the sin of the world."

James Andrew McLees is buried in the Greenwood Cemetery in Ruston between his two wives. It was the wish of my grandmother, his second wife, that this be done. A stained-glass window in the Ruston First Presbyterian Church is dedicated to his memory.

Twenty-six years before his death, he had written on the evening before Easter:

My dearest Cousin Mamie should have had a letter before this, but I trust she will excuse my delay when she hears that I have been unwell for some time, in the midst of numerous college activities. Cousin Mamie, your letter was truly a treat; I assure you that I enjoyed it much. Would that I could send you one so pleasant, but I am feeling dull and more than likely you will find this epistle much after the manner of my feeling.

The weather for the past week has been charming—real Spring days. I enjoy it hugely. After the day's work is over, we have about two hours for recreation, and it is, indeed, pleasant to take the arm of some kind and confiding friend for a walk in the Twilight for, indeed, this is the loveliest time of the day. Then it is that the mind gathers many sweet and fond recollections and recalls the happy hours of bygone days.

Jamie McLees (so he signs himself) writes of the approaching commencement week and urges Cousin Mamie to attend:

> The Societies have elected their speakers and Marshals for the commencement occasions. This excitement makes the time seem very near. I will send you an invitation when they are printed and you will see the names of the speakers and marshals, though I suspect they are all strangers to you, as there is but one from our part of the world . . . And I would be glad to have you here then. I think you would enjoy it <u>muchly</u>. Why not come? The Air Line road will be finished by that time, and it will not be too far. Come . . . and bring Cousin Ella. I was sorry to hear of her sickness with the mumps. I hope that she will soon recover.
>
> Since the completion of the Air Line I will be prevented from visiting you at Greenwood next summer in my route home. This much I don't like, but then it saves a great deal in traveling expenses. How inconvenient it is to be <u>poor</u>."
>
> I fully agree with you, begins the next paragraph, as to your opinion of woman. She is indeed a lovely piece of creation. Nor would I have you believe me to be such a queer soul as never to have loved a lass! Strange, indeed, is that man who has in his soul no love for woman. Though she causes often many a bitter pang, yet "Every Bitter has its sweet." But I believe I shall take the advice of my uncle—"not to be exercised about a <u>sweetheart</u> just now" for he has the experience doubtless of his youthful days to warn me of the folly. And then a sweetheart might get tired of waiting for a student to complete his education and marry some other fellow. And this would cause him to exclaim in the language of the <u>poet:</u> "Tis sweet to love, But Oh! how bitter to love a girl and then not git her." However, one might get a <u>sweetheart quite young</u> who would not think it so long to wait until he could complete his education.

I was pleased to discover this letter and to hear my grandfather's youthful voice full of love, affection, good humor, and the enjoyment of small pleasures of life coming from so many years away, a voice of which his own daughter, my mother, had no recollection.

EASTER SUNDAY, APRIL 13

The day after Jamie McLees, my maternal grandfather, wrote his cousin from the idyllic campus of Davidson, my paternal grandfather, a child of five, witnessed one of the most horrific events in American history since the end of the Civil War.

On Easter Sunday, April 13, 1873, at least 165, and probably more, recently freed Black slaves and three white men perished in a bloody battle at the courthouse in Colfax, Louisiana, one of a number of violent events that followed a contested state election in which freed Black people had won many of the offices. The Colfax Massacre, organized by the Ku Klux Klan and the Knights of the White Camellia, another terrorist organization associated with the Klan, was a violent and successful attempt by white supremacists to take back the total power they had lost during the Civil War. When the recently elected Black men occupied the courthouse, a crowd of heavily armed white men gathered outside and began to assault it. The Black men inside were also armed and returned fire, but after many of them were killed and they ran out of ammunition, the survivors surrendered. As they left the courthouse, waving white flags, one at a time, deliberately, they were shot. Of the three white men who died, it is thought that one of them was killed by friendly fire.

There is an obelisk in the Colfax cemetery "Erected to Honor the Memory of the Heroes . . . who fell in the Colfax Riot fighting for White Supremacy." And it was, most historians agree, the beginning of the end of Reconstruction in the South.

My grandfather, who was five and living with his grandmother on a farm near Colfax, witnessed some of the horrors that were committed in Colfax and the countryside around it. The details of what he saw are lost in the fog of time, but one family story places him on a train in the town watching it all from the windows. In any case he told my father of the horrible things he had seen, and my father told me.

Joel Lafayette Fletcher Sr., not long after he was born on his widowed grandmother's farm near Colfax, had gone with his family by wagon train to a farm near Palestine, Texas. According to a memoir he wrote, he was carried behind the wagon by "Joe Teagle, a bright mulatto fellow I later knew well."

His family did not stay long in Palestine. His mother was unhappy there, my grandfather wrote. She had a premonition of her death and begged her husband to take them back to Louisiana, which he did after less than a year. They returned to the farm on a hill near Colfax where my grandfather had been born, to a house with a mulberry tree that his mother had planted before leaving for Texas. Shortly after they settled back in Louisiana, his mother died giving birth to a son who died a few days later. And so, my grandfather was raised by his grandmother, Rebecca, who had raised fourteen children of her own, all of whom, remarkably, lived to adulthood. She was, my grandfather wrote, "a jolly good soul, loved her big print family bible . . . she was greatly loved and widely known; she assisted in cases of sickness and held full sway at all births in the area for miles around." When my grandfather went to live with his grandmother Rebecca, seven of her children were still at home, and Ann, her youngest child, four years older than my grandfather "slept at the head of the bed and I at my grandmother's feet."

My grandfather adored his grandmother and looked back fondly to the years he spent with her. He wrote: "There was much happiness in that family. I think I caused most of the unhappiness as it was about me that most of the wrangles occurred. . . . I loved every one of them, and strangely enough they all seemed to love me."

When he was about fourteen, his grandmother died, and his father, who had since remarried, came to get him, but he did not get along with his stepmother and did not stay long under his father's roof. He returned to his grandmother's house, which had become the home of his uncle Jesse and aunt Julia, and remained there until he was no longer a child.

Somehow, as he was growing up, my grandfather developed a love of literature, though how he managed to find books, other than his grandmother's bible, is a mystery. He mentions that when she punished him and kept him from playing with his cousins, Walter and Newty, with whom he hunted and explored, she kept him in and made him read to her from her bible. "Soon I forgot the hunt or chase and became wholly absorbed in the story." As he grew older, he may have been able to go to the library in the nearby town of Alexandria. Somehow, in the desolate piney woods of central Louisiana, he found and read books and came to love them and they were always an important part of his life, a love he passed on to his children.

Years later, someone said of him that though he never had the finest home in the several towns he lived in, he always had the finest library, and I have a copy of a letter he wrote in 1940 strongly supporting the passage of a tax in Colfax for the building of a new public library. "Next to the grace of God in our hearts," he wrote, "books, more books are probably the greatest need of the hour."

Like his grandmother Rebecca, he loved his bible, and he loved Shakespeare, and spent a lot of time reading both. He married my grandmother, Leila Craig, in 1893 and took her on a honeymoon to a hotel in Shreveport. As soon as they got to their room, my grandfather went to a window and opened it; my grandmother immediately shut it; my grandfather reopened it, and my grandmother shut it. I don't know who finally won the contest, but my grandfather spent the rest of the honeymoon reading aloud *The Taming of the Shrew* to his bride. It was a foreshadowing of a difficult marriage that, in spite of frequent quarrels, exasperation, and separations, produced seven children and lasted until my grandfather's death fifty years later.

There were no public schools in that part of Louisiana when my grandfather was growing up, but he did attend some kind of academy in the nearby town Verda, and later studied at a private high school in Mount Lebanon, which before the Civil War had been a university founded by Baptists from South Carolina.

When he finished school in Mount Lebanon, my grandfather went to Palestine, Texas, where some of his mother's family lived, and began to study law at the firm of Gregg and Reaves. While there he became re-acquainted with Joe Teagle who told him the story of how he had carried him in his arms behind the wagon on that first trek to Texas twenty years before.

When my grandfather was twenty-one, he took both the Louisiana and Texas bar exams and passed them both, not an easy feat since Louisiana law is based on the Napoleonic Code and Texas law on Anglo-Saxon Common Law. He returned to Louisiana to practice and, over the next few years, lived in Shreveport, then Natchitoches, and for a while in Baton Rouge where he served as Clerk of the Legislature (during which time he devised a system of shorthand that he later taught at the Chautauqua in Ruston). Eventually he returned to Colfax, where he had grown up, and practiced law there for the rest of his life in an impressive brick building with massive columns across from the street from the courthouse. He was also able to have built for his growing family a house with columns, an important symbol of stature in the South, on property he owned, "The Old Place," in the country near Colfax.

In 1909, my grandfather argued before the Supreme Court of Louisiana a case against the D. C. Richardson Taylor Lumber Company, Ltd., representing Pierre and Noeme Antee whose son had died in an accident at one of their sawmills.

Louis Antee, Black and twenty-one, was killed only a few days after he had begun work at the lumber company in central Louisiana in January of 1908. According to an article in the *Southern Reporter*, the young man was killed "in the morning before daylight by coming into contact with the main driving belt where it crossed a narrow alley between the engine house and the mill." The company, my grandfather argued, was negligent because it allowed this dangerous passageway, unlit and unmarked, to exist, and had not given sufficient instruction to the inexperienced young man, who was new to the job. "The evidence shows," he said to the court, "that this belt was almost invisible when it was dark," as it was in the early morning before sunrise when Louis attempted to pass through the alleyway.

While Pierre and Noeme Antee had only my grandfather to argue their case, the lumber company hired two law firms to defend it. Alexander & Wilson, together with Wise, Randolph & Rendall, argued that Louis Antee's death "was caused by his own gross negligence and want of care." "It is hardly possible," they told the court, "that he was ignorant of facts obvious to the dullest perception." They cited an earlier case, *Sauer vs. Union Oil*, in which the court found that "A servant, who without inquiry, selects an improper and dangerous route, assumes the risks of resulting injury." The Louisiana Supreme Court agreed with Alexander & Wilson and Wise, Randolph & Rendall and upheld an earlier ruling that the lumber company had not been at fault. Although my grandfather lost the case for negligence, he did manage to squeeze out a judgment against the sawmill owners for "$4.50 wages due their son at the time of his death."

Not long after the court case, my grandfather's new house near Colfax mysteriously burned to the ground. He moved his family into town, but that house was also soon set on fire, and an attempt was made to torch his office. He decided it would be wiser to move his wife and children to Ruston, eighty miles north of Colfax, where schools were better, and life was a little more civilized than in the rough sawmill town where the sawmill owners, alleged to have ties with the Ku Klux Klan, called all the shots.

He bought the old Presbyterian manse on North Vienna Street in Ruston for his family, and he moved into a boardinghouse in Colfax that became his permanent home. He probably was happy with this arrangement and no doubt enjoyed the quiet and solitude that permitted him to read his beloved books for hours undisturbed and to ignore the hostility that he must have felt from a large portion of the white population of Colfax. Usually on weekends, he went to Ruston to spend time with his family (and to father three more children). But sometimes he went instead to New Orleans to attend the opera.

Like his love for literature, his interest in opera is hard to understand. I once thought it might be genetic, but a family story that we have Italian blood, which seems to have been invented by my grandfather, promoted by my father, and cherished by me, has been proven to be untrue.

The myth of our Italian blood arose from the fact that my great-grandmother's maiden name was Leopard. My grandfather, who never knew his mother, surmised that at some point the name had been changed from the Italian Leopardi and that perhaps we were even kin to the great Italian poet Giacomo Leopardi.

This theory was supported by another family story about my grandfather's grandfather, Green Hill Leopard (who sounds more like an endangered species than an ancestor). When the elders of the Baptist church to which Green Hill Leopard belonged discovered that he drank red wine and played the fiddle, they went to his home to inform him that he was being expelled from the church. However, Green Hill played them some hymn tunes on his fiddle and promised to give up red wine, so he was allowed to remain in the church.

It all sounds very Italian, but, unfortunately, I have recently discovered in public records that Green Hill Leopard was descended from a Johann Jacob Lippert, born in Germany, who emigrated to Pennsylvania in the eighteenth century. His son, Emmanuel Lippert, not wanting to fight in the Revolutionary War, went to live in South Carolina where he became Emmanuel Leopard. So much for my cherished Italian heritage!

My grandfather Fletcher was fascinated by world's fairs, and my father told me that he never missed one. Perhaps the first one he attended was the World Cotton Centennial in New Orleans in 1884 when he would have been sixteen. I don't know if he went to the 1893 Chicago World's Fair; it is likely that he went to the one in Saint Louis in 1904, officially known as the Louisiana Purchase Exposition. I know that he went to the 1933 Chicago World's Fair where he saw and was impressed by Sally Rand, the fan dancer, and to the 1939 New York World's Fair from which brought me back a small paperweight in the shape of its symbol, the Trylon and Perisphere.

My grandfather made a fairly comfortable living as a country lawyer, but real prosperity always eluded him. He was known for taking only those cases that interested him, and too many of his clients were poor, like Pierre and Noeme Antee. He did manage to acquire a good bit of property around Colfax and Natchitoches, about a thousand acres in several different tracts.

His daughter, Sarah, told her son, my cousin Guy, the story of how he acquired one of the tracts of land. She said that one of his clients had shot a man to death on the steps of the Grant Parish courthouse. My grandfather realized that there was no argument he could make in court that would save his client from the gallows. I don't know if there were extenuating circumstances; for instance, if my grandfather thought the murdered man deserved to be shot. But he did not want his client hanged. So, he bought a coffin, had it fitted with airholes, and shipped the guilty man to Mexico. The fee for this service was the title to some acreage the murderer owned outside of town.

Occasionally some of his property was leased for gas and oil exploration, but gas or oil was never found. The nearest he came to striking it rich was in the 1930s when a well was being drilled on one of his properties. He was at work in his Colfax law office when someone came running in to tell him that his well had come in and that it was a gusher. A local tradition held that when a gusher occurred, the property owner was supposed to put on a new suit, stand under the gusher, and give a triumphal whoop. My grandfather rushed back to his boardinghouse to put on the suit he had acquired in hopes of such good fortune, then dashed to the oil well, gave the required whoop, and stood under the gusher until he was well-soaked in "black gold." Shortly thereafter, the oil stopped, and water started flowing out of the wellhead. His gusher supplied just enough oil to ruin the suit. In future years there were other fruitless leases on his land. Oil was discovered nearby, and made of some of his cousins rich, but great wealth was not my grandfather's destiny.

In Colfax, he seems to have had a reputation as an eccentric and a wit. Once when a longtime adversary of my grandfather died—a man with whom he had frequently locked horns—a reporter for the *Colfax Chronicle* asked him if he planned to attend the funeral. "No," he replied, "but I approve," the paper reported.

I saw my grandfather infrequently when I was growing up, mostly on trips to Ruston when our visits to my grandmother coincided with his. My mother found him a little peculiar and did not encourage him to come to stay with us in Lafayette. He was always lean and spry, and well into old age he enjoyed standing on his head, walking on his hands, and doing somersaults, behavior my mother thought the neighbors would think odd. Though I seldom saw him, I was fond of him.

He died when I was eight, and we went to Ruston for the funeral. He was laid out in his coffin in the front parlor of the house on North Vienna Street, the first dead person I had ever seen. The night before the funeral, I slept in a room that adjoined the parlor and, lying in bed in the half-dark, I could see the silhouette of the coffin in the weak light from a streetlamp outside. The next day, his youngest daughter, my aunt Kathleen, wept while she put a small bunch of violets in his lapel just before the coffin lid was closed.

My parents and aunts thought that I was too young to attend the funeral, and my sister Lorraine stayed behind to look after me while the rest of the family went to the First Presbyterian Church and then to Greenwood Cemetery. After my grandmother died a few years later and was buried beside him, their daughters planted a mayhaw tree on their grave and every year used to send me a jar of jelly made from its fruit. I felt a little odd about spreading it on toast.

Even though I did not spend much time with him, I always felt a sympathetic bond with my grandfather. He did not quite fit in, and neither did I. When I was about eighteen, a freshman at Tulane, I wrote the following poem about him:

My grandfather was an ingenious man,
He stood on his hands by an old stone wall
And he didn't care at all what people thought of him.
My grandmother frowned when he did somersaults,
The whole world spinning round on her front lawn,
But he didn't mind at all.
After a quarrel, sometimes
He slept in the horse's stall,
(Newspaper in the straw kept out the cold.)
And, when he was very old, he died.

The world is spinning still the same, Pleased with its surprise,
It spins and spins,
And holds grandmother's buried eyes.

~

There is much about my life that would, no doubt, astonish and appall these ancestors about whom I have written. And yet, I cannot help but feel a comforting kinship with them and gratitude to them for the lives they led. In spite of all our differences, I recognize some of myself in them, and know that, largely because of them, this is who I am, and, more importantly, this is who I should be.

2

HOME

My parents were married on October 15, 1919, in Farmerville, a small town near Ruston, Louisiana, where my mother had been teaching grade school since her graduation from the Mississippi Synodical College for Young Ladies in Holly Springs, Mississippi. The marriage was a great disappointment to my father's sisters who had decided that he should marry Mildred Smith, a banker's daughter.

My mother was the youngest child of the widow of a Presbyterian minister who had died when my mother was only a year old. She and her three sisters and one brother had been brought up poor, almost wholly dependent on the charity of her late father's parishioners and the largesse of her mother's sister, Aunt Fanny, who herself had the good fortune to be married to a banker. My aunts thought my father could have and should have made a more advantageous match.

My father, the son of a country lawyer, had joined the US Navy during the First World War and was finishing his officer training at the Great Lakes Naval Station in Chicago when the war ended. He was given the choice of a commission or an early discharge. He took the discharge and returned to Louisiana where, armed with a degree in agriculture from Louisiana State University, he found a job as assistant county agent with the Union Parish agricultural extension service.

An assistant county agent earned very little money, not really enough to support a wife, so after their marriage, my father decided to try his hand at farming. He and my mother moved to a cabin on family property in central Louisiana, near Colfax.

My father loved many things about farming, and the farm was beautiful, about one hundred acres on the banks of the Red River. With high hopes for success, he planted vegetables and started raising a herd of shorthorn cattle. But the year ahead was difficult. One major problem was a spring flood on the Red River, which destroyed a crop of Bermuda grass my father had planned to sell for hay.

Probably more importantly, my mother was unhappy as a farmer's wife. She hated being alone in a primitive farmhouse all day while my father was out plowing the fields and tending to his few livestock. The last straw was the morning she drew water from the well and found a dead blue jay in the bucket. She gave my father an ultimatum: the farm or the marriage. He wisely chose the latter.

Through someone he had met at a farmer's short course at LSU before he began farming, my father was offered a job as an instructor in agriculture at what was then Southwestern Louisiana Industrial Institute in Lafayette. So, in August of 1920, my parents moved from the red clay hills and piney woods of northern Louisiana to the flat and fertile fields and cypress swamps of southern Louisiana.

My parents often said that moving from north Louisiana to Lafayette was like moving to a foreign country. It was then certainly hard enough to get to. When my father had attended Louisiana State University a few years earlier, in order to travel from his home in Ruston to Baton Rouge by train, he first had to go to Mississippi, spend the night in Natchez, then take another train back to Louisiana the next day. It was on the second leg of his first journey to LSU that he met the legendary politician Earl K. Long, younger brother of the even more notorious Huey. During the overnight stay in Natchez, Earl, also on his way to his first term at LSU, had spent on women and booze all the money his family had given him for the coming semester, and he asked my father's help in composing a pathetic, hopefully persuasive telegram to his father telling him how he had been taken advantage of and robbed. Earl and my father were to cross paths many times after that.

My parents adapted well to their new community in southern Louisiana. They made friends with many of their Cajun neighbors, came to love the strong, black coffee and spicy cooking they had never tasted in the northern part of the state, where food was less important and much less adventurous. They did not seem much to miss their native hills, where the concepts of joie de vivre and laissez-faire, such touchstones of life in French Louisiana, were largely unknown.

My parents' assimilation did not include a change of religion, and they regularly attended services as part of a small congregation of steadfast Presbyterians living among the French Catholic majority. The Presbyterians of Lafayette then met in a modest, somewhat woebegone, clapboard church painted dark green on Buchanan Street in an unimportant downtown neighborhood. I must have been baptized in this church, but my first memories of it, from a few years later, are of sitting with my parents and my sisters on the unforgiving pews Presbyterians are predestined to sit upon.

The First Presbyterian Church of Lafayette was cold and drafty in winter and hot and stuffy in summer, but it had one saving grace: it was next door to the Mello Joy Coffee Company, and the delicious aroma of roasting coffee helped make tedious sermons more tolerable. Years later, when I heard the expression, "the Odor of Sanctity," I thought I knew exactly what it meant.

The first house I remember living in was Whittington Hall on the college farm. My father by then was Dean of the College of Agriculture and had won some fame with his cattle judging team. He had even been pictured with his "boys" and a superior Jersey cow on the cover of *Progressive Farmer* magazine.

Whittington Hall was a handsome two-story house with white columns, surrounded by live oaks and fields and barns. There was ample space to explore and play and ride my Shetland pony, Betsy. Whittington Hall was named after the farm family who had owned it before it was purchased by the state, but I had somehow got the idea from one of my favorite books that it once belonged to Dick Whittington, lord mayor of London, though I really had no clear idea of what a lord mayor was or where London was.

For a time, like Dick Whittington in my book, we even had a cat. But then my father's sisters from Ruston, who were always giving me gifts they hoped would improve my mind and encourage creativity, gave me a set of watercolors and a picture book about a yellow striped tomcat.

Our cat was a very ordinary white barn cat, sometimes more gray than white from spending its days in the barn chasing mice. Compared to the handsome, lemon-hued cat in my new book, I thought it dull and unappealing and so decided to enhance it with the watercolors. I managed to paint only a few bright yellow stripes on its tail before it fled and was never seen again. Undoubtedly it found another barn; there were several in the neighborhood where it could continue unmolested the pursuit of mice. I was not very attached to the cat and don't remember missing it. I was, in any case, much fonder of my pony and my black-and-tan fox terrier, Small Fry.

We lived very happily at Whittington Hall for a few years. I recall occasionally the grown-ups talking solemnly about something called a war that was going on somewhere in a place called Europe, but it did not impinge on our daily lives. I do remember vividly the Sunday my oldest sister, while driving to New Orleans, heard on the car radio the news that the Japanese had bombed Pearl Harbor and returned home in hysterics to tell us.

I had not yet begun school, but I had discovered books and had started learning to read and write. Among the first books I put my hands on were a two-volume set belonging to my father titled *Diseases of the Horse* and *Diseases of Cattle*. The illustrations of horses and cows, showing all their veins, arteries, muscles, and internal organs in vivid color were, like my book about the yellow cat, much more fascinating to look at than the actual animals grazing in the fields behind the house.

One day my parents told me that we were going to move and that Mr. Potter, a Boston bull terrier, Small Fry's successor, would be going with us, but that Betsy the pony was staying behind. We were going to live in a brand new and very large brick house on the college campus. It was the mansion that the then president of the college, Lether Frazar, had built for himself on the site of the more modest frame house of the college's first president, Edwin Louis Stephens. My father, in the wake of the political scandals that rocked the state in the late 1930s, had just been named the third president of the college.

Before Earl Long's powerful brother, Huey, was assassinated in 1935, the month before I was born, he is said to have remarked often that his cronies had better hope that nothing ever happened to him because he was the only one smart enough to keep them out of jail. His words were prophetic.

In 1939 the federal government began an investigation into corruption in Louisiana. According to Richard D. White Jr. in his book *Kingfish: The Reign of Huey P. Long*, the investigation "eventually handed down 250 indictments against Louisiana state officials. The list of indicted covered the state's governing regime and included legislators, major department heads, university officials, contractors, architects, notaries public, and just about any official who could pocket a bribe or kickback." There were many convictions, including that of the governor of Louisiana, Richard Leche, who served five years for mail fraud and other schemes, and James Monroe Smith, president of LSU, who was sentenced to twenty-four years at Angola prison for embezzling half a million dollars from the university and ordering the university print shop to print fake bonds to cover his losses. Frazar, president of Southwestern, escaped prosecution, but lost his job, nevertheless.

I have a copy of a letter my father wrote at the time: "To Whom It May Concern," undoubtedly to protect himself from the wrongdoing he had witnessed during the Frazar administration. It relates how Frazar called him into his office and ordered him to start ordering meat for the farm dining hall from "a certain powerful friend of his in north Louisiana." When the federal investigation began to heat up, Frazar asked to see all the checks that had been passed during the meat transaction. My father went through the files and found them and noticed that one of them had been endorsed by Earl Long. When Frazar returned the checks to my father to be put back in the files, Earl's signature had been erased. The erasure may have saved Frazar from an indictment, but soon, as far as his job was concerned, he was toast.

The State Board of Education chose my father to succeed Frazar in November of 1940. On the day my father was to take office, January 1, 1941, Frazar, whose nickname was "Mule," displeased at having lost his job and having to leave his fine new house, locked all the doors, pocketed the keys, and took the entire campus maintenance staff to the Sugar Bowl game in New Orleans. My mother was impatient to get settled in her new home and persuaded my father to call a fireman friend, a Mr. Broussard, who knew how to pick locks. So, we entered our new home like thieves, which Frazar no doubt considered us. We were able to spend the first night of the New Year there, and it was to be our home for the next twenty-five years. In 2000, back in Lafayette for the celebration of the one hundredth anniversary of the founding of the university, I was introduced to

Frazar's daughter. The first thing she said to me was: "So you're the one who got to live in *my* house!" Sixty years later she still seemed very angry about it.

When we first moved to the campus, I was not happy there. I was a farm boy used to living in a farmhouse, to roaming fields, to riding my pony, and playing with my dog, coming home with clothes that were dirty and shoes, if I were wearing any, encrusted in mud. I was not comfortable in a setting where everything was new and expensive-looking and had to be treated with great care. My mother, worried about the damage I might thoughtlessly do, instructed me always to use the kitchen door when entering and leaving the house, and I was banned from the graceful circular stairway that ascended from the front hall to the second floor. I was restricted to the narrow kitchen stairs so as not to soil the pretty rose-colored carpeting on the front stairway.

One afternoon, thinking my parents were away, I descended the front stairs, feeling guilty about doing so. I was halfway down when my mother emerged from the living room, and my father appeared in the back hall. I was so upset to be caught in forbidden territory that I lost my footing and fell. "Daddy," I sobbed when they ran to see if I was hurt (I wasn't), "let's go home. I don't like this damn house!" It was then my father decreed that the house was to be our home and not a museum, and we were to live in it like a normal home. And after that we did.

What cultural life there was then in Lafayette centered around the college, and over the course of the years my parents entertained a host of interesting visitors: scholars, authors, diplomats, musicians, politicians, scientists. My sisters and I were almost always present on such occasions and thus were given a window on a world that most young people growing up in a small southern town in the 1940s and 50s did not even know existed.

Every Monday morning there was a mandatory assembly of students and faculty in the auditorium on the top floor of old Martin Hall, the main administration building. The assembly always began with a prayer by a local priest or pastor, and after announcements of various kinds and a musical number or two performed by students or faculty, a lecture was given by some distinguished visitor. On one occasion when Rabbi Louis Binstock from Chicago was the speaker, the Southwestern Mixed Chorus thoughtlessly opened the program with an arrangement of "Were You There When They Crucified My Lord?" And then, when Rabbi Binstock rose to make his way to the podium, adding insult to injury, the chorus broke into "Sit Down, Servant." It was a more tolerant, civilized, and kindly era, and Rabbi Binstock, far from being offended, was very amused.

Archduke Otto von Habsburg, on a postwar lecture tour trying to raise money for his perpetually impoverished family, was another of the assembly speakers. After his turn at the lectern, he came over to the house for coffee, as most of the lecturers did, where he was asked to select (from photographs) the "campus beauties" for the college yearbook. After doing so, he patted me on the head before sitting down at our piano to play "The Blue Danube" and "Tales from the Vienna Woods." I was familiar with both pieces from the old records we had inherited from my mother's aunt Fanny, together with a wind-up Victrola that we kept in the attic. However, it was the first time I had heard them without a rhythmic "click, click, click" produced by cracks in our records.

One hot summer morning, a former president of France (Vincent Auriol, I believe) came to the house for coffee after his lecture and asked for a glass of ice water. My mother whispered to our servant, Gus, an elderly fellow who was set in his slightly eccentric ways, to be sure to use "the best silver tray." Soon thereafter Gus appeared carrying the impressive tray on which he had placed an array of the glass jelly jars Mother had collected to protect her fine crystal from the peril posed by me and my playmates who were in and out of the kitchen all summer long consuming enormous amounts of ice water.

When the celebrated soprano Lily Pons came to a reception at the house after a Community Concert, I begged my father to tell her a story I had often heard: a number of years before, when my father had been in charge of a cattle show on one side of the New Orleans Municipal Auditorium, Miss Pons was scheduled to give a recital on the other. She found out about my father's cows and refused to sing a note until they had all been loaded back into the cattle cars. I thought she might be amused by the incident, but when I suggested that he tell her, my father just glared at me and said: "Don't you dare mention that!" I didn't.

After Pulitzer Prize-winning novelist Louis Bromfield spoke on the campus, my father took him and his young male French secretary, who was traveling with him, to lunch at Poor Boy's Riverside Inn, then located on the banks of the Vermilion Bayou, just outside of town. I was invited to come along and remember being fascinated by the secretary, who was very handsome and wearing an elegant three-piece suit. After lunch, my father drove us to New Iberia so Bromfield could visit with his old friend Weeks Hall, the eccentric painter and owner of Shadows-on-the-Teche before it became a National Trust property. In the 1920s, Bromfield had moved to Paris where he became for a time one of the American writers and artists known as the "Lost Generation," and where he and Hall, also part of the exodus, had been drinking buddies. Alas, I was too young to make much sense of their conversation, which probably was fascinating.

Not all the guests my parents entertained were as distinguished as those mentioned above. During the difficult period in the 1950s when segregation was coming to an end, my parents were awakened late one night by a phone call from a prominent Lafayette attorney well known for his virulently racist views, and later even better known for his championing of the preservation of the French language in Louisiana The lawyer insisted that he and a judge from a small town near Lafayette had something extremely important to say to my father and that they had to tell him in person, immediately. The doorbell rang a short time later.

When the lawyer and the judge staggered in reeking of whisky, my father turned to my mother and said, "You better make these people some coffee." While she was so occupied, the lawyer delivered their important message. Using a racial slur, he told my father that if he let Black students into Southwestern, "we're gonna throw your ass in jail." When my mother returned with the coffee, the inebriated judge, mistaking the sugar bowl for a coffee cup, picked it up and tried to drink it. "So much for 'sober as a judge,'" my mother said.

Although the first Black students enrolled at Southwestern encountered many difficulties, thanks to the cool and determined heads among the college administrators, and perhaps to the more tolerant attitudes of the largely Cajun population, integration at Southwestern, occurred without major problems. It was the first southern white college to be successfully integrated, with none of the ugly incidents that marred the process almost everywhere else in the American South. My father and his administration were able to prevent the violence and bloodshed that occurred on other southern campuses, but they were not able to eradicate the bigotry and hatred that existed in so many hearts. Two hundred and fifty years of cruelty and injustice had created a toxic situation that the Black enrollees had to face, and they should always be remembered and honored for their resolve and courage.

My father was under a great deal of pressure, but he stated his position simply: you may or may not approve of integration, but it is now the law, and we are going to follow it. Instead of attempting to aggravate the situation as some of his contemporaries did, he calmly and firmly let it be known that under his watch Southwestern was not going to break the law, no matter how many people disliked it. To prepare the way for a peaceful transition, he called on many influential citizens throughout Louisiana for help. He also established a human relations council made up of both faculty and students to help Black students with problems that might arise. After one of the first council meetings, Dean of Men Glynn Abel, who had conducted it, reported that one of the professors had forced the Black students to sit in the back of the classroom. He told Abel, "Tell the Black students that ten minutes from now that problem will be resolved." And it was.

At some point, *Life* magazine approached my father about doing an article on a successfully integrated southern college. My father refused to let *Life* on the campus. He realized that bringing national attention to the peaceful integration of Southwestern would probably destroy it.

My father's stance was effective in calming the situation, but it made him many enemies, including the editor of the local newspaper and the pastor of the Presbyterian Church in which he had taken an active part for many years.

Our family had in any case got off on the wrong foot with this particular Presbyterian minister a number of years before. By the time he came to preach in

Lafayette in the 1950s, the congregation had grown considerably and had moved from the humble frame building on Buchanan Street to a handsome new edifice of red brick with white columns across from the college campus.

On the first Sunday the new minister was to preach, it was my mother's turn to arrange the flowers for the altar. Arranging flowers was not something she was especially good at, but my mother was determined to do something impressive to welcome the minister. It was early spring, and she created a towering arrangement of dogwood for the altar table in front of the lectern, unaware that the new minister was so short that the base of the lectern had been removed so that he could see over it. All through his first sermon, the pint-sized pastor struggled to make eye contact with his congregants through the swirls of leaf and branch and flower. Mother was embarrassed, but my sisters and I thought it very funny, and we were not altogether successful in suppressing giggles throughout the service.

The preacher was tiny, but he had fierce eyes surmounted by bushy eyebrows and looked like a kind of pocket-sized Old Testament prophet. He had strong opinions, which he expressed with great fervor, accompanied by the raising of hand and the shaking of fist.

I was away at Tulane in New Orleans and then in the US Navy during most of the turmoil brought on by integration, and I was not in church with my family the Sunday the preacher said something from the pulpit about integrating the university that greatly offended my father. I never found out exactly what had transpired. It was a sensitive subject, not to be broached, but I was greatly surprised when I came home one weekend and discovered that my parents had left the church of which they had been members for many years, where my father had been a deacon and then an elder.

Although some members of the community continued to hold a grudge against him because he had permitted Blacks to attend Southwestern, by and large things settled down, and my father continued to be successful in cajoling money from the state legislature to run and expand Southwestern. He was supported by a great number of former students in whom he had taken a personal interest and helped get an education, most notably during the Great Depression when he formed an agricultural co-op that let hundreds of impoverished young pay for their schooling by working on the college farm. By the time the college became a university in 1960, he had a loyal base of former students who had become successful farmers and influential businessmen throughout the state; friends in high places, as it were. He hated politics and politicians—Louisiana has long been famed for its especially unsavory ones—but he became skillful in working with them for the good of the university. He even managed to stay in office when Earl Long was elected governor and his nemesis, Mule Frazar, became lieutenant governor.

His survival at that time may have been due in part to the fact that Earl's baby sister, Lucille, a colorful character in her own right, lived across the street from my grandmother Fletcher in Ruston. Lucille liked to talk, and my grandmother liked to listen to her, and they spent a lot of time together. She and my grandmother became very close, and if he had fired my father, Earl probably would have caught hell from Lucille. When, as a teenager, I visited my grandmother, I sometimes used to cross the street and sit with Lucille in her kitchen while she told me fascinating stories. One that I remember was about a cigar-smoking lesbian from a prominent Lafayette family who went to Chicago during Prohibition and was gunned down by the mob. Lucille's stories were not the kind I usually heard at home.

As my father was approaching retirement in 1964, the US Department of Defense announced the closure of the Naval Auxiliary Air Station at New Iberia, a town twenty miles from Lafayette. My father saw it as an opportunity to greatly expand the holdings of the university and to make good use of what had been essentially a training facility with classrooms and dormitories already in place. It would have assured the university space for expansion in the coming years and would have been the crowning achievement of my father's career, which had been entirely devoted to strengthening the university. At first things went smoothly. The Department of Defense approved the request, saying that Southwestern's plan for the property was the best it had received. And the State Board of Education gave its approval. But then the project began to be criticized by local merchants who were worried about the economic consequences of moving a large part of the university away from Lafayette. And they were joined by partisans of LSU who were afraid that Southwestern might be "getting too big for its britches" and by the various enemies who had never forgiven my father for allowing the integration of the university. The attacks became harsh and personal and took a great toll on him just as he was beginning to experience the vulnerabilities of old age. But he pushed on with his effort to secure the base for Southwestern. When he thought it was a *fait accompli*, he resigned after having had a hand in the appointment of his successor, who, he thought, shared his views about the New Iberia campus. But the day after my father resigned, the new president announced that the university was abandoning the effort to acquire the base. The State Board of Education withdrew its approval, and, in an act of gratuitous pettiness, the legislature rejected a motion to have my father named "President Emeritus."

My father's heart was broken. Throughout his career he had put enormous energy into his vision of building a greater university, and the pursuit of the New Iberia project had completely consumed the last years of his presidency.

In the next few months, he often wrote to me (I was living then in Italy) of his despair and disgust over the way things had turned out and his disappointment in people whom he had long taken to be friends. He was often depressed, and his heart condition worsened. I have no doubt that his life was shortened.

During this unhappy period in their lives, my parents considered returning to the north Louisiana that they had left forty-five years before. With that idea in mind, they made several exploratory trips to Ruston, where they both had grown up. But they returned from each trip more convinced than ever that south Louisiana was their home. For every friend who had proved to be false there were others who remained loyal. In the end they realized that their real home was the place that had once seemed a foreign land.

When they left the president's house on the campus, they moved into a modest brick house they had built some years before in a pecan grove they called "Le Bocage Vert" (The Green Grove), so named by the French consul who had awarded my father the Légion d'honneur many years before. My parents had recently purchased the land and after the ceremony they drove the consul out to see it. "Quel joli bocage vert!" he remarked.

The property became a refuge from the strains and bothers of life on the campus, and they spent many days and many nights there after the small house was built, even while the president's house was still their official residence. For the first time in many decades they had a place that was their own, where they could relax and enjoy life.

On these few acres, in his remaining years, my father worked out his anger and disappointment by cultivating camellias and Louisiana irises, and gradually came out of his depression. He began to write a newspaper column that was carried by several Louisiana newspapers, conveying his thoughts about education and anything else that interested him. His last columns were about the stupidity of the war in Viet Nam and the terrible waste of it all. These columns made him unpopular with conservative readers who supported the war, but he could not have cared less.

During this dark period in his life, he was also buoyed, as he had been for more than half a century, by my mother's basic optimism and bright spirit. During my father's final illness, my oldest sister, who went through life expecting the worst to happen and was a little disappointed when it didn't, asked Mother, "How can you be so cheerful while Daddy is dying?" "Because that is what he would expect me to be," Mother replied.

My father died in Lafayette in the spring of 1972. My mother died there just after Christmas in 1986. They are buried in a cemetery not far from the banks of Bayou Vermilion, about a mile from their beloved Bocage Vert.

3

UNCLE WILL

My uncle William (Will) Robert McLees, my mother's older and only brother, was twelve when his father, Reverend James Andrew McLees, died of a stroke, leaving his widow, a son, and four daughters in near poverty. My grandmother received a pension of fifteen dollars a month from the Ruston Presbyterian Church, which Reverend McLees had founded, some charity from the members of its congregation, and was helped financially by her older sister, Fannie, who had married a well-to-do banker. She also sold Avon products, one of the few ways women of her generation could earn money.

My grandmother's sister, Fannie, paid for my mother's education at the Mississippi Synodical College for Young Ladies. Education was important to my grandmother and her sister, both of whom had studied at a Baptist college in Alabama.

Will had musical talent, and a few years after his father died, he shocked his family by running off to play the trumpet and drums in the band of the I. W. Swain Minstrel Show, one of the largest traveling shows in the South. His sisters never forgave him, and he was shunned by them for the rest of his life.

Because he was considered a pariah, I was barely aware of him when I was growing up. I have only one memory of him. When I was still a child, at a cousin's wedding reception, a gray-haired man, staggering a bit, patted me amiably on the head, then ambled off. "That's your uncle, Will," my mother told me. "He has a drinking problem, as you can see."

At home, his name was seldom mentioned, and when it was, my father always scowled with disapproval. My aunt Frances late in life told me that because I looked so much like my uncle Will as a child, my parents were always deathly afraid that I also might turn out to be a misfit and an alcoholic and thought that I should be shielded from his bad influence. In the few photographs I have seen of Will as young boy, he does look exactly like me in the photos made of me at the same age.

Most of what I know about my uncle Will, I learned long after he was gone. My cousin Joe, grandson of my mother's oldest sister, was curious about him. He did some research and passed on to me what he discovered.

The 1920 census showed Will living in Harris County, Texas. The 1930 census listed him as "divorced," and his occupation as "office clerk, oil refinery." According to his draft registration card, issued in 1942 when he was fifty-five, he was living in Baytown, Texas, and was employed by the Humble Oil Refinery.

He must have read for the law and passed the state bar exam because his death certificate in 1951 described him as an attorney, still employed by Humble Oil. Joe surmised that because Will died in the Houston VA hospital, at some point he must have served in the military. He would have been the right age for the First World War.

Will, Joe learned, divorced his first wife, and his second one predeceased him. His second wife, we had heard, was "an artistic type." She painted pictures and is said to have written a novel but lost the manuscript before she could show it to anyone.

When Will died in 1951, even though he was estranged from my mother, he left her enough money to buy a new blue Buick sedan, and he left me a complete set of the novels of Balzac in English translation. Mother also inherited a small painting in a cheap gold frame, painted by his second wife. It was an oil of a lone, skinny, twisted tree. She hung it in the living room to which the person who painted it had never been invited.

Unlike my uncle Will, I did nothing drastic like running off as a teenager to join a minstrel show, but when I was fully grown and my family members began to realize that I was gay, though most were supportive, I experienced from others disapproval and the shunning that was done to Will. I so wish that I had known him.

4

FANNIE'S GIN SOUP

My mother was educated at the now defunct Mississippi Synodical College for Young Ladies in Holly Springs, Mississippi, where she learned to be a lady, but not to be a cook. Indeed, she was quietly proud of being helpless in the kitchen. It showed that she had never had to do that sort of thing. As a college president's wife, she did a great deal of entertaining, but rarely found herself behind the stove. That was not her place.

When she did find herself behind a stove, she usually burned whatever was in or on it, and she had developed a somewhat fatalistic attitude. When I returned to live near her in the 1970s, she found peculiar an effective remedy I had for an upset stomach, one that was common in Europe, but almost unknown in Lafayette, Louisiana: charcoal tablets that calmed intestinal turbulence and absorbed the poisons. Once when she saw me popping them, she told me: "I don't know why you're wasting all that money buying charcoal when all you have to do is ask me to fix lunch."

In the course of a long, gracious, and, on the whole, very happy life, she did master a few—a very few—recipes for those occasions when a cook was not available.

Late in life she devised this recipe for Gin Soup as a first course. The amount of gin she used depended on her estimate of how palatable she thought the second course was likely to be. If it appeared that it was turning into an unavoidable fiasco, she poured with a heavy hand.

Gin Soup
2 10½ ounce cans of condensed consommé
1 pint of half-and-half
A teaspoon of dried tarragon

A dash of Tabasco
As much gin as deemed necessary
(Optional) tablespoon of fresh chopped tarragon for garnish

Mix ingredients in a saucepan and bring to a brief simmer over medium heat. May be served hot or cold. To serve it cold, chill overnight in the fridge and stir well before ladling into individual bowls. Serves four.

5

THE NEW COACH'S WIFE
My Mother's Story

The young couple, my mother told me, had not been in Ruston very long. He had been hired to coach at the local high school. They had joined the First Presbyterian Church and were just beginning to make friends in the overwhelmingly, rigidly Protestant town in northern Louisiana.

The husband was away at school one weekday afternoon, as he always was. The wife had finished cleaning the house and decided to take a bath. It was a sultry late September day and she had filled the tub in the bathroom with cool water. She was about to lower herself into it when she remembered that she had forgotten to put the card for the ice man in the kitchen window.

In those days, before most people had an electric fridge, one would put a card for the iceman in the kitchen window. Each edge of the card had a number on it: 10, 25, 50, and 100. The number put on top let the iceman know how much ice was required. And each day he would make his rounds, come in the kitchen door (doors were never locked in Ruston), and leave the indicated amount in the ice box.

The coach's wife, wrapped in her towel, went into the kitchen. She was about to put the card in the window when she heard the kitchen door opening. There was no time to run back to the bathroom. She clutched the towel around her and made for the nearby kitchen closet which proved to be a tight fit because it was filled with brooms, mops, buckets, and the gas meter, on which she had to squat. She had only been there for a few uncomfortable seconds when the closet door swung open. It was the gas man come to read the meter. With absolutely no presence of mind, she blurted out: "Oh! I was expecting the ice man!"

By dinnertime, everyone in Ruston had heard about it.

6

BLACK LIVES THAT MATTERED

I grew up as an almost perfect example of southern white male privilege. When I was old enough to walk, but too young to go to school, I had a Black teenager as a paid companion. When I did go to school, I went to a white-only elementary school connected to the local college, by far the best elementary school in town, and until I was old enough to walk to school by myself, I was accompanied by a Black man who held my hand as we walked to school in the morning and met me and walked me home in the afternoon when school was out. The same Black man brought everyone in my family a cup of coffee in bed early every morning, and then cooked breakfast for us all. Our Black cook came a little later in the morning and fixed lunch.

My bed was made up by a Black maid, who also picked up my clothes where I dropped them, washed them, ironed them, folded them, and put them up in my closet and chest of drawers.

For as long as I can remember, there were Black people in my life, but always in the background, and my principal sin against them was that I never fully recognized their humanity. Writing about them is difficult because I realize that I know so little about them. Their lives ran near and parallel to our lives, but my lack of knowledge betrays my lack of curiosity about them as human beings. The only stories I have to tell about them are from where their lives intersected with ours. Amusing things they said and did that are inevitably, unavoidably patronizing.

When I was a young boy, our Black servants always called me "Mistuh Joe." I always called them by their first names, and now, I am ashamed to admit, I did not even know some of their last names.

We were kind to our Black servants and treated them with respect. In a way, we even loved some of them. But they were always our servants and as such only supporting players in our lives, like supporting actors in a play, the maids and butlers, which, of course is exactly what they were. They were our servants, not our friends. It was not until I was grown and far away from home that I knew what it was to have African Americans who were real friends. We were racists without meaning to be, without realizing that we were. The loss was ours.

The first joke I heard, when I was four or five, was a racist joke, and I immediately ran into the kitchen and told it to Lizzie, our Black cook, "What did the worm say when it got to the Negro graveyard? Mmm! Chocolate." I told it in all innocence, but an innocence that reflected the pervasive racism that I was growing up surrounded by, had already absorbed. I wonder now, as I didn't then, what Lizzie must have felt when I blurted it out?

Because of the prevalence of the easy-going Cajun influence in Lafayette, it was never as virulently racist as some other parts of the South. At one time, in the nineteenth century, miscegenation was not illegal nor even totally socially unacceptable. According to Lafayette genealogist Franklin Mouton, two sons of Alexandre Mouton, US senator and later the eleventh governor of Louisiana, were married to Black women.

Alexandre, son of Jean Mouton, the founder of Lafayette, had two wives, and thirteen children by the first, and six by the second.

One of Alexandre's sons, Charles Alexander Mouton, was married to a highly educated, very beautiful, Black Haitian woman named Mathilde Schoal. They were married in 1881 in the Cathedral of St. John the Evangelist and are buried in the same plot in the cathedral graveyard, land that was donated to the church by his grandfather. Many of their descendants live alongside their white cousins today, no doubt some in the predominantly Black neighborhood known as Mouton Addition on the northside of Lafayette.

With the end of Reconstruction in the early 1870s, the rise of white supremacy, reinforced and romanticized by the promotion of the myth of the "Lost Cause," infected even the laissez-faire southern part of the state. The Knights of the White Camellia, an organization with ties to the Ku Klux Klan, was, in fact, formed in 1868 in the south Louisiana town of Franklin, less than fifty miles from Lafayette. It was essentially a terrorist group that was attempting to restore slavery and the primacy of the slaveholders, using tactics of harassment, floggings, and lynchings to terrorize Blacks. Many of its members came from the upper strata of Louisiana white society and included landowners, lawyers, judges, physicians, and journalists. The Knights of the White Camellia, after a few years, more or less fizzled out, perhaps because southern Louisiana did not provide as fertile a ground for hate as other parts of the South.

Miscegenation had been legal in the south for a few years after the Civil War, but gradually the slave states passed laws against it. The laws must have been unenforced in Louisiana at least till the end of the nineteenth century, but by the time I was growing up in Lafayette a marriage such as that of Charles Alexander Mouton and his Haitian bride would have been unthinkable.

However, there was still hidden mingling of the races. The one case that I and everyone else in Lafayette knew about involved Isaac (Ike) Bendel, bachelor brother of the New York milliner and retailer, Henri Bendel, who had been born in Lafayette.

Ike lived in a grand, columned house (today the French House of the university) on Johnston Street where he was looked after by his Black housekeeper. He died in 1952, and shortly thereafter a Black dentist from Los Angeles arrived in Lafayette on the Sunset Limited train to claim his part of the estate as Ike's illegitimate son. His striking resemblance to Ike was undeniable proof that he was his son. The story was not, of course, reported in the *Lafayette Daily Advertiser* but told in whispers around town. While miscegenation was illegal then in Louisiana, it was said that he received some kind of settlement before he took the train back to California.

By the 1940s and 1950s, even if racism was not as pervasive and extreme in Lafayette and much of Cajun Louisiana as it was in other parts of the South, it certainly existed there in various degrees. There were some people like the prominent lawyer who threatened to put my father in jail if he integrated the local college. It was an open secret that another prosperous and respectable lawyer had made his money by regularly cheating his black clients and was proud of it. There was the Presbyterian minister who from the pulpit chided my father for facilitating integration. And there were, no doubt, many others of whom I was not aware. At that time, being a rabid racist was no impediment to social standing in Lafayette. Bigots did not have to worry about expressing strongly racist views in any company. They were never challenged or contradicted.

The most prevalent kind of racism in Lafayette might be described as "polite" racism. It was exemplified by Lafayette's self-appointed grande dame, Mrs. Elisabeth Montgomery.

In 1932, my mother and twenty-three of her friends formed a social club to do good works in the community. Les Vingt Quatre (The Twenty-Four), dubbed by some of their children "The Vain Cats," did make a valuable contribution to Lafayette, the most important being the creation of the first public library, and later the Lafayette Museum. Elisabeth Montgomery was also a charter member of the club and a cornerstone of what passed in Lafayette for society.

Mrs. Montgomery's attitudes toward Blacks were typical of generations of well-to-do white southern women. She lived with a vision of Blacks that had nothing to do with reality, but that let her believe that she was a benevolent Christian who treated her inferiors kindly. There was never any question in her mind that Blacks were her inferiors.

After segregation was declared illegal throughout the country in 1964, and as painful progress was being slowly made toward Black equality, she and many of her ilk became more and more afraid that the "Nigras" were getting too uppity.

They were not like the wonderful "Darkies" she had known in her youth, who had always known their place.

When she entertained at Shadow Lawn, her home on Lafayette Street that she and many of her friends considered the center of Lafayette's social universe, her Black servants, immaculately clad in white, would be serving drinks and refreshments to her white guests who might well be discussing "the Nigra problem," as if the Black faces in front of them were not there.

In 1988, she recorded an oral history titled: "Personal Reflections of Early Lafayette" in which she writes of "adorable pickaninnys" and

> shoeshine boys . . . the little negro boys made money nearly any way they could in those days . . . when you got off the train, there were three or four, "Shoeshine, Mister"? Shoeshine, Mister"? All around. You could pick whichever one you wanted. Around the courthouse, if a man stopped, it was, "Shoeshine, Mister"? And these little negro boys were wonderful and danced, tap-danced, and the one who could tap the best, usually got the job. So, it was fun to watch them. Lots of my friends from the north who came down to see us, when they got off the train, couldn't stop looking at all the little negro boys dancing the way they do. So, it was fun.

The most telling passage in her book of recollections is what she wrote about the cotton crop: "Every negro in the country picked cotton. When September came, every white woman was without help. The Blacks were all in the fields. They picked all day long and didn't mind picking, they had a wonderful time . . . they would get in those fields and sing and laugh and I don't believe I have ever seen them in my life as happy as they were then. That was a gala time. . . . That was like a big picnic."

I have no doubt that Elisabeth believed every word of these horrible lies. Such self-deception permitted her to live unbothered by her Methodist conscience.

Sometime shortly after the 1964 Civil Rights Act had been passed, and Blacks could finally go to places that they never had been able to enter before, I was home on a visit from Italy and went with my mother to have lunch with Elisabeth at Don's Seafood Inn, a downtown restaurant. Shortly after we were seated, a Black couple was shown to a table near ours. Elisabeth was livid! Off she went on a tirade about "the Nigras," which I hoped the couple could not hear. I tried my best to ignore her, and she eventually finished her anti-Black rant, but then immediately began on the Puerto Ricans. At one point, she turned to me and asked, "Do you all have a Puerto Rican problem in Florence?" With as straight a face as I could manage, I told her, "Yes, we certainly do. I don't know *what* we're going to do about him." Elisabeth was not amused. I had never been one of her favorite people, and had I had the horrid luck to have been born her child, she would have been sorely disappointed in me. She no doubt pitied my mother for having such a "different" son.

Although I may not have realized it at the time, the Blacks whom I knew and grew up with were an important influence on me, and to some degree shaped the person I was destined to become. I did not know it then, but I know it now. They taught me by example, by being good and kind in spite of the lives they were forced to lead. They gave us so much. We gave them so little.

WILBERT SAM

Wilbert Sam, ten years older than I, was my hired companion and playmate before I started school. We were always together, and Wilbert's principal task was to keep me from getting into mischief. He had a wonderful imagination and made up stories to entertain me. One was about a rabbit that could transform itself into a P-38, the World War II fighter plane. The rabbit would pull its nose and the nose would become a propeller, pull its ears, and the ears would become wings, pull its tail, and the tail would become a rudder, and then it would fly off to fight Nazis, something that Wilbert himself did some years later. Wilbert was also very polite and well-spoken. It was always said around the family that "Wilbert Sam taught Joel his manners."

It is apparent from a photograph of Wilbert and me playing with a football that I was not at all interested in the game. Instead of focusing on the ball, I am mugging for the camera. It is not surprising that in spite of Wilbert's best efforts I did not become anything resembling a jock. I remember my dismay when at my birthday party about the time this photo was taken, I received five footballs as gifts. My mother had warned me ahead of time to be gracious if I received a present I did not want. I tried my best and told what was probably my first social lie. "I've always wanted five footballs," I said.

EDNA SAM

Wilbert's aunt Edna was a cook at the Southwestern dining hall and sometimes for us. She often babysat us. She was kind and calm, and we all adored her. Years later, when my sister Lorraine was working as a food chemist in San Francisco and living in Berkeley, she got a telephone call from Edna who was visiting her daughter in Oakland.

She asked Lorraine if she could come to see her. Lorraine was delighted and said, "Of course!"

Edna took the bus from Oakland to Berkeley, and when she arrived at Lorraine's apartment, she would not sit down, would not accept the coffee, a Coke, or even a glass of water that Lorraine offered her. "I just came to make sure you were all right," she said, and then took the bus back to Oakland.

GUS

In January of 1941, my father became the third president of Southwestern, and we moved from Whittington Hall on the school farm into the large, brick house that the previous president had built for himself. Gus, who came with the house, was already quite elderly and lived in an unpainted cabin in someone's backyard just a few blocks away.

Gus arrived every morning at 6 a.m., made coffee, and then brought a demitasse of black Mello Joy or Créole Belle, with cream and sugar on the side, to each member of the household, except for my father, an early riser, who was often already awake and drinking coffee he had made himself.

About 7 a.m., Gus, an inattentive and careless cook, managed to put breakfast on the table for all of us. I joked with my sisters that Gus treated us like Greek gods, putting burnt offerings before us, and often it was true.

When no one was at home and the phone rang, Gus would answer it: "The president's residence. The butler speaking." We never thought of him as a butler and we never referred to him as such, unconsciously depriving him of the bit of dignity that such a position would have implied.

Gus retired while I was away at Tulane and lived on for a number of years with his common-law wife, who was much younger, in his little cabin. We heard that after he died, it turned out that he had owned for many years a lot in downtown Houston which, by the time he passed away, was worth a great deal of money, and his companion was left well provided for.

LIZZIE PILETTE

Lizzie Pilette was our cook for most of the years that we lived in the house on the campus. She was barely four feet tall, as was her husband, Joseph. It was said that she and Joseph, and a number of their relatives in Lafayette, were descended from a tribe of Pygmies who had been brought as slaves from Africa. They had a diminutive son they called "T-Put" and a cousin named "Shorty," who worked on the campus.

Every morning before I left for school, it was my job to take down from the shelves of the kitchen cabinets everything Lizzie needed to prepare lunch. When I began Tulane, my parents bought a stool with steps so she could retrieve the items herself.

Our main meal was at noon. My father would come home from the office, and I would come home from school. Lizzie did not prepare a wide variety of dishes, but what she cooked was always good. A roast chicken or chicken fricassee, a maybe too well done, but still tender steak, green beans or collard greens, always rice, and always biscuits or cornbread. Dessert was usually ice cream from the college dairy, delivered weekly, together with blocks of yellow cheese and gallons of fresh milk, by Mr. Higginbotham, who had been one of my father's agriculture students and who managed the farm dairy. Lizzie always had coffee ready to serve him.

LOUISA GIRARD

Louisa, who cooked for us on special occasions, was a leader of local Black society that centered around St. Paul the Apostle Church on South Washington Street in a predominantly Black neighborhood. It was founded in 1911, the oldest African American Catholic church in Lafayette. According to her obituary published in the *Lafayette Daily Advertiser* upon her death at the age of ninety-five in January of 1991, she was an organizer and charter member of "the Little Theresa Court No. 11 of the St. Paul Altar Society."

She was also a charter member of the Lafayette Mardi Gras Festival, Inc., which organized parades and balls for Lafayette's Black community. The last time I saw Louisa she was proudly riding on a float in a Mardi Gras parade, elegantly dressed with a fox fur draped over her shoulders.

Louisa was famous for her specialty, a delicious pastry called *oreilles de cochon* (pig's ears), crisp and light and decorated with a swirl of cane syrup. If they were not eaten within twelve hours of being plucked from the hot oil in which they were fried, they became limp and soggy. Once when my parents were taking a morning flight to San Francisco to visit me and my sister Lorraine, Louisa was in her kitchen at 4 a.m. to make a batch of *oreilles de cochon* for them to take to us. They were still crunchy and delectable when we ate them, ignoring crumbs and sticky fingers, on the way from the airport to Lorraine's apartment.

In 1960, Southwestern Louisiana Institute became the University of Southwestern Louisiana, and that summer I was working in the university's news bureau, researching and writing articles about the history of the institution. Going through old files, I found a photograph of Crow Girard, the prominent Lafayette banker who gave the original twenty-five acres for the college campus. Somehow, he looked very familiar. He looked like someone I knew, but I couldn't figure out who. That evening, I mentioned this to my mother. She smiled and said, "You're thinking of Louisa's husband, Johnny Girard. Everyone knows that Crow was his father."

When Louisa died in 1991, the *Lafayette Daily Advertiser* printed her obituary and listed as her survivors "one son, Claude Girard of Washington, D.C., and two nieces." Revealing something of the spirit of that time and that place, it made no mention of her husband, Johnny, who had predeceased her, but did state, not entirely accurately, that "She was employed by past president Joel Fletcher at USL as his housekeeper for many years."

Louisa was known and respected by many people in Lafayette, both Black and white. But only one white man was listed among the pall bearers listed in her obituary. J. C. Chargois was a prominent local decorator who made no effort to pretend that he was anything but gay and thus, like Louisa, belonged to a minority that was usually tolerated, but not really accepted. They must have been kindred souls.

DR. RALPH WALDO EMERSON JONES

I never met Dr. Ralph Waldo Emerson Jones, but I heard his name many times. Like my father, he was the president of one of the Louisiana state colleges and, in my father's opinion, the smartest and best educated one. Jones was both president and baseball coach of Grambling State, an historically Black college a few miles outside of Ruston, the town in northern Louisiana where both my parents had grown up. The grandson of a slave, his father was the first dean of historically Black Southern University in Baton Rouge, and Jones received his master's degree from Columbia University. He was Grambling's president for forty-one years and oversaw its development from the modest two-year Louisiana Negro Normal and Industrial Institute with 120 students to an accredited state university with an enrollment of over 4,000 and a multimillion-dollar physical plant.

He and my father had a warm relationship, and Jones invited him several times to give the commencement address at Grambling. On one of these occasions, my father was presented with a dark suit custom-made by the Grambling home economics department that, my mother said, made him look like a preacher. Her opinion was confirmed one day when, while wearing his Grambling suit, my father stopped by the side of the road to repair a flat tire. He was jacking up his blue Pontiac when another car pulled up beside him. The driver rolled down the window and enquired: "Do you need some help, Reverend?"

Going before the appropriations committee of the Louisiana state legislature to plead for funds to run the college was the thing my father hated most about his job. He would always get very depressed for days beforehand while he and his deans plotted their strategy. He developed a deep loathing and scorn for many of the politicians he had to work with, and yet he was largely successful in his efforts. This task must have been infinitely more difficult for Dr. Jones in that so many of the white Louisiana legislators at that time were unapologetic bigots and racists. But still he did what he had to do. I can only imagine the humiliations and compromises this good, smart, dedicated man must have had to endure to achieve what he did.

In the 1980s, years after my father had passed away, one day my mother told me, "I've just been remembering something that I can hardly believe happened, and yet I know that it did." Occasionally, the Louisiana state college presidents would hold their annual meeting at Southwestern. When they were finished with the meeting in Martin Hall, the administration building, they would all come over to the president's home to have coffee together in our living room. All except Dr. Jones. "No one ever told him he had to," Mother said, "but while everyone else went to the living room to be served demitasses of strong coffee from a silver tray by Gus, Dr. Jones would go straight to the kitchen and have his coffee with our cook. Can you believe that?" asked Mother. Unfortunately, I could.

Dr. Jones lived a life that greatly mattered, even though some of those around him were blind to it. He accomplished an enormous amount at Grambling, and yet he was strongly criticized in his later years by younger Blacks for being too much of "an Uncle Tom" figure. But the question is: could he have succeeded had he not been so accommodating?

Judged from where we are today, Dr. Jones and my father would be far from perfect college presidents. But they were both good men. They had vision, courage, and a sense of what is just and what is unjust. They worked with what they were given, did what they were able to do, and both left important legacies for those who came after them to build on.

7

FRICASSEE, GUMBO, AND OTHER BEASTS

One Easter before I was born, my father gave my sisters a pair of baby chicks that he had named, ominously for them, Fricassee and Gumbo. According to my sister Lorraine, Gumbo was, alas, soon petted to death. But Fricassee lived to be a Methuselah among chickens. She was still alive when I arrived a few years later, and I remember her well.

When I was an infant and Fricassee was still a young hen, our family lived in a small frame house on Brashear Street, near the college. It was an exceedingly quiet neighborhood, and there was so little traffic that Fricassee was allowed to play unsupervised in the front yard. Soon she struck up a friendship with Connie, a neighbor's pet duck on the other side of the street. Lorraine tells me that every morning Fricassee would cross the street to get her friend Connie and then accompany her back to our yard where they would spend the day clucking and quacking and scratching for bugs. At sunset, Fricassee would take Connie back to her yard and then return home to the pen in the backyard where she slept each night.

When my father became dean of Agriculture, we moved from Brashear Street to the Southwestern farm. Fricassee came with us and led a privileged life among the other barnyard fowl. A few years later, when my father was named president of the college, we moved from the farm to the newly constructed President's House on the campus which was not the place, my mother decided, for a pet chicken. She asked Mr. Landry, the grocer, if he would mind keeping Fricassee in his chicken coop. Mr. Landry said that would be fine. We often accompanied mother to Landry's Grocery on Cherry Street and always went to the coop behind the store to say hi to Fricassee. This continued for some time until the Saturday my mother telephoned Mr. Landry to order a chicken for our Sunday dinner. The chicken he sent was Fricassee. Mother, fortunately, came out the back door just as Gus, our servant, was about to wring Fricassee's neck. Mother screamed, and Gus dropped Fricassee. She was not sent back to Mr. Landry. A pen was found, and Fricassee lived out the rest of her life, not in the Groves, but in the bushes of Academe in our backyard.

We always had dogs, often more than one. The first I remember was a rat terrier named Small Fry. Next was Mr. Potter, a Boston bull terrier named after the family friend who gave him to us when we moved to the house on the campus. Swabby was a part collie we had during the war. He was named in honor of the V-12 unit of sailors who were sent to Southwestern as part of a program to train naval officers. He became their unofficial mascot and was well-known around the campus. He took a fancy to Dr. Albert Pettigrew Elliott, the dapper head of the English Department, started following him to class every day, and sat in on several semesters of Shakespeare.

My youngest sister usually named the pets and always gave them, to my mind, embarrassing names: among them Elmer, Andrew, and Clarence Lee. The one dog I got to name was Inky, a sweet black mongrel with a perpetually wagging tail who was devoted to me.

Elmer was a jimmy-jawed fox terrier with a hernia and a penchant for wandering off. Sometimes when I went around the campus calling his name, trying to persuade him to come home, instead of Elmer the dog, Dr. Elmer Feusse, the eccentric head of chemistry, appeared. Elmer Feusse was one of the banes of my father's existence. He had strong opinions about how the college should be run, ideas that always clashed with my father's. Once when my father went to Baton Rouge to testify before the legislature as to why the school should be given funds to build the graceful brick arcades that now join the main buildings on what is known as "The Rectangle," Dr. Feusse showed up at the hearing with charts and graphs that proved, he maintained, that it would be much cheaper just to buy all the students umbrellas.

Clarence Lee was the most memorable of our dogs. He was a short-haired, highly intelligent, highly strung Chihuahua with one droopy ear. He was loved by all except my father, who thought a Chihuahua an unmanly dog. Clarence sensed this and began to tremble and twitch whenever he and my father were in the same room. It did not help that my father sneeringly called him "Alligator Bait."

Clarence was my constant companion; we slept in twin beds in my room, his head on the pillow just as if he were a human. And each morning when Gus brought me a cup of café au lait, Clarence drank his portion from the saucer.

Clarence also had a talent that made him a local celebrity after Lydia Krauss, society editor of the *Lafayette Daily Advertiser*, wrote a feature article about him.

Whenever someone sat down to play at the Steinway grand in our living room, Clarence would hop up on the piano and begin to howl his head off. Most people thought it cute. "CHIHUAHUA LIKES TO SING" read the headline of the article in the *Daily Advertiser*.

The piano served another purpose in Clarence's life. Although mostly housebroken, when he occasionally forgot himself or just could not hold it any longer, he always piddled in the same place under the piano (For years after his demise we referred to the ineradicable stain beneath the Steinway as "The Clarence Lee Memorial Spot.") Whenever this happened, Mother would be furious and let Clarence know that he was "in disgrace." She would send him to spend the rest of the day in his box in my closet.

One morning when Clarence Lee had piddled and been banished, my father brought home for morning coffee an oil man, one of the first ever in Lafayette, who had just moved to town from Texas. Ten o'clock coffee in the living room was an established part of our household routine, and my mother knew to have the silver service, the demitasses, and a large pot of coffee waiting for the arrival of my father and his guests. She never knew how many there would be.

Clarence Noble was the only guest that morning, and soon after Gus had served him his steaming black demitasse of Mello Joy, Clarence Lee sneaked into the living room. Knowing that he would be unwelcome, perhaps he thought he would be safe hiding under the guest's chair. And it was there Mother spotted him. She put down her demitasse, glared at Mr. Noble's chair, and not remembering or perhaps never knowing that his first name was also Clarence, said very sharply: "Clarence! Go get in your box this instant!" Clarence Noble was so startled that he dropped his coffee on the rug.

Clarence Lee was gone like a shot. Mr. Noble never saw him, which did not help matters when my father began to explain that my mother was talking to a dog.

We heard a few months later that Mr. Noble had unexpectedly passed away with cardiac arrest. We were grateful that it had not happened, as it well could have, in our living room.

There were always dogs around and sometimes there were parakeets. A lovebird named Bill almost went to church on my mother's hat one Sunday. And then there were my two alligators, much less menacing than the ones in Robert Flaherty's *Louisiana Story*, though the first one did develop a mean streak after being teased by the grocery boy. The unnamed beast . . . he was simply called "the alligator" . . . lived in a cage in the backyard and was less than a foot long when we first got him but was growing. At some point, my parents decided it would be a good idea to get rid of him and gave him to a man from Chicago who was passing through, allowing me to believe that he had been stolen or had escaped. I was devastated and asked all my friends in the fourth grade of the F. M. Hamilton Training School to help me look for him. We scoured the campus and the nearby neighborhoods and, of course, found nothing. I penned a sad note about my loss to my oldest sister who was working in New Orleans. About a week later, as we were having lunch, to the dismay of my parents, a package from my sister arrived containing a baby alligator. In those days, when highways were being built through the swamps, baby alligators were often found and sold on Canal Street for two dollars each. The new alligator, which I named Hercules, proved to be more companionate than his predecessor. For one thing, he was much smaller, only about six inches in length. Who could feel threatened by a six-inch alligator? I took him almost everywhere. Curved into a U-shape, he fitted neatly in my shirt pocket. We even bathed together. He did not have much of a personality, but in an alligator that is not necessarily a bad thing. He was, in fact, so docile that I did not keep as vigilant a watch on him as I should have.

One day while my attention was elsewhere, he wandered off in the house, and by the time I realized he had decamped he was nowhere to be found. He was missing for several weeks, and I had just about given up hope of ever finding him again when early one morning I heard a piercing scream. It came from a friend of one of my sisters who had stayed the night and was putting on her make-up at a vanity table when Hercules crawled across her naked foot. I promised to be more attentive to his whereabouts in the future, but Mother insisted that he no longer be allowed to spend the night in the house, so I fixed up a box for him in the garage. One winter night the temperature plunged below freezing, and the next morning I found poor Hercules stiff and dead.

I had a few other nontraditional pets in the house on the campus. In 1948, while the Progressive Party candidate for president, Henry Wallace, was making a radio address, a baby squirrel fell out of the oak tree in our side yard. ("Must be a red-squirrel," my father, who was supporting Dewey, remarked.) I found him and fed him sugar water with an eyedropper until he was old enough to feed himself. I named him Timmy and he became as tame as a cat. He sometimes had the run of the house, but most of the time lived in a cage in the backyard that, after my experience with Hercules, I had provided with a warm bed for chilly nights.

From time to time, I also had flying squirrels which were easily tamed by rubbing their bellies. I would tie one end of a string to the squirrel's leg and the other to a belt loop, allowing just enough string for the flying squirrel to be able to crawl around my body while I bicycled around town.

One Saturday I squandered my entire one-dollar weekly allowance at a one-cent sale of goldfish at Woolworth's. I thought the one hundred goldfish looked spectacular in the blue porcelain tub in my oldest sister's bathroom, but she did not, and soon I had to transport them to Cypress Lake, the ornamental pond in the middle of the campus, where their descendants perhaps still live.

I have probably forgotten a few of the pets we had over the years. I have a vague memory of a horned toad that did not last long. And lizards that were pets for only a little while. By the time I left for Tulane in the autumn of 1953, the last pet left at home was Inky, his black coat spotted with gray, his tail still wagging.

8

MY DECISIVE MOMENT?

In the photograph, I am sitting on the steps at the bottom of the stairs at Whittington Hall, on the farm in Lafayette, Louisiana, where we lived when my father was dean of Agriculture at the local state college. I am wearing short pants and shoes that are badly scuffed and muddy from play. My chin is cupped in my right hand, and my right arm is resting on my right knee. My left arm is around my dog, Small Fry. The dark-haired terrier is barely visible against my dark jacket. I am staring wide-eyed at the person who is taking the photograph, though I have absolutely no memory of the man I was observing so intently. I only remember what my mother told me later: my parents had company for dinner that night.

Sitting on the steps with Small Fry, Whittington Hall, late 1930s. Collection of the author by an anonymous French photographer.

I had been sent up to bed, but then I sneaked back down to see what was going on. The dinner guest, a French photographer traveling on assignment for *Life* magazine, snapped the photograph and later sent a print of it to my mother as a thank you for the dinner she had served him. He told her that it might appear in *Life*, but it never did. My mother was convinced it was because she had done such a bad job of arranging the daisies in the bowl on the Victorian table to the left of me and Small Fry.

In spite of the evidence it offered of her lack of proficiency in flower arrangement, my mother loved the photograph, had several copies made for relatives, and kept it framed on her desk where it was part of the visual background for the rest of my growing up. Now it hangs over my desk where it catches my attention every now and then and reminds me of that distant time when I was a child in a house on a farm in Louisiana.

In New Orleans some years ago, I met Alain Desvergnes, director of the *École Nationale de la Photographie* in Arles. I asked him if he knew of any French photographers who had been on assignment for *Life* magazine in America in the late 1930s or early 1940s. There was only one, he said: Henri Cartier-Bresson.

9

THE CAMELLIA PAGEANT

In January of 1940, I made my first public appearance. Clad in green velvet and lace, wearing shiny patent leather shoes, I was the crown bearer for the Camellia Pageant, part of the annual Mid-Winter Fair put on by the local college. The pageant had been the idea of my father, then dean of Agriculture, to supplement the livestock shows that were the main feature of the fair. My father loved camellias and eventually hybridizing them was to become a beloved pursuit. Their glorious blooms always gave color to the gray and damp winter months in southern Louisiana and were usually at their peak in January when the fair took place.

The first Camellia Pageant was held in 1934. In addition to the presentation of the queen and her court, the music and dance departments of the college provided the entertainment. To be chosen Queen of Camellias was considered one of the highest honors a coed could hope for.

The pageant in 1940 was in the Earl K. Long Men's Gymnasium which had been built the year before and named for the new governor. Earl had been lieutenant governor under Richard W. Leche, who had been elected governor in 1936, after the assassination of in 1935 of Earl's brother, Senator Huey Long. Shortly after Leche's inauguration, he famously declared: "When I took the oath of office, I didn't take a vow of poverty." He resigned in 1939 after he was accused of fraud and subsequently convicted and sent to prison for stealing federal funds, the first (but not the last) governor of Louisiana to be sent to prison.

The 1940 Camellia Pageant was the last public appearance of Walter J. Burke, grandfather of celebrated crime novelist James Lee Burke. A state senator and a great patron of Southwestern, is seen here crowning Margaret Prudhomme, Queen of Camellias.

The final Camellia Pageant was in 1962. It was becoming very expensive to stage, funds were scarce, and the burgeoning Lafayette Mardi Gras, seeking to rival the one in New Orleans, overwhelmed it.

Reverend James Andrew McLees, my maternal grandfather.

Jeannie McBride McLees, first wife of James Andrew McLees.

Ellen McMurray McLees, second wife of James Andrew McLees, my grandmother.

Joel Lafayette Fletcher Sr., Joel Lafayette Fletcher Jr., Joel Lafayette Fletcher III, Ruston, Louisiana, circa 1937.

Fannie McLees Fletcher, circa 1918.

With the white barn cat before my creativity spoiled our relationship, as photographed by my sister Lorraine for her high school chemistry class.

President's Home, Southwestern. Built by my father's predecessor who lived in it only a short time before he lost his job in the wake of the scandals that sent the governor of Louisiana and the president of Louisiana State University to federal prison. We moved in on January 1, 1941, and my parents lived there for the next twenty-five years.

I barely made it into the frame of this photograph with my father in front of the President's Home at Southwestern shortly after it became our home. My grim-faced father may have been thinking about the Louisiana politicians he would have to deal with in the coming years. What one can see of my expression indicates that I was not happy in the confines of the new mansion.

My father in the study of the President's Home, 1940s.

With my parents in front of the President's Home, Southwestern, circa 1960.

My mother's older siblings, Jeannie and Will. Will became the "black sheep" of the family when he ran off to play the trumpet and drums with a traveling minstrel show.

My mother, Frances Allen McLees, circa 1900.

Mrs. Joel L. Fletcher, front hall of the President's Home, 1947.

In this photograph, taken at the Whittington Farm around 1940, I am standing in front of Edna Sam. Her nephew, Wilbert, my paid companion, is on her right. I do not recognize the woman with the hat who must have been one of the other servants employed by the college who worked for us from time to time.

With Wilbert Sam in front of the house on Whittington Farm about 1940.

Gus and Lizzie dressed to serve Christmas dinner at the house on the campus, 1951.

Louisa Girard, right, wearing her fox fur, riding on a float in the parade of the Lafayette Mardi Gras Association, the Black Mardi Gras Krewe, in which she played an important part. This is the last time I remember seeing Louisa, around 1980.

The last public appearance of Walter J. Burke, grandfather of celebrated crime novelist James Lee Burke, crowning the Queen of Camellias, January 1940. As Crown Bearer, it was my first public appearance.

My father receiving the Legion of Honor, France's highest decoration.

Aunt Bill and Aunt Frances with Lonzo, who was abandoned by his parents in Ruston when he was an infant. The aunts saw to it that he was always fed, clothed, educated, and loved. In their old age he repaid their kindness and devotion by diligently looking after them. At Aunt Bill's burial in Ruston's Greenwood Cemetery, at her request, so that she could be sure it was done properly, he put the first shovel of dirt in her grave.

Aunt Kathleen and Aunt Frances on a cruise where pink leis and pink and white plastic hats must have been de rigueur, though they do not seem entirely convinced.

Guinevere, my 1923 Ford Model T, preparing to take part in the 1952 Lafayette High School homecoming parade.

Elizabeth (Lizzie) Snyder Glide.

Lorraine on the deck at Brickyard Cove.

Roy Elliott Jr. at the helm of a sailboat, probably the *Rani*, the forty-foot sloop that he designed and had built.

Sunset at Brickyard Cove, Mt. Tamalpais, across San Francisco Bay.

With Stephen (left) and Gordon (right) in a sampan on our way to a floating restaurant in Kowloon, on liberty from the USS *Bennington* (CVA 20), anchored in Hong Kong Harbor.

With Simonetta at the American School of Languages, Florence, 1964.

Carl Selph, poet, friend, and my business partner in the American School of Languages.

"Imparate L'Inglese di Oggi" (Learn the English of Today) poster advertising the American School, Florence.

10

MY FATHER IS KISSED BY A FRENCHMAN WHILE THE BISHOP WATCHES, AND I BECOME A FRANCOPHILE

At the end of the Second World War, General Charles de Gaulle, who had been the leader of the Free French in opposition to the Nazi occupation of France, was excluded as an equal from the peace talks. My father, president of what was then Southwestern Louisiana Institute (now the University of Louisiana at Lafayette), was a great admirer of de Gaulle. He thought the exclusion unjust and wrote a letter about it to the New Orleans *Times-Picayune*. The letter must have been eloquent and persuasive because it was picked up and published by papers across the country, and eventually was read into the *Congressional Record*. It also must have been noticed in France because, much to my father's surprise, when the first French honors were awarded after the war, his name was on the list to become a chevalier of the Legion of Honor.

La Légion d'honneur, France's highest decoration, was created by Napoleon Bonaparte in 1802 and first bestowed in 1804. It is awarded for gallantry in military action or for distinguished service in the military, and in civilian life "for work that enhances the reputation of France through scholarship, arts, sciences, politics, etc." It can be awarded to nationals of countries other than France, and among the many Americans who have been given the honor are, to name but a few, John Singer Sargent, Julia Child, Jerry Lewis, and Neil Armstrong.

Dr. Hosea Phillips, a professor of French at Southwestern, volunteered to instruct my father in the protocol attending the ceremony. "Philippe," as he was known, had studied at the Sorbonne and had a reputation on the campus for flamboyance, excitability, and unpredictability. He excelled at getting his students' attention. Once while teaching in a second-floor classroom, he told a student that if she made one more mistake while reading aloud, he would jump out the window. She soon grievously mispronounced a word. Philippe ran and leaped, as he said he would, out the window. There was a collective gasp from the class, and all rushed over to look for the body on the lawn two stories below. What they saw was Philippe crouching just beneath the window on a wide ledge that only he realized was there.

The French consul in New Orleans was to drive over to make the presentation to my father. Philippe, describing the ceremony that was to take place, told my father that after the consul pinned the medal on his lapel, he would then kiss him on both cheeks. This prospect so horrified my father that he later said he seriously considered turning down the honor if it meant he had to be kissed by a Frenchman. I don't know how Philippe persuaded him that this was an established and acceptable tradition among men in France and therefore had to be endured. In northern Louisiana, where my father came from, it was probably considered a felony.

The photograph of the ceremony shows, from left to right: Philippe; Claude Colomb, who was then the mayor of Lafayette; my father stoically awaiting the buss, resolutely not making eye contact with the consul; Lionel Vasse, who is gripping both his shoulders; a military man I do not recognize; and Lafayette's bishop Jules Jeanmard.

It was not clear to my ten-year-old mind why my father had been decorated. I thought it had something to do with fighting the Nazis, though I was not sure exactly where he had done this or how he had found the time to do so in his busy life of faculty meetings, state board meetings, and other administrative duties. I must have got the idea from a war movie about the O.S.S. which had made a great impression on me. And at times the war had seemed very close to Lafayette. There had been reports of U-boats in the Gulf of Mexico, and when KVOL broadcast the news that Abbeville in France had fallen to the Germans, panic swept through southwest Louisiana. Many assumed that the Abbeville in question was the town twenty miles from Lafayette where we often went to eat raw oysters. In any case, since my father was the most important and powerful person I knew, the idea that he somehow had killed a few Nazis did not seem unreasonable.

In July of 1946, I went with my father to the Bastille Day celebration in New Orleans. Our party included M'sieur Perot, a Frenchman who taught French at Southwestern. M'sieur Perot had been giving me private lessons in conversational French, and for the occasion he had taught me the words to the French national anthem, "La Marseillaise."

We left Lafayette long before dawn and arrived at St. Louis Cathedral in time for an early morning mass. The French aircraft carrier, *Béarn*, which had fought with the Free French during the war, was in New Orleans, and the cathedral was filled with sailors.

When the mass was over, the sailors streamed out of the cathedral, putting on their white hats with little red pom-poms. We then went to a reception at the French consul's residence in the Garden District where I was very taken by the marzipan made in the shape of apples, oranges, bananas, and bunches of grapes. Afterwards, we were given a tour of the *Béarn*. On the bridge the captain pointed out in the glass windshield the bullet holes made by Nazi strafing.

After the visit to the *Béarn*, there was a sumptuous lunch in the banquet room at La Louisiane, a prominent restaurant on Iberville Street in the French Quarter. Because this was the first Bastille Day after the terrible war, it was a very emotional event. We were seated at the head table, facing a sea of sailors. Heartfelt toasts were made with pink champagne (though my glass had only ginger ale), and I stood on a chair to join in the singing of the French national anthem. All the sailors rose to sing, tears streaming down their cheeks. Spurred on by the intensity of feeling in the room and the sight of so many grown men weeping, I soon had tears streaming down my cheeks as well. After the last verse of "La Marseillaise" was sung, while I was still standing on the chair, encouraged by M. Perot, I shouted out the first complete sentence in French that he had taught me: "Vive La Belle France Libre!" The room broke into cheers, and we all wept for a beautiful and free France.

That was the moment my abiding love for France began.

Before he was awarded the Légion d'honneur, my father received a lesser honor, the Reconnaissance Française, a bronze medal given in recognition of his work in setting up student exchanges between France and the United States. The first French exchange student who came to Lafayette was the daughter of an admiral from Bordeaux and, to my eyes, very glamorous. She looked a lot like the actress Danielle Darrieux. I remember her vividly because several times she was my babysitter, and I was enthralled. Years later Philippe went to Bordeaux and looked her up. He returned to report (could he be believed?) that she had become the madame of the most exclusive bordello in Bordeaux.

In 1960 or thereabouts, I saw my father's hero, de Gaulle, at a reception at the Palace of the Legion of Honor in San Francisco, a three-quarter-scale adaptation of the eighteenth-century Palais de la Légion d'honneur in Paris. What I remember most about the occasion is that de Gaulle and I were the two tallest people in the room. We nodded to each other over the heads of the shorter Frenchmen, who all seemed to be shoving and pushing to get closer to *le général*.

That evening, with a group of French friends, I watched on television the dinner that was given in de Gaulle's honor. He was obviously fatigued, and during long speeches by Governor Brown of California and Mayor Christopher of San

Francisco, he kept dozing off. Each time he did, his wife, Yvonne, leaned over the person sitting between them and poked him awake. Finally, it was his turn to speak. He rose majestically, raised his arms in the air, and proclaimed: "Vive Chicago!" The translator quickly translated. "The General has just said 'Long Live San Francisco!'"

11

GROWING UP NERVOUS

Everyone else in my immediate family was calm, slow-speaking, and very southern-sounding. My father moved with an impressive deliberateness and had a deep and authoritative drawl. My mother spoke more softly, but her voice also had a lovely southern lilt. My sisters drawled and glided through life. Only I, from an early age, was a fidget who always spoke too quickly to sound truly southern.

This may have been caused by an overdose of sulfa drugs that were new and experimental when they were given to me as a cure for scarlet fever when I was very young. I read somewhere a few years ago that nervousness could be a side effect, sometimes long-lasting, of the "miracle drug" of the 1940s, an overdose of which came close to killing me. But I have always suspected that I may have just been born this way. Today when people remark that I do not sound very southern, I give them various reasons, none of which I really believe: growing up in southwestern Louisiana, I heard a mix of southern and Cajun accents; I went to Tulane and have a kind of hybrid New Orleans accent; I lived abroad for many years. I can usually see the skepticism in their eyes as they conclude that my way of speaking is just an affectation. But I have never spoken any other way. When I taught English as a foreign language in Italy my students used to complain that I spoke too fast for them to understand and begged me to slow down. I tried. But I have always spoken and moved more quickly than most of the people I grew up with.

I not only spoke more quickly and was generally more hyper than the majority of people I was surrounded by in Cajun and Catholic southwestern Louisiana, I was also taller and Presbyterian. My parents, of mostly Anglo-Saxon stock, moved from north to south Louisiana many years before I was born. My genes, encouraged by my father's strong belief in good nutrition, made me the tallest boy in my class from grammar through high school where, perversely, I refused even to consider the idea of going out for basketball.

Almost all my classmates had names like Boudreau, Broussard, or LeBlanc, and were short of stature. While I was growing up, it was impossible for me to find a pair of trousers that were long enough at either Gaidry's or Abdalla's, the only two men's shops in Lafayette. "Those are perfect," the salesman would insist, as I stared at myself in the fitting room mirror, the cuffs of the pants he was selling me riding slightly above my ankles. When I got to the eighth grade I was already taller than my father who was a hair over six feet tall. By the time I graduated from high school and went off to Tulane, I was just under six foot five.

There were many positive and enjoyable things about my childhood and youth, but I was always conscious of being rather a misfit among my classmates: a tall, skinny, nervous misfit who spoke too fast and seemed to be set at a different speed. I was a like a 33 1/3 rpm record played at 45 rpm.

A few years after my bout with scarlet fever, my nervousness got out of hand. When I was nine or ten years old, I developed a number of serious "tics." My head would jerk, my arms would twitch, and occasionally my hands would flutter uncontrollably. My parents were very concerned. I remember waking one night to find them standing in the doorway of my bedroom waiting to see if my tics and twitchings occurred while I slept. Pretending to still be asleep, I obliged them with a couple of twitches.

Our local doctor, the same who had prescribed the too large dose of sulfa that had almost done me in, could give them no explanation for my aberrant behavior. He suggested that they take me to Oschner Clinic in New Orleans for tests. This they soon did. I spent a day there being jabbed, pricked, listened to with stethoscopes, and attached to various machines. The results of the tests, when my parents received them a few days later, showed nothing physically wrong with me. "It's probably psychological," a doctor at Oschner told them and recommended that they make an appointment for me with a child psychologist. There were, of course, no child psychologists in what was then the little town of Lafayette. So, I was taken to one who had a practice in a pretty building with a wrought-iron balcony on Prytania Street in New Orleans.

Every week for the next few months, my parents and I would get up before dawn and drive eastward for three hours along bayous and through cane fields and swamps. (This was long before the construction of the Interstate.) We would wend our way on old Highway 90 through the tiny towns of New Iberia, Jeanerette, Franklin, Morgan City, eventually drive across the high and somewhat scary Huey P. Long Bridge, and make our way to the Garden District.

Before these trips to the psychologist, I had loved going to New Orleans. It had meant staying at the Monteleone Hotel in the French Quarter where a deluxe room then cost nine dollars a night, shopping with my mother at D. H. Holmes, Maison Blanche, and Godchaux's, the large department stores that offered an array of goods unavailable in provincial Lafayette, and where I could find trousers that actually fit. New Orleans also meant coffee and beignets at the Morning Call or the Café du Monde, lunch at Kolb's or Galatoire's where I can still remember the first time horseradish sauce thrilled my taste buds and cleared my sinuses. I adored New Orleans until I started going there for medical reasons and the sessions with the child psychologist began to sour me on the city. To keep me in a good humor, my parents would indulge me with gifts of my own choosing each time we went for a session on Prytania Street.

The treatment must have begun in summer because I remember that the crêpe myrtle trees outside the clinic were in full glorious bloom and were the last pleasing thing I saw before entering the dreary hall on the ground floor of the clinic where we sat waiting for our appointment, surrounded by other worried looking parents and their impaired offspring.

As I recall, the first session with Dr. Kirkpatrick included my parents who described in embarrassing detail the behavior that had brought us to this sorry pass. I squirmed and looked at the floor and out the window as they told the doctor about my tics and twitches and jerks. Dr. Kirkpatrick was a grave-looking man, bald and humorless, who peered at us through thick glasses and spoke in a deadly monotone. After my parents had finished their woeful tale, he asked that they wait downstairs while we finished the session in private. I was relieved when they left the room, but I was also uneasy about being alone with Dr. Kirkpatrick.

He began by asking me a number of embarrassing questions. I did my best to avoid giving honest answers. The worst question was "Has anyone ever told you that you must not play with your wee-wee?" I knew exactly what he meant but pretended not to. "With my what?" I asked. "Your wee-wee. You know, the thing you make water with." "Make water with?" I attempted to sound baffled. He tried a few more euphemisms before he gave up and pointed at it. "Why, no," I said, "Not that I remember." I sensed that he believed my evasions, and I felt slightly empowered. The future sessions would not be pleasant, but I was not going to let him intimidate me. He was the enemy, but, as much as I disliked it, I was up to the fight. In any case, I could tell that his heart was not in his work, and that he was not really giving me his full attention. There were long pauses in our sessions. He would stop asking questions and stare unhappily out the window while I sat fidgeting, eager to get out of his depressing presence. I had the impression that he was as uncomfortable as I was.

It was after the third session that something truly dreadful happened. As I came down the stairs from his office to rejoin my parents, I saw among those waiting to see Dr. Kirkpatrick, a girl in my class at elementary school who had acquired the nickname: "Scissors Sally the Sad Sack" because she was given to sudden rages and had once during art class chased a classmate out the door and down the hall with a pair of scissors. I was aware that she was seriously disturbed and at school had always made sure to give her as wide a berth as possible. And now here she was. Unavoidable! She spotted me just as I spotted her. She jumped out of her chair and came toward me. "Joel! What are you doing here? Are you here to see Dr. Kirkpatrick too?" I must have gone white, and I don't know what I mumbled. I grabbed my father's hand and led my parents out to their Plymouth as quickly as I could. I was deeply depressed all the way back to Lafayette as I mulled over the implications of being treated by the same doctor as Scissors Sally. I must be in a far worse state than I had imagined. Fortunately, it was still summer vacation, and I did not have to face the prospect of seeing Sally at school in the immediate future.

After the painful encounter with Scissors Sally, I began to choose more important and expensive bribes in exchange for my compliance and good humor during the trips to the psychologist. We always arrived early enough to stop at the Katz and Besthoff drugstore on the corner of St. Charles and Broadway where my parents obligingly told me I could choose any gift I wanted. Once I found a complete photo kit that included a Brownie camera with a flash attachment, several rolls of film, and a home laboratory for developing and printing the photographs. This was an extravagant choice, but my parents must have realized how badly I needed something to take my mind off Dr. Kirkpatrick. My father bought it without a complaint. While we were driving over to Prytania Street, I loaded a roll of film in the tiny camera. I took it with me up to Dr. Kirkpatrick's office. I asked him if he minded if I photographed him and he seemed pleased. I took the entire roll, using up the little package of blue flash bulbs. I don't remember much about that particular session, but it must have gone the way the others did, with Dr. Kirkpatrick asking me questions and I trying hard not to give honest answers. My parents were pleased that I had wanted to photograph Dr. Kirkpatrick. They seemed to think it was some sort of positive breakthrough.

That evening when we got back to Lafayette, I took the camera kit up to my bathroom and carefully finished reading the instructions. Working only by the dim light of a red bulb that had been provided, I did everything the brochure told me to do. I unloaded the film, developed it, then exposed it in the little metal light box. I put the exposed sheets in the tray of nasty smelling liquid and watched Dr. Kirkpatrick's detested face slowly appear. I hung the prints up to dry, and then did something that was completely unpremeditated. I went to my mother's desk and found her scissors. After inspecting the prints, I cut them up into the smallest possible pieces. All of them. And then I flushed the pieces down the toilet.

Before I went to bed, my mother said. "I heard you working in the bathroom. Have you developed the pictures you took today?" "Not yet." I lied. "I'd love to see them when you do," she told me. "Sure." I said. "I'll show them to you."

I didn't know it then, but there were to be no more sessions with Dr. Kirkpatrick. A few days later my mother and father and I were in the sitting room after breakfast. My father and mother were sharing a copy of a day-old New Orleans *Times-Picayune*, and I was sprawled on the floor on the other side of the room reading a comic book. "My goodness!" my mother suddenly exclaimed. "Daddy, look at this!" "What?" he asked. She lowered her voice. "Here's an article about that child psychologist. Dr. Kirkpatrick." "What does it say?" Mother put the paper down, stared at my father, and whispered: "He's committed suicide!"

I pretended not to hear and concentrated on the adventures of Prince Valiant. I realized that my parents were staring at me. As with so many topics that they sheltered me from, they must have felt that Dr. Kirkpatrick's suicide was not something that should be discussed in front of me, and they never mentioned it to me, though I did overhear my mother saying something about it on the phone to one of her friends.

My parents, probably shaken by Dr. Kirkpatrick's unexpected demise, did not pursue any other treatment options for me. From a few things they had said, I gathered that they had always been a little skeptical about psychology and psychologists. His suicide must have only confirmed to them that psychology was not to be taken seriously. They did not consider it a real discipline based solidly on science like, for instance, animal husbandry in which my father had earned two degrees.

After the termination of my sessions with Dr. Kirkpatrick, I still had one thing to worry about. How was I going to cope with Scissors Sally when school reopened? I was convinced that she would confront me in her hysterical way at school where it would be almost impossible to avoid her. In the waning days of that summer, it was often the last thing I thought about at night and the first thing I thought about in the morning. As school was about to begin again that September, I tried not to worry about it, nor to think about the probable consequences of my bond with the school maniac. I would be exposed in front of all my classmates and made to feel even more of an outsider, a misfit.

But my fears turned out to be unfounded. When school did start up, I soon noticed that Sally seemed to be avoiding me as resolutely as I was avoiding her. It had never occurred to me that she might be as embarrassed about having to see a child psychologist as I was. She never spoke to me. I never spoke to her. And her violent temper became less apparent. Had Dr. Kirkpatrick actually helped her?

As for my own nervous condition, it took a few years, but the tics and jerks almost completely disappeared on their own, and I became very expert at concealing their vestiges. Whenever I felt an uncontrollable urge to jerk my head, I would give in to it and then pretend that I had intentionally turned to look at something. In any case, in the context of my being such a fidget, the tics were not terribly obvious. They have never completely gone away. I perhaps have a very mild case of Tourette's syndrome, not serious enough to cause any real disruption in my life. And I eventually moved away from south Louisiana. I have lived much of my life in places where tall, nervous people are more the norm than they were in the Louisiana of my youth.

12

AUNT BILL'S BISCUITS

My aunt Bill's real name was Leila Willie, the latter a corruption of Wilhelmina, but she was seldom called that. Born in 1899, she was the oldest of my three maiden aunts, the others being Frances and Kathleen, all of whom loomed large in the lives of their nephews and nieces. Kathleen, the youngest, who served As a WAF during the Second World War, ventured farthest afield. She earned several degrees in library science and spent much of her working life as a librarian at the University of Southern Illinois. Frances, with a master's degree in English literature from the University of Virginia and a PhD from Louisiana State University, returned to her family home in Ruston and taught on the English faculty at Louisiana Tech. Bill received her bachelor's degree from Louisiana Tech in 1932 and her master's degree from Iowa State College in 1938. Her field was early childhood education. For many years she ran the Tech nursery school and helped civilize generations of young Rustonians. Early in the 1960s, she was called to Washington, DC, to take part in the planning of the Head Start Program, the purpose of which is to help with the education of low-income children.

My maiden aunts were always trying to improve my mind and raise my standard of culture, which could be very annoying, but eventually left me with much to be grateful for. They all had strong personalities and were always referred to as "The Aunts," almost as if they were a sports team.

They sometimes descended on us in Lafayette; always at Christmas which we celebrated at our house on the campus. It was a long, noisy meal with always too much to eat, and lots of opinions expressed, some shouted. Once when I was a teenager, I hid a tape recorder under the table to capture the conversation. When I played it back, there was not one intelligible word, just a constant babble of voices.

Several times a year we would drive up to Ruston to see them. Leaving southern Louisiana to spend four boring hours in the back seat of a Plymouth, while driving up to the red clay hills and piney woods of northern Louisiana, was never an unalloyed pleasure. There were things about visiting Ruston that I enjoyed, but my aunts had strongly held, sometimes contradictory, ideas about how a child should be raised and a visit to their home on "Presbyterian Hill" in Ruston was always stressful. I never knew when suddenly one or all of them would proclaim some well-meaning dogma that would destroy my peace of mind. I particularly remember the time they found me reading a comic book and raised holy hell, telling me that I was ruining my mind and polluting my soul by wasting time on such trash. Aunt Kathleen, the librarian, who had the highest decibel level of the three, ranted on and on until I was a nervous wreck and remained one until we were safely back in laissez-faire Lafayette.

But the food was always delicious and helped soothe my nerves. The fried chicken was sublime and there were luscious, pickled peaches and fresh peach ice cream that I remember eating in an arbor covered with blooming wisteria in the backyard. There were delicate "sand tarts" made from an ethereal shortbread, and always the light, crisp, and delicious biscuits with lots of butter and cane syrup. "Take two and butter them while they're hot" was a family saying, but who could stop at just two?

My late cousin Kathleen, named after our aunt Kathleen, vividly remembered the Fletcher sisters' tradition of baking powder biscuits and how they cut them out with a small biscuit cutter that made half-dollar size or even smaller biscuits. Cousin Kathleen's mother, Sarah, the only one of the sisters to get married, was also a formidable biscuit maker and had definite opinions about them. For example, she maintained that "drop biscuits" were déclassé because they showed an unwillingness to roll and cut biscuits properly.

Cousin Kathleen's husband, Stephen, remembers Aunt Frances daintily eating Aunt Bill's small biscuits. "Because they were tiny, there would be no uncouth biting into a large biscuit and then putting the biscuit with a big, curved bite-mark back on the plate. Also, there would be less possibility of crumbs falling or, even worse, sticking to the lips and the sides of the mouth."

My cousin Kathleen also remembered her mother, Sarah, and Aunt Bill describing the proper mixing technique for biscuits: "All the dough must be removed from the bottom and sides of the bowl and incorporated into the biscuits. There must be absolutely no waste! No man would marry a woman who wasted biscuit dough. It would indicate a careless woman who was probably careless about other things as well." Sarah was the only one of the sisters who seems to have profited from this adage. She married a handsome Cajun schoolteacher named Belazaire Josephus Bordelon and moved to Kaplan, a tiny town in a flat and desolate part of the state, very near the Gulf.

After moving to south Louisiana, Aunt Sarah became an even better cook, mastering many of the fiery Cajun dishes that were unknown on Presbyterian Hill. However, even though the food was sure to be delicious, I dreaded meals at

Uncle B. J. and Aunt Sarah's house because of the quantities that were forced on their guests. I was happy enough to accept seconds, but Sarah always insisted that we have thirds or fourths, and if I refused, she would look hurt and say "What's the matter? Don't you like my cooking?" By the time I left her table I was always sated and convinced that I would never want to eat again.

But Aunt Sarah's fig preserves were the best I have ever tasted and slathered on her excellent biscuits were a real treat. After she passed away, I called my cousin Kathleen and asked her if Sarah had given her the recipe before she died. "Are you kidding," said Kathleen, "She didn't want anyone else making her fig preserves. She took that recipe with her to the grave."

It is no exaggeration to say that Bill and Frances were pillars of the First Presbyterian Church in Ruston and, next to their family, it was the most important thing in their lives. They were instrumental in choosing the pastors and projects that the church pursued. No initiatives were undertaken without their approval and support.

The Ruston Presbyterian Church was founded in 1884 by my maternal grandfather, James Andrew McLees, and the present red brick building in late gothic revival style, which dates from 1924, features a large lancet stained-glass window dedicated to him.

When my paternal grandfather moved his family from Colfax to Ruston, he bought the former Presbyterian manse at 1102 North Vienna Street on "Presbyterian Hill," and it became the family home.

My father was ten years old when his family moved to Ruston. He soon met the little girl who was to become my mother: Fannie McLees, who was nine and lived with her widowed mother, her four sisters, and one brother on the other side of North Vienna Street.

There were staunch Presbyterians on both sides of my grandparents' house in Ruston. The Smiths at 1100 North Vienna Street and the Grahams at 1104. The Graham house was an impressive two-story white frame house with a large front porch, set far back from the street. A low stone wall ran in front of it, and whenever we visited Ruston, the first thing I did was walk on top of the wall from one end to the other and back again. Bachelor John P. Graham and his spinster sister, Helen, lived in the house which they had inherited from their parents. Both were very active in the Ruston First Presbyterian. John was for many years the clerk of session and also served as the historian of the church. Helen, if I remember correctly, played the organ at services, and John sang in the choir. They also hosted musical evenings at their home.

They lived long, decorous, pious, and proper Presbyterian lives, respected by their peers, and loved by many, including my aunts. Helen died first, followed a few years later by her brother. When the house was being cleaned out after John's death, the packers discovered in his closet a sizeable cache of women's dresses, all in his size.

When my aunt Kathleen retired from the University of Southern Illinois, she moved back to Ruston and the three of them spent their last years on North Vienna Street. All three aunts loved to travel and most summers after they retired, they were off to Europe or destinations more exotic. They came to see me several times during the years I lived in Europe. When they were in their eighties, they spent a month on an extensive trip around the world. During this last, long adventure, Aunt Kathleen sent me a post card from Venice that read: "We <u>loved</u> Venice. It wasn't nearly as dirty as India."

Shortly after she retired from teaching at Tech, Aunt Frances had an unexpected romance. Many years before, when she was a young student, she and her history professor, a Dr. Butler, who was a decade older than she, fell in love and became engaged. When she announced her engagement to her mother and her sisters, they just laughed. "Don't be ridiculous, Frances," One of them told her. "You can't marry that man!" "Why not?" she asked. "For one thing, you are much taller than he is!" She allowed herself to be bullied out of the engagement and broke it off. Dr. Butler left Tech, and she had no idea what happened to him.

As far as I know, Frances never had another relationship. When I was at Tulane, I started a poem about her, but never finished it. It began: "I had an aunt who was beautiful / But never married / In time she tarried / While the muscadine grew tightly round the pear / Shutting out both light and air."

One day, when Frances was almost seventy, while she had gone to do some shopping at the Piggly Wiggly supermarket, the telephone at 1102 North Vienna Street rang and Bill picked it up. "Is Mary Frances Fletcher there?" the caller asked. "No, she is not," Bill said. "Do you know when she will be back?" he asked. "No, I do not," Bill said. When Frances returned a few minutes later, Bill told her, "Someone called and asked for you, but I don't know who it was." It was not until a year later that Dr. Butler phoned again, and this time Frances answered the phone. He told her that he had married after he left Tech and that he had spent his life teaching at a college in Mississippi, not that far from Ruston. He told her that his wife had died. She told him that she was very sorry to hear it. "I've never forgotten you," he said. "And I've never forgotten you," she replied. Could he come to visit her? he asked. "I would like that very much, she said.

It was the beginning of an affair of the heart that lasted until he passed away about five years later. Frances told me that he had asked again to marry her. "I told him no, it was too late for that, but that I would be happy to be his friend." They began to take little trips together, with Frances driving. Their guardian angels must have been watching over them because she suffered from narcolepsy and often fell asleep in mid-sentence and probably never should have been behind the wheel of a car. They listened to music together and read books to each other. One of them, Frances told me, was an English translation of Manzoni's *I Promessi Sposi* (*The Betrothed*), a novel set during the plague that tells of the struggles of an engaged couple who finally after many years are able to wed.

I met Dr. Butler once when he and Frances visited Lafayette. He was very dapper, wearing a three-piece tweed suit, his Phi Beta Kappa dangling on a gold chain in front of his vest. He looked like he might have fallen out of the pages of a novel by Henry James. His language was as formal as his suit, and he always referred to Frances as "Dr. Mary Frances Fletcher." And he was still almost a foot shorter than she.

Aunt Kathleen, the youngest of the three maiden aunts and an unrepentant smoker, was the first to die. Then Aunt Bill, the oldest. When Aunt Frances was left living alone in the house on North Vienna Street, I tried to visit her as often as possible, though, since I was living at the time in North Carolina, it was not that often.

On my last visit, I mentioned that I had to be in Jackson, Mississippi, rather early the next day. I was sleeping in the front bedroom where I had slept on visits for more than half a century. I woke about 2 a.m. and went to use the bathroom that was next to the back porch, where Frances slept.

She heard me stirring and assumed that I was getting up to leave for Jackson. When I came out of the bathroom, she was already in the kitchen fixing me breakfast: eggs, bacon, toast, and coffee. There was nothing to do but eat it, thank her, get dressed, and drive off in the dark. As I maneuvered out of the driveway, she stood under the light on the front porch waving goodbye. It occurred to me that there was no one else left of the face of the earth who would get up uncomplainingly at that hour to make sure I had a good breakfast. She always signed her letters to me: "Devotedly, Frances," and devoted she always was.

Aunt Bill's Biscuits

Preheat oven to 425 degrees Fahrenheit.

Ingredients:
2 cups all-purpose flour
4 teaspoons of baking powder
1 teaspoon salt
1 tablespoon of unsalted butter
1 tablespoon of Crisco
1 cup of milk
About three drops of white vinegar
A board generously sprinkled with flour on which to roll out the flour
A rolling pin
A baking sheet or pan well-greased with cooking oil or melted butter.

Chill in the fridge the flour, baking powder, and the bowl they are to be mixed in for at least half an hour before making the biscuits.

Mix the dry ingredients and sift them twice. If you do not have a real sifter, you can accomplish this by putting the flour and baking powder and salt through a large sieve with the help of a spoon into a large measuring cup, then back into the bowl.

Cut the butter and Crisco into small pieces and gently work them into the dry mixture with your fingertips. Gradually add the milk and vinegar and mix it with a broad-bladed knife to produce a soft dough. Do not overwork.

Put the lump of dough on the floured board, pat it down and lightly roll until the dough is about ¼ inch thick. Use a small circular cutter, perhaps an egg cup, and cut out the biscuits.

Arrange them on a baking sheet or in a pan so that they do not touch. Brush them with the melted butter.

Put the biscuits in the fridge for about ten minutes before putting them in the 450-degree oven.

Bake for 12 to 15 minutes, carefully watching, until they are golden brown.

Makes about 24 tiny biscuits. If you end up with fewer, your biscuits are too large.

13

THE LONG AND SHORT LIFE OF GUINEVERE

When I was fifteen, I got my driver's license and bought my first car. I paid twelve dollars to a family friend for a 1923 Ford Model T that had seen better days. My parents did not object, believing the car safer than the motor scooters many of my friends and classmates were acquiring.

They were wrong, of course. For one thing, the exhaust pipe was broken off beneath the wooden floorboard and regularly set it on fire. I kept a bucket of water in reach behind the driver's seat with which to douse the flames before they reached the gas tank upon which I was sitting. I suspect the car was the first major challenge for my guardian angel. The car was not easy to start, and I often had a sore right arm from cranking to no avail. And sometimes it just stopped running without warning. I named it Guinevere, after the unfaithful English queen.

My parents banned me from using it on highways, so I stuck to back roads, roads that were not really roads at all, and the tops of levees along the bayou, places where there were even more challenges for my guardian angel.

A photograph shows Guinevere decorated for the 1952 Lafayette High School Homecoming Parade with three of my classmates in drag as the queen and court of Crowley High School, our rival in the big game.

Some months after this photograph was taken, while I was driving in a neighborhood behind the high school, I was amazed to see a tire rolling down the road in front of me and briefly wondered where it had come from before the car lurched forward and I realized it had broken off from the front axle.

I sold Guinevere as junk for fifteen dollars, which I used to buy a rhinestone bracelet as a Christmas present for my then high school girlfriend, probably the worst investment I have ever made.

14

ROBERT RAUSCHENBERG AND THE SWEET POTATO QUEEN

The first painting I saw by Robert Rauschenberg, an artist best known for his combines made with stuffed goats, old tires, and other *détritus trouvé*, looked very much like a Renoir. It was a portrait of his sister, my friend and classmate Janet, who looked exceedingly like a Renoir. She was certainly one of the most beautiful and voluptuous girls at Lafayette High School where she had been chosen the Sweetheart of the Future Teachers of America before going on to greater glory as the reigning monarch of the Opelousas Yambilee, the annual festival celebrating the sweet potato, one of southwest Louisiana's most important crops.

One year my father, who was president of the state college in nearby Lafayette, gave the opening speech at this event and an error in a headline in the Opelousas *Daily World* ended up in the *New Yorker*. The headline should have read: FLETCHER ADDRESS MARKS OPENING OF YAMBILEE, but the typesetter omitted a crucial letter so that it read instead: FLETCHER ADDRESS MARS OPENING OF YAMBILEE.

My father, who had a somewhat contentious relationship with a number of conservative local newspapers in southwestern Louisiana after having presided over the successful integration of the college in the 1950s, always felt that the mistake had been deliberate and that the typesetter himself had probably sent the headline to the magazine in order to collect the ten-dollar fee it paid for such items.

Janet Rauschenberg and I became friends in a Latin class taught by Dr. Grace Agate, the only PhD on the high school faculty. Dr. Agate seemed to think that because of her advanced degree her pupils could learn from her by some kind of intellectual osmosis, and she made little effort to instruct us. Usually, she spent our thrice-weekly hour together knitting or preparing a lesson for the Methodist Sunday School, leaving us in peace to translate (or not) passages from the textbook. Since she was quite deaf, chatting with other students was a pursuit that presented little peril. The class functioned as a social hour in which to get caught up on school gossip and develop friendships.

One morning Janet brought to Latin class a copy of *Life* magazine with a photo-essay about her brother and the work he was then doing. It consisted of arranging his wife, seaweed, and other objects on blueprint paper and exposing it to make collage-like prints. In the mid-1950s, to someone growing up is southwestern Louisiana, this seemed terribly avant-garde. I was very impressed.

Janet lived with her parents a few blocks from the high school in a neighborhood known as "the Saints" because many of the streets are named after prominent Catholic saints: Saint Francis, Saint Catherine, Saint Patrick, Saint Joseph, Saint Louis, and finally Saint Mary who, because of her greater importance, was given not a mere street, but a boulevard.

The house on Brookside Drive, between saints, had been designed for them by Robert, and it was like no other house in town. It resembled a stage set. The front of the house, facing the street, had a huge rectangular window made of many panes of glass. Behind it was a two-story living room with a balcony and, at one end of the room, a large white brick fireplace that went from floor to ceiling. Though it was a modest house, I found it very glamorous; the kind of house, to my mind, in which someone like Greta Garbo might live. On a living room wall hung the Renoir-esque Rauschenberg of Janet.

In 1968 I was living on the Avenue d'Eylau in Paris, within sight of the Eiffel Tower and only a few blocks from the Musée d'Art Moderne de la Ville de Paris. One October day I read in *Le Monde* that the vernissage of a large Rauschenberg exhibition was taking place at the museum that very evening. I had no invitation but decided to go anyway and try to crash the party. This proved very easy to do, and Rauschenberg was indeed present, looking amiable and obviously quite high on something.

I waited until he was more-or-less alone and then went up to him and said: "You don't remember me, I'm sure, but I'm from Lafayette and I met you several times when I was growing up. I was a good friend of your sister Janet." He looked startled and pleased. He grabbed my arm, held it tightly, and loudly proclaimed: "My sister!" Heads turned. I blushed. Fortunately, no flashbulbs went off. We chatted pleasantly about Lafayette for a few minutes, and then he got down on his knees and signed the exhibition poster I had bought for ten francs, greatly enhancing its value.

When I again lived in Lafayette in the 1970s and '80s, I saw Janet from time to time. I told her the story of my poster, and she gave me another. It is from Rauschenberg's 1988 Overseas Cultural Interchange Series. Janet told me that whenever Robert stayed in a hotel room, he always took down whatever was hanging on the walls and replaced it with some of his own art. This poster, she told me, he put up in his hotel room in Havana during the exhibition's stop in Cuba. It is not signed, but it does have four thumbtack holes made by the master.

Once I ran into Janet shortly after she had given a party to celebrate their mother's 80th birthday. Robert was not able to attend, but he had telephoned to ask what Janet thought their mother might like as a gift. "Milton (his first name by which he was known in the family), Mother has always wanted you to paint her a conventional pretty painting of flowers in a vase." "I'll do it!" he exclaimed.

He did do it and shipped the painting to Janet in a sleek and handsome, beautifully crafted wooden crate. At the party, Janet presented the crate to her mother and said: "Here is your present from Milton." Mrs. Rauschenberg eyed the crate unenthusiastically and said what she had been saying for years and years about her son's art. "My, isn't that interesting." "No, Mother," Janet said. "This is the box. The present's inside!"

15

THE REPUBLICAN PARTY COMES TO LOUISIANA

It came in the person of John Davis Lodge, the handsome Republican governor of Connecticut, invited by my father to speak to an assembly of students at Southwestern in the 1950s when Republicans in southern Louisiana were as rare as hens' teeth. According to an article in the *Lafayette Daily Advertiser*, Governor Lodge, from a distinguished New England family, told the students that knowledge, discipline, and faith were the virtues that they should cultivate. "The United States possess the talent, vitality and moral impulse to create enduring traditions and institutions," he declared. "We possess the means to knowledge and the capacity for self-discipline. But without faith, these two great virtues will be as swords that shiver in our hands." It was, according to the *Advertiser*, a very inspiring talk. Unfortunately, "Knowledge" was misspelled in the headline.

Lodge had been, just like Ronald Reagan, a Hollywood actor, and was married to a glamorous actress and ballet dancer. Between 1933 and 1938 he appeared in a dozen movies. In 1934, in what was probably the apogee of his screen career, he played opposite Marlene Dietrich in the Josef von Sternberg classic *The Scarlet Empress*. The next year, in *The Little Colonel*, he played the father of another future Republican politician: Shirley Temple.

The Second World War ended Lodge's Hollywood career and during the war he served as an officer in the US Navy. Because of his fluent French and his knowledge of Europe, where he had studied before entering Harvard, he was made a liaison officer between the American and French fleets. He seems to have served with distinction because after the war he was awarded both the Croix de Guerre and the Légion d'honneur by the French government.

And then he went into the family business: politics. He was the grandson of Henry Cabot Lodge, the Republican senator from Massachusetts who single-handedly kept the United States out of the League of Nations after the First World War, and the brother of Henry Cabot Lodge, Jr., a US Senator, ambassador, and Nixon's running mate in the 1960 presidential election.

When John Davis Lodge came to Lafayette, he was serving as the sixty-fourth governor of Connecticut.

My parents met Governor Lodge at the airport and were somewhat dismayed when he was also met and whisked away by a young blonde woman in a red Cadillac convertible who informed them that she was from Lake Charles and was the head of the Republican Party in Louisiana.

My parents were shocked when they discovered that Governor Lodge and the head of the Louisiana GOP had checked into the Gordon Hotel on Jefferson Street.

The next morning, Governor Lodge gave his inspiring talk to the Southwestern student body and faculty and then came to our house for coffee where he so impressed Gus, our servant, a lifelong Democrat, that he became a Republican on the spot, one of the very first in Lafayette.

After coffee, the blonde in the Cadillac drove Governor Lodge back to the airport to catch his plane, but evidently he missed it because he and the blonde and the Cadillac were spotted in several other locales in southern Louisiana over the course of the next week and appeared together at a Mardi Gras ball in Lafayette a full seven days after he was supposed to have returned to Connecticut.

In those days, what happened in Lafayette, stayed in Lafayette, and eventually Governor Lodge returned to his home state where he served out his term as governor and then had a long and distinguished career as a diplomat, serving as US ambassador to Spain, Argentina, and Switzerland. Today the portion of Interstate 95 that runs through Connecticut is named in his honor.

It also should be noted that while in Louisiana in the 1950s, John Davis Lodge may have laid, in addition to the head of the Louisiana Republican Party, the groundwork for the emergence of the GOP as the dominant party it is today.

16

LOUISIANA LIVE OAK SOCIETY

Dr. Edwin Lewis Stephens, the first president of what was then Southwestern Louisiana Industrial Institute (today the University of Louisiana at Lafayette), founded the Louisiana Live Oak Society to promote "the culture, distribution, preservation and appreciation" of the live oak tree (Quercus virginiana).

Dr. Stephens wrote an article for the April 1934 issue of the *Louisiana Conservation Review*, using as a title the first line of the famous poem by Walt Whitman: "I Saw in Louisiana a Live Oak Growing." In it he first suggested that such a society be formed. He wrote:

> I have been considering the live oak for some time and am coming to believe that the world does not realize what a splendid possession it holds in this tree. Why do we not form a Louisiana Live Oak Association? Let the membership be composed of the trees themselves.... I will volunteer my service for a time as Acting Secretary.... I suggest that the members of the Association shall consist of trees whose age is not less than a hundred years.... I, at present, number among my personal acquaintance forty-three such live oaks in Louisiana eligible for charter membership.

The first president of the society was the magnificent Locke Breaux Oak in Taft, not far from New Orleans, between Lake Pontchartrain and Lac des Allemands. It held the office until it was felled in 1968 by air and groundwater pollution. It was succeeded by The Seven Sisters Oak in Mandeville on the northern shore of Lake Pontchartrain. The current president has a girth of more than thirty-eight feet and is estimated to be about 1,200 years old.

Dr. Stephens should be pleasantly surprised at the evolution of his idea. The Louisiana Live Oak Society eventually changed its name to The Live Oak Society because its members are scatted over fourteen states and now number 6,757 ancient oaks.

When Dr. Stephens died, my father for a time took his place as secretary of the organization. His main duty, as the only human member, was to collect the "dues" from the membership, one hundred acorns from each tree, and see that they were planted somewhere.

In 1963, when the Joyce Kilmer Oak, the tree on the Rutgers campus that was said to have inspired Kilmer to write his famous piece of doggerel, died, as my friend Carl Selph remarked "probably of cumulative embarrassment," my father sent a replacement oak to the president of Rutgers, a Dr. Gross. The *Lafayette Daily Advertiser*, never my father's friend, ran a story about it under the headline: "Fletcher Sends Gross Present."

My father's gift was no doubt well-meaning but probably ill-advised. Whenever I drive on the New Jersey Turnpike, I am tempted to turn off at the Rutgers exit to see if the Louisiana oak survived. I doubt that it has.

17

LES VACHES DE M. MOUTON

When I was growing up in Lafayette, Louisiana, in the heart of Cajun country, it never struck me as odd that the most prominent family in town was named Mouton. It was only many years later, when I was explaining to a friend in France that the main street of my hometown, according to local legend, had been laid out by the cows of Mr. Mouton as they ambled from his plantation to the Bayou Vermilion, that I realized that "les vaches de Monsieur Mouton," which translates to "the cows of Mr. Sheep," did sound a little peculiar.

I grew up among many Cajun names: Arceneaux, Boudreaux, Broussard, Guidry, LeBlanc, Landry, but the name "Mouton" had a special resonance. Lafayette was founded by a Jean Mouton who had been expelled from Nova Scotia with his fellow Acadians by the British in 1754. On some early maps of the area, the town even appears as "Moutonville."

Jean Mouton's son, Alexandre, was the ninth governor of Louisiana, and Alexandre's son, Alfred, was the town hero, a brigadier general in the Confederate army. A statue in white marble of General Mouton, high on a pedestal, his arms proudly crossed and his beard longer than Robert E. Lee's, stood, until recently, in front of the old city hall.

For much of my youth, the mayor of Lafayette was another of Jean's descendants: Ashton Mouton, who rose to national prominence, not through his political acumen, but because in 1953 his twin daughters, born joined at their spines, were successfully separated at Oschner Clinic in New Orleans. It was the first time in my lifetime that someone from Lafayette made the national news. An article in *Time* magazine gave all the details, and I believe there was also a photograph in *Life*.

The doctor who delivered me had the very English name of Hamilton, but he was married to one of the most formidable Moutons in the history of Lafayette. "Tante Ruth," as she was known by all, was a pillar of the Catholic Church and was celebrated for both her piety and her strong personality. The Hamiltons lived not far from St. John's Cathedral, and Tante Ruth was thick with the bishop and all the priests of the diocese. She was generous with donations to the church and favors for the local clergy, who were constantly saying prayers and masses for her soul. They also helped her with more worldly matters, like allowing her to buy wine with a clerical discount from the same distributor who supplied sacramental wine for the Parish.

This led to an unfortunate event the summer that Tante Ruth decided, without mentioning it to her husband, to have a fine family tomb built for them in St. John's Cemetery.

Shortly after the plans had been drawn up and the material ordered, she received a phone call from the railway express agent telling her that a shipment had arrived for her at the station. "That must be the marble for the tomb," she thought and requested that it be delivered to her cemetery plot. It was not until she got another phone call from the cathedral sacristan telling her that three gravediggers were in a drunken stupor on her plot that she realized the shipment had not been the marble but her monthly allotment of wine.

The marble eventually did arrive, and the tomb was erected with the correct names and dates of birth prominently engraved on it, but Tante Ruth never got around to informing her husband of its existence. Then, shortly after the tomb was completed, one of her cousins died and was laid to rest in an adjoining plot. On a scorching August day under a blinding Louisiana sun, Dr. Hamilton looked up from the graveside service and was terribly shocked to see an impressive monument bearing his own name. He thought for a moment that he was having a heat stroke with accompanying delusions, and had he been of a more fragile constitution, the new tomb might soon have been put to the use for which it was intended.

My favorite story about the Moutons and death (Les Moutons et la mort), is the one the noted genealogist and calligrapher, Franklin Mouton, tells of his cousin, Alice, the youngest daughter of one of the many large Catholic families in Lafayette. According to established tradition, the youngest female in a family was expected to remain unmarried in order to look after her parents as they declined into old age. Alice, pious and obedient, never protesting, did exactly what she was supposed to do. Later rather than sooner, her parents passed, and after they were gone, Alice, by then quite elderly herself, continued to live alone in the family home, never wearing anything but black, never leaving the house except to go to mass and the grocery store. For these brief excursions she always covered her head with a shawl and may have lightly powdered her nose, but probably did not even own a lipstick. The years went by, and finally Alice also departed this life. Her death occurred soon after Mr. Delhomme, the local funeral director, returned from a week-long cosmetics seminar in Chicago eager to display his newly acquired skills. When Alice's relatives arrived for the wake, they thought they were in the wrong chapel. Alice was unrecognizable in her coffin. Her hair was permed and dyed red, her cheeks brightly rouged, her lips a slash of scarlet. "She looked," Franklin said, "like a hooker in a box."

18

THE PINK DRESS

My sister Lorraine was the smart one in the family. Rheumatic fever almost finished her off when she was a child, but she survived it and went on to become Valedictorian of her high school class.

When, in the 1940s, she enrolled as a freshman in the state college of which our father was president, he insisted that, in spite of her academic ability, she major in home economics. It was what girls were supposed to do in that day and age. It prepared them for their expected role as wife and mother and, if they had the misfortune not to find a husband, they would be equipped to support themselves by teaching the subject to younger hopefuls in high schools throughout the state.

She signed up without much enthusiasm for Miss Marie Caillet's dressmaking 101. One of her first assignments was, of course, to make a dress. She must have gone either to Heymann's or Saloom's, the two stores in Lafayette that sold yard goods, and picked out sufficient pink material for her project. She designed the dress, cut it out, sewed it together, and handed it in to Miss Caillet.

Miss Caillet returned it with a grade of D. Lorraine, who had never in her life made anything lower than an A minus, was so shocked that, without telling anyone, she went to the registrar's office and changed her major to chemistry.

Four years later she graduated and was accepted to LSU Medical School in New Orleans, but during the first semester, she discovered that she liked dissecting corpses even less than she had making dresses. So she dropped out and found a job as a chemist with Shell Oil in Houston.

One morning while riding to the Shell refinery on the company bus, she struck up a conversation with a handsome young engineer from California. We were all a little surprised when she announced the next year that she was leaving Shell to do graduate work in chemistry at the University of California. Soon she was enrolled at UC and living in International House in Berkeley, which just happened to be the hometown of the handsome young engineer on the bus.

Lorraine eventually married the young engineer, who was not only movie-star handsome, but as smart as she, and from an old and wealthy California family. They had a wonderful and exciting life together until his death from cancer in 2004.

"If Miss Caillet had given me even a C on that dress," Lorraine told me, "I probably wouldn't have had the courage to change my major and would have ended up teaching home economics for the rest of my life in some place like Gueydan or Eunice" (small towns in south Louisiana).

As things turned out, even the pink dress had a happy ending. My sister gave it to our aunt Maude Digby who had it altered and took it with her to Washington when President Eisenhower appointed her husband, Judge Sebe Digby, to the Federal Power Commission. Aunt Maud wore the dress to cocktail parties in Georgetown and possibly even to dinner at the White House. Wouldn't Miss Caillet have been astonished!

Roy Elliott Jr., Lorraine's husband, was the grandson of Joseph Henry Glide who was born in 1835 in Somerset, England, and grew up on his father's farm near the town of Taunton. Because he was a younger son and prevented by primogeniture from inheriting family property, he decided to immigrate to America. About the time of the California Gold Rush, he left Bristol on a ship named *The Manchester*, bound for Philadelphia. Once there he joined a party that was planning to travel overland to California, a trip that took six months. On the way he stopped in Denver and, in a poker game, won some California farmland. When he arrived in California, already a small landowner, he first found employment as a livestock buyer for a wealthy farmer in Grass Valley, north of Sacramento. A few years later he went into business for himself, gradually adding acres to the farm he had won in the poker game. By the late 1860s, he was a major landholder and cattleman in the state. By the time he died in 1906, according to his obituary in the *Woodland Daily Democrat*, Glide "owned more than 30,000 acres of land in Yolo county." He had also been a pioneer in reclaiming swamp lands along the Sacramento River and "owned at the time of his death about 3000 acres of reclaimed land—as fine as any that the sun shines on . . . [and] also owned many acres of land and many head of stock in Colusa, Glenn, Solano, Kern and Tulare counties."

Glide specialized in thoroughbred Shorthorn cattle and Merino sheep, both of which he imported from Europe. He raised them on a very large scale and soon began exporting them back to Europe and elsewhere. An article in the *Woodland Daily Democrat* of July 13, 1906, under the headline: "SHEEP FOR AUSTRALIA/ Registered French Merinos to be Sent from Glide Farm," reported that "C.E. Binnie of Sydney, Australia" had arrived to visit the Glide farm and "arrange for the purchase of a number of French Merino sheep, to be used for breeding purposes in Australia." The article continued: "It is but a short time since Mr. Glide exported to South Africa 60 head of sheep. . . . Another large shipment will be made to

Honolulu next week. Mr. Glide exports 500 head of sheep annually to France, England, Germany, Africa and Australia."

Glide exhibited his sheep and cattle at state and county agricultural fairs, including the California State Fair in Sacramento, and, according to his obituary, "always carried off the first prizes."

In 1871, Glide married Elizabeth (Lizzie) Snider, who had been born in northern Louisiana. Her father, a graduate of the Medical College of the University of Louisiana (which later became Tulane Medical School), had trouble earning a living in Louisiana after the Civil War and moved his family to California in 1868, settling in Sacramento where he soon became one of the leading physicians of the city.

Lizzie was a devout Methodist and became an ardent supporter of Methodist charities to which she generously donated her husband's money. Mr. Glide, who was far less philanthropic than she, once refused to give her the money for a charitable endeavor, so without telling him, she hocked all her jewels. One evening Mr. Glide happened to pass the window of a jewelry store in Sacramento and recognized his wife's gems. He purchased them back and thereafter kept them in a safe in his office. Whenever Lizzie wanted to wear them for an evening out, she had to go to his office to get them and then return them to the safe when the evening was over.

Mr. Glide, after a rather lengthy illness, died in October of 1906. When his will was read, the Glide's five children (Joseph Jr., Elizabeth, Mary, Thornton, and Eula) were horrified to learn that all of his "real, personal and mixed property" was left to his wife. The children were given $5 each.

They, of course, had visions of the family fortune disappearing into the coffers of the Methodist Church. The two boys, Joseph and Thornton, sued their mother, accusing her of exercising undue influence on her husband while he was of unsound mind. A lengthy court case followed, covered in detail by the local press. Finally, in July of 1907 the will was broken. Mrs. Glide was given "the widow's share, or half the community property and the residue of the estate . . . divided among the five children."

But the Methodist Church need not have worried about diminished sums flowing from its great benefactress. Shortly after the case was settled, oil and gas, lots of it, were found on land the Glides owned near Bakersfield. Lizzie proved to be surprisingly adept at negotiating leases with the oil companies that wished to extract it, and she greatly increased the already considerable wealth of her family. Soon there was more than enough money to go around. Even with her excessive (or so her family thought) philanthropy, there was enough left to make her descendants rich for generations to come.

Lizzie Glide's first major project with her new-found wealth was the Mary Elizabeth Inn, a Methodist residence in San Francisco for young women who came to the city looking for work.

The Mary Elizabeth Inn, named after the Glides' two older daughters, opened in 1914 at 1040 Bush Street in San Francisco and, fulfilling Mrs. Glide's dream, was quickly filled with young working women, even though, as it turned out, according to her great-granddaughter, most were not engaged in the kind of work Mrs. Glide had in mind. In 1929, Lizzie bought a parcel of land on the corner of Ellis and Taylor Streets in San Francisco and began construction of a Methodist church that she conceived of as a memorial to her late husband. Two years later Glide Memorial Methodist Church opened its doors to serve a wealthy and conservative congregation, many of them friends and relatives of Mrs. Glide.

For the next three decades, Glide Memorial served the congregation that Lizzie intended it to serve and, as the pastor who was going to change that, wrote, "well-to-do congregants followed Lizzie's vision for a traditional Sunday church where people dressed up, sang hymns, and read scripture." But by the early 1960s, that congregation was dying out or had moved away. In 1963, when the Methodist bishop of San Francisco invited a young African American pastor named Cecil Williams to take over the church, the congregation had dwindled to just thirty-five white members. What happened next is described on the church's website:

> Cecil changed both policies and practices of the conservative church, helping to create the Council on Religion and Homosexuality in 1964. In 1967, Cecil ordered the cross removed from the sanctuary, exhorting the congregation instead to celebrate life and living. "We must all be the cross," he explained. As the conservative members of the original congregation left, they were replaced by San Francisco's diverse communities of hippies, addicts, gays, the poor, and the marginalized. By 1968, the energetic, jazz-filled Celebrations were packed with people from all classes, hues, and lifestyles.

Sometime in the early 1960s, I remember getting a phone call from my mother who, with astonishment, asked: "Did you know that homosexuals are getting married in Roy's grandmother's church?" I did not and was also astonished. They still are, of course, and Glide Memorial is still the vibrant, unorthodox force for good in San Francisco that it has been since the 1960s.

Lorraine's husband, Roy, the son of Lizzie Glide's youngest child, Eula, grew up with a sister and two brothers on Eucalyptus Road in the Claremont neighborhood of Berkeley in a handsome brick mansion designed by Julia Morgan, the celebrated woman architect who is best remembered as the architect of William Randolph Hearst's San Simeon. Morgan was a family friend and designed houses for all of Lizzie's children.

Roy's father, Roy Sr., had been a star football player at the University of California where he also acquired a very un-Methodist reputation for partying which perhaps presaged his descent into alcoholism. When he was in his seventies, his wife finally had enough and banished him from the family home. He went to live in a residential club until the end of his days.

Roy's older brother, John, died fighting in the Second World War. His younger, brother, Thornton, together with his wife and two children, died in a boating accident on Lake Tahoe in November of 1950. He had been an aspiring photographer, a protégé of Ansel Adams, and at one time managed his photography shop in Yosemite.

Thornton's daughter, Linda, five months old at the time of the accident, had been left at home with her grandmother who, with the help of her daughter Elizabeth, raised Linda in the house on Eucalyptus Road.

Linda was too young to have any memory of her parents and siblings, and perhaps because the memories were too painful, her grandmother and aunt never mentioned them. It was only after she was an adult that she began to ask questions and found in a newspaper archive an article about the accident. The article mentioned that the sailing party included a friend from Chicago, also drowned, who had just arrived with about three hundred pounds of photographic equipment, which they had taken on the boat. Perhaps, she thinks, this unwieldy cargo contributed to the accident.

Roy Jr., Lorraine's husband, played rugby instead of football at UC, graduated with a degree in engineering, and served during the Second World War in the US Army Corps of Engineers, helping to build bridges in England.

After the war, Roy, like Lorraine, worked briefly at Shell before beginning full time to manage his family property. When he inherited vast tracts of farmland around Sacramento, he decided to sell it all and buy instead property that he could enjoy. The first piece was a thousand-acre ranch on top of Sonoma Mountain, bordering Jack London's ranch. The ranch came with a sprawling, one-story house with swimming pool and pond where Lorraine and Roy entertained friends on many weekends through the decades. With the help of a resident foreman, Roy raised cattle, though never profitably. A more profitable investment was a vineyard in the Napa Valley where Roy, even though himself a teetotaler, grew pinot noir grapes, which Lorraine insisted he sell to the Schramsberg Winery because they always gave the best annual party for their growers.

Somewhere near the Elliott family home on Eucalyptus Road in Berkeley lived an elderly widow with a small, ugly, unpleasant dog. Roy's mother often ran into her neighbor walking the dog and always had a treat in her purse for the little beast. In a ritual that developed over the years, Mrs. Elliott would give the dog a treat, pat it on the head, and say something along the lines of "What a nice little dog!" The widow was so grateful for the attention given to her *antipatico* canine companion that when she passed away, she left a large pear ranch near Sacramento to Roy and his sister. Roy worked with an architect to design and build a small house for an overseer, and for many years Lorraine and Roy sold the abundant pear crop to the Blue Anchor California Fruit Exchange.

Roy was a passionate sailor and grew up sailing in San Francisco Bay. He designed his own boats and had them built to order. The first one I knew was the *Pari II*. (There must have been a *Pari I* before my time.) Then he built the *Rani* (Lorraine's nickname, of course) a sleek forty-seven footer that once he sailed in the great TransPac Yacht Race from Los Angeles to Hawaii, finishing with a respectable time. Lorraine went on the voyage as cook and, as she had always done on shorter races, managed to pull a freshly baked apple pie out of the oven just as they crossed the finish line.

While looking for a place to keep their sailboats in the early 1960s, Roy and Bert Clausen, a friend from college days, found a recently abandoned brick factory in Point Richmond, on San Francisco Bay just north of Berkeley. The factory had made the famous "Richmond Red Bricks" from the red clay soil that lay around it and which were used in many buildings in the area, in the paving projects of the Bay bridges, and in the construction of the Palace Hotel in San Francisco.

Roy and Bert and were able to buy the factory for not very much money and together they built the Brickyard Cove Marina with spits of land extending into the Bay. It is a thriving upscale community of 200 houses with their own docks, a few apartment buildings, 250 boat slips, and the Richmond Yacht Club. The house that Roy and Lorraine built at the end of Sanderling Island, one of the spits, stands on pilings extending eighty feet into the floor of the bay. A retractable roof covers the dining room and a wall of windows faces the Bay, affording spectacular views, when the fog allows, of San Francisco and Angel Island. It is a handsome house, not an elegant house; an engineer's house in which everything works. The toilets always flush and there is always more than enough hot water.

The boat dock was torn away by the remnants of the tsunami that followed the Japanese earthquake of September 2011, perhaps the only casualty in San Francisco Bay of that disaster. The dock has been rebuilt but is empty now. After Roy died, Lorraine gave the *Rani* to the Richmond Yacht Club which sold it to help finance their young sailors' classes. Renamed, it is sailing out of Australia.

For a decade after Roy's death in 2004 from a recurrence of prostate cancer, Lorraine continued to live in the house and lead an active life. She loved seeing her friends, some of whom were from her days at International House in the 1940s. She often entertained at home, at the ranch on Sonoma Mountain, at the Richmond Yacht Club, and the tonier St. Francis Yacht Club across the bay in San Francisco. She was also very generous to her nephews and nieces, as well as to me. We had always had a special bond. Even when our jealous oldest sister tried to turn her against me, using the fact that I was gay as a weapon, Lorraine remained steadfast and supportive. We spoke by telephone several times a week, sometimes almost every day.

We spoke on the day before Christmas in 2013, when she was ninety, and she told me that she was preparing Christmas dinner for five of her friends . . . no turkey ... an early job in a food laboratory where she spent most of her days working on turkeys had left her with a permanent aversion to eating them. No, she was going to broil steaks with all the fixings, including our mother's recipe for cranberry dressing made with raw cranberries, oranges, marshmallows, pecans, and enough sugar to induce a coma.

We spoke on the day after Christmas and though I could not quite put my finger on it, I sensed that something was wrong. She told me, however, that her Christmas dinner had been a great success and all her guests seemed to have enjoyed the meal and had a fine time.

It was only the next time we spoke a few days later that she mentioned she had spilled boiling water on her leg while she was cooking Christmas dinner. "I didn't want to spoil Christmas," she said, "so I just wore a long skirt and didn't mention it." By then the burn was much worse and she finally went to see a doctor about it. But that incident marked the beginning of her decline. She was able to remain in her home with round-the-clock care for the next two years and peacefully passed away in her own bed in 2015.

When I was fifteen years old and had just finished my junior year at Lafayette High School, my parents let me spend the summer with Lorraine in Berkeley. She had finished her studies at Cal and, not yet married to Roy, was working at a food laboratory in San Francisco. For me it was an amazing summer. In the mornings I took chemistry at the Berkeley High summer school, and in the afternoons, I explored Berkeley. Telegraph Avenue was so very unlike Jefferson Street in Lafayette! There were fantastic bookstores and record shops and the cinema run by movie critic Pauline Kael where I was able to see art movies that never, ever made it to Louisiana. On weekends, we often made little excursions to places like Yosemite and Lake Tahoe, and occasionally went into San Francisco for a meal or to the theater or concerts. It was a summer that changed my life, and when summer was at an end, I wanted more than anything to remain in Berkeley. I thought I could never live happily in Lafayette again. I was given no choice. A dean at Southwestern was doing his naval reserve summer training at Treasure Island, and I was ordered to drive back to Louisiana with him and his family. Reluctantly, I did so. But that summer in Berkeley gave me taste of how I wanted to live my life. And it was but one of a multitude of gifts my generous, loving sister Lorraine gave me over her lifetime. I will miss her for the rest of mine.

19

MY BEAUTIFUL SISTER

My youngest sister, Flo, eight years older than I, was beautiful from birth. In a photograph of her as a child, in a silver frame on my mother's desk, she strongly resembled Shirley Temple, curls and all. When she grew older, I thought she looked a lot like Susan Hayward, a movie star I admired. Flo was the apple of my father's eye, and if he was overprotective of all of us, he was especially so of Flo.

When she was in high school, Flo always had dates on Saturday nights, and on Saturday afternoons our house smelled of the shampoo she was using to wash her hair. She devoted several hours to bathing, washing and drying her hair, and then primping at a vanity table to get ready the evening.

Flo, when she was young, could probably be described as "boy crazy." Once during the war, when an army convoy drove down the street by the side of our yard, she and her best friend, Nicky Nichols, wrote their names and addresses on pieces of paper, wadded them up, then stood by the side of the road, and threw them at the cutest looking guys in the open trucks. I don't know if she ever heard from any of them.

When she graduated from Lafayette High School, she enrolled in Southwestern but soon decided that she was not interested in getting a college education and, without telling anyone, dropped out. Of course, my parents soon found out and tried hard to persuade her to return. But she dug her heels in and refused.

"You'll end up with some horrible job, like working in a laundry," my father thundered at her. But she could not be persuaded.

When she was seventeen, she became engaged to Craig Clark, a young Mormon who was one of the cadets in a wartime officer training program at Southwestern. The cadets were allowed one free night each week to attend a church service and since there was no Mormon church in Lafayette, Craig would sign out for church but come over to our house instead. After a number of Wednesdays, he and Flo fell in love. The engagement was short-lived and ended when Flo went out to meet his family in Salt Lake City, where one of his uncles was a high-up in the Church of Latter-day Saints. After a week in Salt Lake, she decided that she really did not want to be a Mormon.

The next year she eloped with a sexy college student who was on the Southwestern basketball team. Glen Powell was tall, handsome, and moody. My one clear memory of Glen is of him sitting on kitchen steps pouting. My father was very upset by the marriage and did not try to hide his disapproval. Not surprisingly, the marriage lasted only a short time.

While Flo was getting a divorce, a quickie in Arkansas, she met her second husband who was there for the same reason. Charles Dupree Nevels turned out to be a much better choice than her first husband and was well liked by all the family. Smart, quiet, and easy-going, he had a degree in geology from LSU, was a veteran, and as part of the First Marine Division had fought in some of the major battles of World War II, including Guadalcanal and Okinawa.

After the marriage, unable to find a job as a geologist, Dupree, as everyone called him, found a job with Texas-based company that supplied equipment and services to oil fields in Texas and Louisiana. Within a decade, he was vice president of the company, and he and Flo and their two sons and two daughters were living in an upscale neighborhood in Houston. His future looked very promising.

But one day in 1959, he and the company president flew in the company plane to a meeting in New Orleans. The story we heard later was that the pilot remained in the bar at the airport drinking while Dupree and his boss went into the city, and later that day, when they took off for the return flight to Houston, the plane crashed into Ponchartrain Lake and disappeared into its muddy bottom. Flo, who had given birth to her fourth child just a short time before, spent several days and nights on the shore of Lake Ponchartrain waiting and watching until the wreckage and Dupree's body were finally pulled out of the mud. About a month after that, she had a hysterectomy. Three life-changing events in a row that affected her profoundly.

My father insisted that she and the children move back to Lafayette where he and mother could help look after them. Flo must have had mixed feelings about the move, but soon she gave in and returned to Lafayette.

She bought a modest frame house in one of the older neighborhoods, a definite step down from the gracious, comfortable brick house that Dupree recently had bought for his family in Houston.

Her oldest child, Paul, was just nine years old when Dupree was killed. Her older daughter was eight; her younger son was three, and her last-born, a daughter, was only two months old when her father was killed.

I was in California on active duty in the US Navy at this time, so I was not a witness to any of the difficult times she and her family were having, but I heard something about the understandable problems she was having adjusting to her new life, including her struggle to remain independent of the smothering love of our father.

I knew that eventually she started dating and that the men she was seeing, including, if I am remembering correctly, a plumber, were considered unsuitable by my parents.

They were, therefore, very relieved when she started seeing Ed Kyle, a wealthy bachelor oilman from a prominent south Louisiana family. And they were delighted when Flo and Ed eventually announced their engagement. He sold a modern dwelling he had built that suited his bachelor lifestyle and bought a conventional, columned mansion on the Bayou Teche to provide a comfortable home for his new wife and her four children. The date was set, and all seemed to be proceeding smoothly, but the day before the scheduled wedding, Ed's uncle died, so they decided to postpone the ceremony.

It never happened. Instead, Flo went to Texas and married a man she had met at a dude ranch the summer before.

My parents were in such a state of shock that they decided to leave town and visit me and Lorraine in California. Lorraine and I met them at the San Francisco airport and on the way to the car, Mother started telling us a rather garbled account of the elopement. At one point, she turned to Daddy and asked: "What was the name of that man Flo married?"

His name was Maurice Rimkus and he, too, was an oilman, though much less successful than Dupree had been and was looking for a way to get out of a business he really did not like. He was originally from the town of Uvalde in West Texas and wanted to move back there and be his own boss. His marriage to Flo was a ticket to do so. Using the insurance money that Flo had received from Dupree's death, they bought a large tract of farmland near Uvalde, and Maurice became the farmer he wanted to be with an everchanging team of immigrant Mexican workers he treated badly and housed in substandard buildings on the property. The one time I visited them, on my way to California, I stopped to ask directions from a man I saw working in a field. When I asked about the "Rimkus place," instead of giving me directions, he unleashed a string of profanities about "that son-of-a-bitch." I gathered that Maurice must not be too popular with his neighbors. I was not surprised. The few times I had been in his company, I sensed that he had a mean streak. I gathered from his remarks about his Mexican workers that he was a racist and guessed that he was probably also a homophobe, even though he was polite enough to me.

He and Flo lived on the farm for the next forty years, first in a rather ramshackle old farmhouse and eventually in a more modern house that they built on the property. When Maurice became too old and feeble to farm, they turned over the property to Flo's youngest daughter and moved into Uvalde. Flo decided that she could no longer stand to live under the same roof as her disagreeable spouse, so they built nearly identical small brick houses next to each other.

My main point of contact with Flo's family was with her firstborn, Paul, who grew up to be smart, kind, and thoughtful. He was very close to my parents, and they were major influences on his life. Armed with a bachelor's degree from LSU and an MBA from Stephen F. Austin State University, Paul had a very successful career in banking. And even when I was estranged from many of the other members of his family, we always stayed in touch.

In 2016, when Flo was eighty-nine years old, Paul told me that she had recently heard from her first fiancé, Craig Clark, the Mormon, and that he wanted to come to see her. Paul suspected that Craig, in his early nineties, was dying and wanted to see Flo one last time. Maurice, also in his nineties, had been in and out of the hospital and was also believed to be dying.

A few weeks later, I heard from Paul again. "Craig is in Uvalde seeing Mother and he's not dying at all. His wife died some time ago and he has just asked Mother to marry him." Flo accepted the proposal and told Maurice she wanted a divorce. He was furious and his anger seemed to bring him back from death's door. He refused to go along with it. But that was not going to stop Flo. She and Craig fled Uvalde in a rented SUV, driven by Craig's adult son, and headed for Salt Lake City. Not wanting people to talk, Flo moved into an upscale retirement home instead of going to live with Craig on his ranch.

Months went by, and finally Maurice died in September of 2017. I wondered if Craig and Flo were finally going to tie the knot. The news from Paul was not encouraging. Flo had not found any friends in the nursing home, did not like living there, and Craig terrified her by driving too fast in his Cadillac convertible on the country roads around Salt Lake City.

After a bit more than a year, Paul told me that Flo had decided to move back to Lafayette. He did not think it was a good idea. For one thing, it was completely changed from the town she had left almost sixty years before, and all of her friends there were dead. But she had her heart set on it, and Paul finally agreed to help her with the move. He found a well-run nursing home in Lafayette, made all the arrangements, supervised her move, and saw that she got settled in. He later told me that the only person coming to see her regularly was my former high school girlfriend.

I loved and always thought I had a special bond with Flo, though not as strong as I had with my middle sister, Lorraine. Sadly, we have not spoken since our mother's funeral more than thirty years ago. Influenced by the virulent homophobia of our oldest sister, and probably by Maurice, she cut me out of her life because I am gay.

Flo deserved to have a much happier, more fulfilling life than she has had. I like to remember her as the beautiful, boy crazy, feckless girl she once was before life and bad choices dealt her so many tragic blows.

20

HULLABALOO

—For V. B.

"Stay away from those," my father exclaimed, pointing at a billboard with a larger-than-life-sized image of a French Quarter stripper. It was late August of 1953, and he was driving me from our home in Lafayette to my freshman year at Tulane University to which I had been awarded an NROTC scholarship. His admonition, delivered on the Airline Highway on the outskirts of New Orleans, was the only talk about sex that I ever had with my father. I replied, "Yes, sir," and we let it go at that.

He dropped me off at Paterson House, the dorm to which I had been assigned, and shortly thereafter I met my roommate, a business major from San Antonio, Texas. He had a pimply face, greasy hair, a concave chest, a seemingly permanent scowl, and an unpleasant nasal twang. I immediately knew that we were never going to be friends.

Our room was on the second floor of Paterson House, a new brick men's dormitory presided over by our housemother, Mrs. Duncan, a widow of a certain age from Tidewater, Virginia, who with her Tidewater accent pronounced it: "Paterson Hoose." Many of us soon did the same.

I had received a number of invitations to fraternity rush parties, and even though I had decided that I was not interested in this frivolous and superficial side of college life—I was going to be a serious student—out of curiosity, I accepted a couple of them.

The first party was at the Phi Delta Theta house. I was instructed that I would be picked up at the dorm by one of the members. He was late and I grew very thirsty while waiting for him in the un-air-conditioned dorm room on a sultry late August evening in New Orleans. He finally arrived and I was herded with several other freshmen into his car. When we arrived at the frat house, the first thing I saw was an enormous glass punchbowl filled with purple liquid, a huge lump of ice, and floating pieces of fruit. It looked very enticing. "Kickapoo Joy Juice, the specialty of the house," one of the bros told me. My mouth by then was like cotton, and I quickly drank two full cups. That is all I remembered about the party when I woke up the next morning in my dorm bed with a throbbing head. One of the Phi Delts must have kindly returned me to my room and put me safely to bed. I did not, of course, receive a bid from Phi Delta Theta.

I behaved more responsibly the next night at the Sigma Alpha Epsilon house on Broadway, surrounded by mostly clean-cut and attractive young men who were from places like Lake Charles, Alexandria, Shreveport, Jackson, Mississippi, and Little Rock, Arkansas. SAE was the largest fraternity on campus, and its members came overwhelmingly from cities other than New Orleans.

The most prestigious fraternities for students from New Orleans were Delta Kappa Epsilon, Beta Theta Pi, and Alpha Tau Omega, and their members considered themselves, and on the whole they were, more cosmopolitan and sophisticated and were generally known as "the bad boys" on campus. The Dekes, in fact, a few years later, were banned from the campus when they hired a stripper as a summer replacement for their housemother.

The SAEs were as wholesome as students got at Tulane, where the celebrated joie de vivre and decadence of New Orleans infected the entire university, including, and perhaps especially, the faculty. For example, the lectures of Dr. Taylor, a specialist in eighteenth-century English literature, were said to be particularly brilliant on the days (rather frequent) when he showed up in class slightly inebriated. I once saw him cheerfully pedaling his bicycle across the campus, a half-empty whisky bottle bouncing in the basket.

I must have made a decent impression at the SAE house because I continued to receive their invitations, and I was definitely charmed by a number of the handsome young men who eventually asked me to be their brother. When a sexy freshman from Texas, whom I had met during rush, confided to me that if he got a bid to SAE, he was going to accept it, all my high-minded resolve to eschew fraternity life dissolved, and when I was asked to join them, I unhesitatingly said "yes."

As a pledge, I was assigned a "big brother," an active member who was supposed to look out for me, educate me in the ways of fraternal life, and keep me in line. Johnny Yarborough, my "big brother," was a junior in premed from Jackson, Mississippi. He was brilliant, a gifted musician, an ardent Baptist, and, even to my inexperienced eyes, an obvious queen, though no one else, even Johnny, seemed to recognize this. He enthusiastically dated campus beauties and extolled their charms like any normal heterosexual, though perhaps a tad less convincingly. Some of the active members were concerned that I was too quiet and introverted, and Johnny told me, without a hint of double entendre, that they thought he was the right one "to bring me out."

Johnny's efforts were probably not very successful, but I made it through pledge year and became an active member. However, early on I realized that I was not cut out for fraternity life, could not take it as seriously as I was expected to, and the proximity to good-looking guys was more frustrating than fulfilling. I knew well a lesson I had learned long before: a part of the real me must always be carefully hidden. I made myself fit in, while knowing that I did not fit in.

SAEs were expected to be "Big Men on the Campus," to play a large part in student government, be officers of various student organizations, and bring glory to their chapter by being visibly important. They were also expected to date Chi Omegas, their feminine counterparts, from the sorority house just down Broadway. Kappa Kappa Gammas were also acceptable, as were Pi Phis, but dating girls from other, lesser sororities was not encouraged.

I found it easy enough to date Chi Omegas, but I had no desire to shine on campus as a BMOC. What I enjoyed was the time I spent alone, studying, reading, listening to classical music on my phonograph, riding my bike to the levee, dreaming, and avoiding my roommate, which meant spending many hours at the Howard Tilton Memorial Library. Many years later, I was surprised to hear that it was a hot gay cruising spot, with horny guys driving from all over the state and even from Mississippi in hopes of an assignation. But in all the hours I spent there, hunched over books in the reading room, I was never aware of any untoward activity. For me it was a chaste and welcome refuge.

My freshman English teacher was a fey teaching assistant named Mr. Blouin. Our first assignment was to write an essay on the clichéd subject: "what I did last summer." I chose to write about a summer I had spent living with my sister in Berkeley, studying chemistry at Berkeley High. Hoping to impress with my sophistication, I focused on the evening we went into San Francisco to see Josephine Baker at the Geary Theater. I wrote about how I was blown away by the spectacle, and described how after the performance I made my sister wait in the alley by the stage door so that I could get Miss Baker's autograph, and how amazed I was when I realized that the tiny, almost-dowdy figure with no make-up, wearing a beret and a shapeless topcoat, who eventually exited the stage door and signed my program, was the towering, glamorous persona in feathers and jewels who had dominated the stage. I got an A on the paper and was launched as an English major.

During my sophomore year at Tulane, as an active member, I was still faithfully attending Monday night chapter meetings at the SAE house on Broadway, still taking most of my meals there, still hanging out with my bros, still going to their drunken parties.

That autumn, as usual, a new pledge class was inducted. Among them was a young man from Shreveport named John Slaughter who was quiet, dark-haired, attractive, laid-back, a little shy. I had a few conversations with him and found him pleasant enough and smart enough, yet I did not get to know him well. Soon, Felix, the pledge master, a premed major from Montgomery, Alabama, begin to pick on him and complain about him. I never knew why Felix took against John, but he started giving him a hard time, making sure that anyone who happened to be around heard his shrill attacks. John submitted quietly, but he was obviously bothered and embarrassed.

Just before we went home for the Christmas holidays, Felix hauled him before a chapter meeting and totally humiliated him. He recited a list of John's offenses, most of which boiled down to his not being enthusiastic enough a pledge, not spending enough time at the house, not having enough "Phi Alpha juice," a mysterious liquid that was supposed to course through all SAE veins. He held up John as an example of everything a pledge should not be. By the end of the meeting, John was in tears. I remember thinking when the meeting ended that John would probably drop out of the fraternity. Surely, he had had enough of Felix's constant bullying. I felt very bad for him and identified with him. His lack of fraternity spirit echoed my own. I was just a little more skilled at pretending.

Later that week, I was back in Lafayette and went to a Christmas party at The Town House, a social club that played a big part in the local Mardi Gras. My family did not belong, but I was often invited to their functions. Shortly after the festivities began, one of my fraternity brothers from Alexandria, who was dating a girl from Lafayette, arrived with the news that John Slaughter had been killed in a one-car auto accident that afternoon. He didn't know the details.

When classes resumed in January, John's mourning parents descended on the SAE house. They wanted to meet John's friends at Tulane and learn all they could about his life there. Everyone, of course, especially Felix, politely lied and told them what a great guy everyone thought John was and how he was one of the most popular and outstanding pledges, admired by everyone. The officers even decided that he should be initiated posthumously into the fraternity, which so pleased his parents that they donated a diamond-encrusted SAE pin to be given each year to "the best pledge." The ceremony was duly held, and John became in death something he probably would never have become in life: a full-fledged SAE. He was laid to rest in a cemetery in Shreveport under a granite tombstone on which was engraved his name, his dates, and in large letters: "S.A.E." His parents sent the fraternity a framed photograph of his grave, and it was hung in one of the front rooms of the house so that John would always be remembered by his brothers. I, for one, have never forgotten him.

The cruelty and hypocrisy made my stomach turn, and my drift away from the fraternity accelerated. I had already realized that I did not truly belong. I'd accepted their invitation for a wrong and hopeless reason. They were not really my tribe.

In any case, I'd begun make a few friends outside the fraternity. The main one was Nicholas Polites. I must have first laid eyes on Nick in the autumn of 1953 when we both began our freshman year at Tulane and were in several of the same classes. But we were not to speak until several years later.

I had heard of Nick from his aunt Mario (Yes, that was her name. It is not a typo.) who lived in Lafayette and was a family friend. She had told me about her nephew and said that we *must* become friends because we had so many interests in common. She had told Nick the same thing about me. Therefore, we both carefully avoided each other until we were brought together in a philosophy class during our junior year. The class was taught, if what transpired in the classroom can be described as teaching, by the egotistical chairman of the philosophy department, James K. Feibleman. His lectures consisted largely of name-dropping anecdotes about his interactions with famous people. One that I remember began: "When Albert and I were discussing the Theory of Relativity...." Autodidact Feibleman came from a wealthy New Orleans family, had never finished college, but had published a card catalogue drawer full of books: novels, poetry, tomes on philosophy, and other erudite subjects. He had recently married Pulitzer Prize-winning New Orleans author Shirley Ann Grau, a former student who was half his age.

His lectures were excruciatingly boring, and Nick and I out of desperation finally began to talk to each other. Soon we were kicked out of class for it. We discovered that we really did have a lot in common and that is when our friendship began.

For my junior year, I decided to live off campus and moved into a basement room that I shared with thousands of cockroaches on Robert Street, half a block off St. Charles Avenue and a dozen blocks from Tulane. Nick was living with his family on nearby Arabella Street. We both had bicycles and often rode them together to the Latter Memorial Library on St. Charles to listen to and check out classical LP records. We had long, high-minded conversations about music and literature, shared a number of the same enthusiasms and, to be truthful, were both cultural snobs, proud of our rarified and precocious tastes that we thought set us apart from the usual Tulane undergraduates.

Nick's father owned a restaurant on St. Charles Avenue, not far below Lee Circle, on a block that was visibly in decline. The Polites Grill was not a fancy eatery, more of a diner really, with a menu that reflected the Greek heritage of Nick's father.

Their house, on oak-lined Arabella Street in the heart of the fashionable Garden District, was rather grand, but its double garage held only one ancient Plymouth. I suspect it was Nick's mother, Eugenia, who always pushed her husband to live a bit beyond their means, a character flaw she passed on to Nick.

Eugenia was very unlike her sister in Lafayette. Mario was a short, smart, no-nonsense, closeted lesbian who ran the public relations office for the university. Eugenia, her younger sister, was tall, hyper-feminine, and high strung. She was also a celebrated Mrs. Malaprop and Nick enjoyed recounting her manglings of the English language. Once she let out a loud scream while she was looking in a mirror. "What's wrong?" an alarmed Nick asked. "I have a conjunctive eye!" she told him. Another time, when she was planning a cocktail party, she sent Nick out to buy some "agnostic bitters." One summer, Nick and I went with Mario and Eugenia to spend a day on the beach of Ship Island in the Gulf of Mexico off Biloxi. I was lying on a towel next to Eugenia when a motorboat went by. She raised up off her towel, peered at it and said, "Look, Joel. There goes a P. T. A. boat." A few years later, I was having lunch with Nick and Eugenia at the Polites Grill. A seedy looking waitress was leaning up against the counter chewing on a toothpick. Eugenia, to get her attention, snapped her fingers and shouted: "Garçonnière!" Nick would always say the same thing after one of his mother's malapropisms: "Isn't she marvelous!"

In the living room of the house on Arabella Street, above a Steinway grand, was a full-length portrait of Eugenia by a noted New Orleans artist. It was reminiscent of the nineteenth-century German painter Franz Xavier Winterhalter, famous for his depictions of the Empress Eugénie. After the death of their parents, Nicholas and his brother, Demetri, donated the portrait to the Louisiana State Museum. When racketeer Edwin Edwards beat racist David Duke ("Vote for the Crook," the bumper stickers read) for governor of the state, he chose it from the works in the museum to hang in the Governor's Mansion in Baton Rouge. Nick and Demetri were amused; Eugenia would have been thrilled.

For my senior year, I moved back into a campus dormitory but continued to spend much time with Nick. Although I had grown away from the fraternity, I still attended some of its functions and felt its pressures to conform. And I still pretended to others, if not to myself, that I was heterosexual.

Just before my senior year began, I had an unnerving experience. Under a hot and blinding September sun in the French Quarter, I nervously paced up and down trying to get my courage up to enter Laffite's Blacksmith Shop, then a notorious gay bar I had heard whispers about. I finally plunged in. While I was standing just inside the doorway, waiting for my eyes to adjust to the dark, a fruity voice came out of it: "Well, if it isn't Joel Lafayette Fletcher the Third!" Thoroughly traumatized, I turned and fled back to my dorm room and back into the closet. (Many years later, when I returned to live in Lafayette for a decade after my repatriation from Europe, I finally figured out who must have outed me in Laffite's: a flamboyant queen named Beverly Broussard who worked for the Southern Pacific Railroad. He would have known of me, though I wouldn't have known him. His mama had wanted a little girl instead of a little boy and had done everything in her power to transform him into one. When Beverly was a teenager, he and his mama used to take the Sunset Limited to New Orleans for the weekend. They would check into the Roosevelt Hotel and then go shopping on Canal Street for matching outfits. Later, wearing their new apparel, together they would cruise the Sazerac Bar trying to pick up men.)

The autumn of my senior year, still trying to become what I was not, I began to date a Newcomb coed from Cincinnati, largely encouraged by Nick who liked her and thought she was very intelligent. She also looked a lot like one of my idols: Lotte Lenya, whose recording of her husband Kurt Weil's *Three Penny Opera*, I had l almost worn out. As a German major, she shared my enthusiasm for Weil and Lenya, but I am sure she would have been horrified to learn that her resemblance to "Pirate Jenny" was part of her attraction. She was also the great-grandniece of Ralph Waldo Emerson, whose essays I had just been reading in a course on American transcendentalism. It was another real plus for someone majoring in English. And I realized it also enhanced her standing in the eyes of my family, especially my literary aunt Frances who had a PhD in English literature and taught it at Louisiana Tech in Ruston.

When I brought Ellen home to meet my parents, my maiden aunts were also visiting, perhaps on purpose to inspect my new and seemingly serious girlfriend. When I introduced Ellen to them, Aunt Frances grasped her hand and said: "My dear, you look *just* like Ralph Waldo Emerson!" I doubt that Ellen was pleased but at least she did not react as my high school girlfriend, Rhonda, did when she met Frances for the first time. Frances demanded: "My dear, do you know who lived in Dove Cottage?" Rhonda burst into tears and ran out of the room.

Ellen was a Kappa Alpha Theta, and even though she had joined when she attended another university before transferring to Newcomb, my fraternity brothers were silently (and some not so silently) disapproving. SAEs simply did not date girls from that sorority!

Undeterred by the scorn of my bros, of whom I was seeing less and less, by the time we graduated that spring, I had given Ellen my diamond SAE pin, and she considered us engaged. We cuddled and smooched a lot but never went "all the way," not unusual for those puritanical and hypocritical times when much was made of girls saving themselves for their wedding night. I was secretly thankful for the excuse.

Upon graduation, I received an NROTC commission as an ensign and was assigned to an aircraft carrier based in San Francisco, then as now a city of irresistible gay temptations. Although I kept up the pretense of being a butch young naval officer, when I was away from my ship I began to have a few gay adventures. A surprise visit from my "fiancée" ended our relationship. I explained nothing, but my lack of interest was obvious. Baffled and in tears, she flew back to Ohio.

For the three years that I was on active duty, I corresponded sporadically with Nick but had really lost touch with him by the time I was honorably discharged in spring of 1960.

He showed up in San Francisco some months later with an old address he had for me. It was the apartment of a by-then ex-lover. He knocked on the door and found a gathering of people who knew me. When he said that he was "looking for Joel Fletcher," he was surprised to hear some of the places they suggested that I might be found. When we did manage to connect, he told me: "You were my *last* straight friend! I've been telling people about you for years!"

Our friendship was rekindled on a more honest and solid basis. There was no reason to keep secrets anymore. We remained friends until his death more than half a century later.

And little by little, I discovered that I was not the only SAE from Tulane who was hiding his private life. A few years after graduation and out of the Navy, I was showing an English friend the sights of New Orleans during Mardi Gras. One afternoon we squeezed our way into the orgiastic crowd at Dixie's Bar of Music. After a few minutes, I spotted Buddy Bass, who during my senior year had been our "Eminent Archon," the fancy title, borrowed from ancient Greece, given the president of SAE chapters. He was talking to someone at the bar. I panicked and told my friend: "We've got to get out of here right away." When he asked why and I told him, he laughed. "And why do you think he's here?" In the end, my English friend went back to Lake Charles with Buddy for a romantic post-carnival week-long affair.

And among all those clean-cut and handsome young SAEs, dating Chi-Os and striving to be BMOCs, there must have been others in the same dark closet. Through the years I have come across a few, some of whom even married Chi-Os and lived, as best they could, their double lives. I consider myself to be one of the lucky ones who managed to escape and lived to tell the tale.

21

INFORMATION FROM THE OTHER SIDE

—For S. S. L., with love

I met Gordon and Stephen in the late 1950s on board the aircraft carrier USS *Bennington*, then known as the unluckiest ship in the US fleet because of a series of explosions and other tragic events on board. Gordon, Stephen, and I had received our commissions through NROTC scholarships: Gordon at UC Berkeley, Stephen at Stanford, and I at Tulane. There were quite a few NROTC officers on board the *Bennington*, and we made a strong contrast to the other young officers who had graduated from the Naval Academy or come up through the ranks. For one thing, we were all much more knowledgeable about the world outside the navy and felt that we were vastly more sophisticated and interesting than our brother officers who had not had the same exposure to the wider world. They, on the other hand, considered us amateurs, dilettantes in a life they took very seriously. Some of us were no doubt truly insufferable. Most of us, with no thought of making a naval career, were marking time till our release from the navy. Probably because the world was at peace, we did not take our mission all that seriously. We tried to be competent officers, but most of us were far from "gung ho." We joked among ourselves that the *Bennington*, which was actually named for a Revolutionary War battle, was the only ship in the US Navy named after a girl's college.

    I reported aboard the *Bennington* in June of 1957, just after it had returned from a cruise to the western Pacific and entered the Hunter's Point Shipyard for a complete overhaul. An unfortunate, if not tragic, event had occurred during the cruise that confirmed its status a jinxed ship. While it was docked in Sydney, Australia, a group of college students dressed as pirates sneaked aboard the afterbrow, made their way undetected to the bridge, found and pulled an alarm, and declared the ship captured. It was merely a college prank, but the US Navy was not amused. The captain of the ship at the time never made admiral, and the young lieutenant (a graduate of the US Naval Academy who had intended to make a career in the navy) who that fateful evening had been the officer of the deck, last I heard had become a used car salesman in Southern California.

The day I reported aboard the *Bennington*, I was assigned to the gunnery department, given a cabin, and completely forgotten for the next three months while the interior of the ship was noisily torn apart and put back together again. For most of that time I sat in my cabin wearing a pair of earplugs while reading Proust and a great deal of Henry James, something I had long wanted to do. In the evenings, I was usually free to leave the ship and explore nearby San Francisco, which I did with great enthusiasm and less discretion than was wise.

The overhaul was finished, and the *Bennington* was engaged in doing air operation exercises out of San Diego when Gordon and Stephen reported for duty. By that time, I had already been aboard for a year, and more or less knew the ropes. There were quite a few *simpatici* junior officers on board with whom I had become friendly, but it soon became apparent that I shared a special bond with Gordon and Stephen.

They were posted to the *Bennington* just in time for a cruise to the western Pacific, with Tokyo, Subic Bay, and Hong Kong the ports of call. Gordon soon organized a class in spoken Japanese, one of the six or seven languages in which he was allegedly fluent. Stephen and I both signed up for it, and that was where we got to know each other. Gordon was a patient teacher. He seemed always in a good humor, had an infectious laugh, and a great enthusiasm for life and learning.

The classes were lots of fun, though I did not learn much Japanese, just a few basic phrases, and upon arrival in Yokosuka, my initial attempt to communicate was so discouraging that I did not try again. The first person I encountered on leaving the ship was a tiny, stooped, and ancient-looking shipyard worker wearing overalls. "Ohayou gozaimasu," I greeted him warmly. He looked at me blankly for a moment, then turned, unzipped his overalls, and began to urinate on the pier.

As soon as we had a chance, Gordon, Stephen, and I contrived to go on liberty together, and it was in Japan that our friendship began to flourish. Our first excursion was by train to Kamakura where, under a drizzle from a leaden sky, we walked down a broad graveled path, lined with firs and crêpe myrtles, to gaze at the monumental bronze Daibutsu Buddha. After we had had our fill of the Buddha and were thoroughly soaked by the rain, we went back to the station and waited for a train to Tokyo.

It was still drizzling when we arrived at Tokyo Station an hour or so later. We were surrounded by a sea of waist-high umbrellas as we walked, dodging cars and umbrellas, to the Ginza where the willow trees looked unreal and out of place in the glare of neon lights. By that time, it was early evening. We found a restaurant and feasted on *sukiyaki*. After the meal, we came upon a Kabuki theater where a performance had just begun. Gordon insisted that we buy tickets and go in. The performance was fascinating and not altogether mystifying because the mime was so beautifully performed.

When the performance finished, we decided to make a night of it and take an early train the next morning back to Yokosuka and the *Bennington*. We strolled along the Ginza until we came to the Shirobasha Tea Room, a large faux-Victorian establishment with stained glass windows and classical statuary. We found a table next to a stone basin filled with water and well-stocked with carp. Two attractive young women seated on a balcony were watching us. Since liquor was not served at the Shirobasha Tea Room, we ordered flavored ices. Soon the young women from the balcony were standing beside the basin, laughing and throwing bits of bread to the fish. They both wore sheath dresses with high collars. The older one had lighter colored hair and a plumper face.

She sat beside me. The younger one sat next to Stephen. One of them called out to a friend, and soon the friend joined us and sat next to Gordon. We finished our ices and then, at the suggestion of one of them, we left the tea room, and the six of us crowded into a taxi. We soon left the brightly lit Ginza and turned down a very dark street and drove for what must have been several miles.

The older girl put her head on my shoulder and softly sang American songs in my ear. She took a small vial out of her purse and put a silver bead in her mouth. "Sen-Sen," she said and put one in my mouth. I did not let her see it roll from my lips to the floor of the cab. "This is the Meguro district," she told me. The cab stopped and we went into one of the many tiny bars lining the street, the Kilroy Bar. There were two American soldiers sitting at the bar with two Japanese girls who were not as attractive nor as well-dressed as the girls we were with. The music of George Shearing and Erroll Garner was playing on a radio. "I like cool jazz," the girl told me. Stephen's girl was making quite a to-do over him. "She very young and not know anything," my girl told me. "She think he look like popular singer, Paul Anka." After a pause, she added: "I think you look like Alec Guinness." I was not particularly flattered. The jazz program ended, and the radio began to play rock 'n' roll. "You know that Elvis the Pelvis have brother named Enis the Penis?" she asked. She led me to the dance floor, and as we danced, she slid her leg between my legs. Then we went back to the bar and she sat on my lap and we kissed, and, innocent that I was, I wondered if I was going to catch VD. I swished the beer I was drinking around in my mouth, hoping it would serve as a disinfectant. She told me that she liked me because I was polite to her and spoke to her in a soft voice.

"No, we cannot stay with you tonight. We have to be back on-board ship," we lied, and they were disappointed because, they said, they really liked us and thought that we really liked them. But we were not going to sleep with them. "We will take you to a station near here where you can catch a train to Yokosuka. It is a Japanese custom; the girls see the boys away." "No, we must go back to Tokyo Station to meet some friends," we lied again for we knew that the next train for Yokosuka did not leave until early in the morning, and it was just half past eleven. But we had to leave them because their drinks were costing us too much money, and we were not going to go to bed with them. We went to get coffee at a little coffee stand next door, and in the brighter light I looked at the girl I was with and saw the heavy pencil lines beneath well-plucked eyebrows, the imperfections in her complexion, the age in her eyes. "I like you," she told me again. "You come back to see me?" "In four weeks," I lied yet once again. "In four weeks, you meet me again? I give you my address." She wrote it on the back of one of my cards. Her room number and two telephone numbers.

We took a taxi to the Imperial Hotel, the Frank Lloyd Wright masterpiece now destroyed, where we had arranged to meet some of our other officer friends. We explored the public spaces and then slept for a while in the comfortable chairs in the lobby. Before dawn, Gordon, Stephen, and I woke and spent an hour prowling through the streets around the hotel. We found a little café that was open, went in, and had a bowl of soup. And then it was time to head for the station.

The *Bennington* called in a few other ports before heading back to the States. While we were in Subic Bay in the Philippines, Gordon and I signed up for a bus tour to the resort town of Baguio. About thirty sailors and just a few officers were along for the ride through the green and mountainous countryside north of Manila. Gordon and I roomed together in a simple guesthouse and took long walks around the town and by the lagoon in Burnham Park. He confided in me his plans to attend a Lutheran seminary when he was released from the navy. As a seriously lapsed Presbyterian, I respected his strong beliefs, but could not really understand them. And his religion did not seem to lessen his appetite for life. I wrote in a journal that I kept at the time about how much I enjoyed his company, his spontaneity, his apparent and infectious enjoyment of the material world. I recorded that he told me "Each day is something new!"

When the ship anchored off Hong Kong, Gordon, Stephen, and I spent a few days exploring. In the late 1950s it seemed a quiet, provincial city that still retained a very British flavor. It did not then have the prosperity and bustle we had seen in Tokyo. We bought cheap tailor-made suits and trousers and jackets which came apart at the seams soon after we got back to San Diego. We took a rickshaw ride up to the romantically situated Foreign Correspondents' Club in which all the naval officers were given an honorary membership and had a meal together on one of the floating restaurants in Kowloon. I have a postcard photograph of the three of us on our way to the restaurant, smiling broadly and wearing our new suits that had not yet begun to disintegrate.

We also found a bookshop and browsed for an hour or so. I came out with what I thought of as curiosities: a copy of Mao's *Little Red Book* and a thin volume titled *Saturday Afternoon at the Mill and Other One-Act Plays*. The latter had a note that described the themes and methods of the plays as reflecting "the tremendous strength, and the progress made, in China today." In other words, they were blatant propaganda.

On the ferry back to the ship that evening, we ran into Ltjg Krog, a dedicated and gung-ho Naval Academy man who had the misfortune to have me as his junior officer of the deck and Stephen as his junior officer of the watch. He did not disguise his scorn for our lack of enthusiasm for the navy, and it seemed to gall him that we performed quite competently, giving him little to complain about. But on long, dull watches in the middle of the night or early morning when there was not much to do while steaming through a seemingly calm and empty sea, Stephen and I had a great deal to say to each other but had very little to say to Ltjg Krog. We discussed literature, quoted favorite poems to each other, laughed at arcane literary jokes and allusions. We must have seemed real smart-asses to Krog. When we ran into him that night on the ferry, we exchanged a polite, if curt, greeting. Then he spied the little package I was carrying with the logo of the bookshop. "What's that you're reading, Fletcher?" Krog asked. I pulled the two books out and showed them to him and was taken aback by his reaction. "Communist propaganda!" he shouted. He fixed me with a stern look: "Don't you know that you could be court-martialed for bringing that stuff on board." "Well, I just bought it to see what it was like. I promise I'll destroy it," I lied, "as soon as I've looked through it. We have to know what the enemy is thinking if we are going to defeat them," I said, trying to look as sternly at him as he was looking at me. He seemed somewhat mollified. A few weeks later, on one of the long, dull night watches, while Krog studied a leadership manual, Stephen taught me the words to the Italian Communist Party marching song. "Avanti popolo! Avanti popolo! Bandiera Rossa, trionfera!" On the rest of the voyage home, we often crooned it softly under Krog's nose.

On the cruise back to the United States, even though I did not feel myself fully qualified, I received my letter of qualification as officer of the deck, and I was given a watch section which included Gordon as my junior officer of the watch. My immediate assistant, the junior officer of the deck, was an Ensign Wynne who was clumsy, nervous, and had both BO and halitosis. It was hard not to notice his unpleasant smells because he had a way of getting up very close whenever he had something to tell you. He stepped on toes both literally and figuratively. Gordon was good company, but he was not an ideal watch officer. He had excelled in seminars at Berkeley where he had time to consider all sides of a question and thoroughly discuss them. It was very different on the bridge where decisions had to be made instantly and wrong choices could mean disaster. He was obviously very uncomfortable. But in spite of these handicaps, we managed to stand our watches on the return voyage without mishap.

When we got back to the States, we spent a few weeks tied up at Alameda, across the bay from San Francisco. One night when Gordon, Stephen, and I had liberty, we planned to meet for a drink at the Buena Vista Café near Fisherman's Wharf before going out to dinner. Stephen and I were there at the appointed time. Gordon showed up more than an hour later. "I'm sorry that I'm so late," he apologized, "but I was having an important conversation with my grandmother, and I couldn't get away." "Where does your grandmother live?" I asked. As best I could remember, he had never before mentioned his grandmother. Gordon gave a hearty laugh. "She doesn't," he said. "She's been dead for twelve years." After spending so much time with me and Stephen on our cruise to the Orient, Gordon finally felt comfortable enough with us to share his secret: he was often in contact with relatives, friends, and even strangers who had passed on. Stephen and I listened without comment as Gordon related how he had discovered his gift for communicating with the departed and had been doing so since he was very young. Somehow, coming from Gordon, Stephen and I agreed later, it all sounded very believable. The Gordon we had got to know in the past few months was always so literate and articulate and sane.

In the future, whenever Gordon mentioned a conversation he had had with someone, it was not always clear if the person was living or dead, and I always thought it rude to ask.

Soon the ship went back to San Diego and started the boring routine of spending Monday to Friday cruising around Catalina Island doing air ops and various training exercises. The more I got used to being on the bridge, the more relaxed I became about it. Gordon, on the other hand, seemed to grow more apprehensive and depressed. Weeks and weeks passed. And then one evening he knocked at my stateroom.

"I've something important to tell you."

"What is it?"

"God wants me off the watch bill."

There was a pause while I tried to find something to say. Finally, I got out, "Well, Gordon, you better tell the navigator. He's the one who takes care of watch bill assignments." After Gordon left, I went to find Stephen and told him what Gordon had told me. "What do you think will happen to him?" I asked Stephen. "They'll probably take him off the ship and send him somewhere for psychological evaluation," Stephen said. "We know and love Gordon and can accept his little quirks, but I don't think the US Navy will be as understanding." "Probably not," I agreed.

Gordon did inform the navigator of his conversation with God. And an amazing thing occurred. He was, just as God wished, taken off the watch bill, and, logically, I suppose, since he had a direct line to God, was made the ship's assistant chaplain. The senior chaplain on the *Bennington* did need a lot of help. He was an alcoholic Catholic priest who was often drunk on board. Someone had joked that one morning after he finished saying mass he blurted out: "Lesh run through the sacraments jes' one more time!"

Gordon took his new assignment seriously and went around with an "all's right with the world" smile on his face. We heard his infectious laugh, which sometimes became a cackle, much more often than we had during his tenure as a watch officer. A more competent but less interesting young ensign from the Middle West was assigned to my watch section. Round and round Catalina Island we cruised during the week. On weekends when we did not have duty, Stephen and Gordon and I still hung out. Whenever I was in their company, I felt more alive, connected, was able to forget the isolating experience of being in a place I did not want to be, doing something I did not really want to do. San Diego did not have the magic of San Francisco, but we found places to go. We had meals together, many of them at Mexican Village, a restaurant next to the ferry landing on North Island, sometimes preceded by drinks at the elegant and mirrored bar of the nearby Del Coronado Hotel. I bought a second-hand sports car, a Simca convertible that from a distance looked almost like a Porsche. In it we made excursions to La Jolla to lie on the beach or drink at a joint called the Pour House, where a parody of Goya's *The Nude Maja* hung above the bar: a reclining female nude in the same pose as in Goya's famous painting, but with crossed eyes, curly blonde hair, and a fly crawling up her abdomen. It was signed: "Irving Goya."

We also went to performances at the Globe Theater in Balboa Park, to concerts, and often to one of the several new coffee houses that were beginning to be the fashion, and where entertainment was too often untalented poets reading bad poems or ungifted but sincere folk singers singing doleful songs. Sometimes we just sat around the pool at the Officer's Club on the base, drinking beer and talking about what we would do when we were released from service. Gordon, of course, was going to seminary, Stephen to Columbia to continue his study of Russian. At this time, I had a fantasy, inspired by our recent cruise to Asia, of returning to Japan to teach English.

Month after dull month went by in this Southern California limbo. And then one morning there was an exciting announcement in the *Bennington*'s daily news release: We were scheduled for an overhaul at Hunter's Point Shipyard in San Francisco. I had reported aboard the ship during an overhaul at Hunter's Point and now, nearly three years later, as I was nearing the end of my active duty, the ship was ready to be overhauled once more. Gordon, Stephen, and I were elated at the prospect of several months in San Francisco.

This time the work that was going to be done on the ship was much more extensive. Almost the entire interior was going to be gutted, including all of the officers' quarters. We were informed that the unmarried officers would be moving into the Bachelor Officer's Quarters on the base. One of my fellow gunnery officers, a seasoned lieutenant commander, gave me some good advice: "The BOQ has limited space. Don't rush to sign up for it. When it is full, they will give you an allowance to rent a place off base." I did as he suggested and by the time I went over to sign in, there were no more rooms left. The housing allowance for bachelor officers was very small, but rents in San Francisco then were absurdly low. A friend I had made during that first yard period in the Bay Area was leaving the city temporarily and offered to sublet me his apartment on Telegraph Hill. It was perfect. In the 1100 block of Montgomery Street, it had one bedroom, a living room, and a kitchen. The john was behind a door at the end of the entrance hall, and the shower and fridge were both in a tiny space off the kitchen. There was garage space for my Simca, and all the tenants had access to a kind of rough terrace on the roof that provided splendid views of the Embarcadero and the Bay Bridge. My rent was $40 a month. Best of all, the apartment was in the heart of an interesting and varied neighborhood. Broadway with its bars and cafés was just a block down the street; the City Lights Bookstore was a few blocks away, as were the night clubs the Hungry Eye and the Purple Onion, where one night I saw a young and very funny comedienne at the beginning of her career. "What I like about San Francisco," Phyllis Diller cracked, "is that it is such an *intellectual* city, and as I often say, there's nothing like going to bed with a good book, or with a friend who's read one."

The neighborhood had also been the epicenter of the Beat Generation, which by the time I moved to Montgomery Street had begun to peter out and move elsewhere. Allen Ginsberg had written *Howl* in a room just a few doors up the street from my sublet. Ginsberg was gone, and his room was occupied by a gentle artist named Peter who, when he was not making clever pen-and-ink drawings of the people he saw on the streets, wandered around with a calico cat draped on his shoulder.

My apartment became an off-the-ship hangout for Gordon, Stephen, and a few other young officers with whom I had become friendly. We often met there for drinks, or one of us prepared some kind of meal or had one delivered by a deli. The cast of characters varied from evening to evening, but Gordon and Stephen were regulars.

One evening just Gordon was coming over for dinner. I was going to prepare our meal from a cookbook I had found in a used bookshop on Telegraph Avenue in Berkeley: *Aromas and Flavors*, the second and lesser-known cookbook of Alice B. Toklas. I had chosen a lurid dish named "Nymph Aurora" that was made from shrimp cooked in cream with green food coloring, served over rice. I had decided not to start cooking the meal until Gordon actually arrived, and I was sure that he was not somewhere, oblivious to the time most mortals lived by, chatting with a dead friend.

That evening, he was more or less on time. I started boiling the rice and cooking the shrimp. "Do you mind if I go into your bedroom and pray before dinner?" he asked. "Be my guest," I said.

Gordon went into the bedroom and closed the door. I waited and watched the rice cook, then overcook, and the shrimp turn from succulent to leathery. After what seemed a very long time, Gordon emerged. He had a radiant smile on his face. "I've been talking with God," he explained. "He wants me back on the watch bill. He wants to test me!" Gordon said with enthusiasm. I considered this for a moment. "Gordon, would you do me a big favor?" "What?" "If they put you back on the watch bill, would you please request someone else's section?" "Why?" He looked a little hurt. "Well, Gordon, I really don't want God testing *you* while I am officer of the deck!"

A few weeks later, the *Bennington* returned to San Diego and began the usual routine of operations and exercises off Catalina Island. Gordon, under orders from God, was put back on the watch bill, and not in my section, for which I was grateful. In any case, my time on active duty was almost at an end. In March of 1960, I received an honorable discharge and headed for San Francisco, ready to start a new life, though I was not clear about what that would be.

For months after my release from the service, each morning I opened the newspaper to see if some catastrophe or near catastrophe had occurred on the *Bennington*. None had. If God were testing Gordon, he was doing so very quietly.

Eventually, when I was on a visit to Louisiana, I did see a photograph of the *Bennington* in the New Orleans *Times-Picayune*. "U. S. Carrier Heads for Laos." read the caption. It was the beginning of the Vietnam War and of a much darker period of history. The light-hearted days of going in circles around Catalina Island pretending to be at war were over.

By then, Gordon and Stephen were also out of the navy. Gordon was at the Lutheran seminary, just as he had planned; Stephen was studying Russian at Columbia. I was in San Francisco trying to decide what I wanted to be when I grew up. In the years that followed, there were times when Gordon and Stephen and I almost lost touch, but never quite.

Stephen and his new wife and I spent time together in Paris a few years later when I was there on a trip with my parents. Stephen had been studying in Moscow and was spending the summer in Paris in a friend's apartment. We got together on Bastille Day, and that night went out looking for dancing in the streets, but because of the war in Algeria there was none.

I received occasional letters and cards from Gordon. After a year, he left the Lutheran seminary. The next time I heard from him, he was teaching in a Christian Brothers school and considering becoming a priest. This was the first time he was to change religion in the course of the next twenty or so years. Some of the sects he joined and then left were well out of the mainstream.

I did not see Gordon again until the spring of 1968. I was by then working in Paris for a federation of American universities. My main task was to travel around Europe to visit study abroad programs and write reports on them.

Gordon had planned to spend some time with me in Paris, but that May hell broke loose as students and workers joined forces for what became known as *les événements du Mai*. All France was shut down by the ensuing strikes, and I was sent to Brussels to keep communications open with our New York office. Instead of coming to visit me in Paris, Gordon came to Brussels. The afternoon he showed up at my hotel, I was busy writing a report for my colleagues in New York describing the effects the events in France would probably have on our summer programs.

Gordon decided to take a nap while I was scribbling at the desk. When I finished the report, I looked over to see that Gordon was lying on the bed with his eyes open and a broad smile on his face. "I've just had a very interesting visitor," he told me. "The eighteenth-century French translator of Martin Luther, with whom I've been in contact with for some time, came to welcome me to Europe. We had a wonderful chat!" Gordon was still very much Gordon.

Gordon and I eventually made it back to Paris. When we had last seen each other, we were both playing the role of butch young naval officers, but since at that time I was sleeping in my bedroom with my French boyfriend, and Gordon was sleeping on the sofa in the living room, it was not possible to maintain that fiction. I was fairly certain that Gordon would understand. But even better, he confessed that he too was gay, and we were able to continue our friendship on a more open and honest basis.

If Gordon received visitors from the other side while he was visiting me in Paris, he never mentioned them. When I was free during the day, and in the evenings, I took him around to see the city. His enthusiasm was infectious.

It was several years before I saw Gordon again. By then I had left Paris and was working in London, "on secondment" to a bureau of the British Ministry of Education to set up exchanges between American and British schools.

Gordon called me from Gatwick Airport to tell me that he was on his way to Zaire with a planeload of Peace Corps volunteers and that he had a layover in England. A few hours later, I met him at Victoria Station, and we had a lovely day together. I caught Gordon up on what had been happening in my life, and he filled me in on what had been happening in his, on both sides of the mortal divide. After disillusioning experiences with a variety of organized religions, he had decided to abandon them all and listen only to his own inner voices on matters of morality and the hereafter. I agreed with him that it sounded like a sensible idea.

We had a good Indian meal that evening before I took him back to Victoria and put him on a train to Gatwick. The next morning when I turned on the radio, the first thing I heard on the BBC early news was that a planeload of American

Peace Corps volunteers had been forced down in Uganda by Idi Amin and were being held hostage. I knew that it had to be Gordon's group, and it was. I worried until a few days later when I heard on the BBC that all the volunteers had been released and were on their way to Zaire. I eventually had a letter from Gordon describing the ordeal that had begun in fear of prison or execution and ended with a banquet for the volunteers given by the erratic dictator who had decided that the captive volunteers were all dear friends.

I had several more letters from Gordon while he was in Zaire, and then communication ended. When I moved back to the United States in 1975 after a dozen years of living in Europe, I thought I had lost contact with him altogether. I had sporadically kept track of Stephen who was teaching at an eastern university and separated from his wife.

During one of our infrequent telephone conversations in the early eighties, I asked Stephen when he had last heard from Gordon. "It was several years ago. He told me that he had some medical problem and was thinking about going to Switzerland to have it treated." I remembered that in one of his letters from Zaire, Gordon had hinted that he had found his sex life surprisingly fulfilling. I mentioned this to Stephen. We both had read that the newly discovered AIDS virus was believed to have originated in Africa, and we sadly came to the same conclusion as why we had not heard from Gordon. Over the next few years, whenever I spoke to Stephen, I always asked if he had had any word of Gordon. And I was never surprised when he said that he hadn't. For us, Gordon was sadly no longer among the living. He had, there was little doubt in my mind, permanently crossed over to the other side where he had been a frequent visitor.

In the mid-eighties, Stephen gave up his academic career and moved to Wyoming where, after spending too many years in a dreary suburb of Boston, he rediscovered the outdoors and began to lead an intensely physical life: hiking, skiing, snowboarding. After so many years, we began to speak more often.

In the early 1990s, thanks to a neighbor who knew a lot about computers, I discovered the Internet and began to search for lost friends and acquaintances. I found one in France, another in Holland, several in the United States. And then I found Gordon in San Francisco. He had been living and teaching there since we had lost contact so many years before. I did not mention to him that Stephen and I had decided that he was another of the many victims of AIDS. I did tell him that Stephen recalled his having had a medical problem and his considering going to Switzerland for treatment. Gordon remembered. "It was an allergy that finally went away by itself." Gordon explained that he had not been in touch because, since we had always been friends, and were going to continue to be friends for millennia, even though he had often thought of me, he had not bothered trying to get in touch because there was no sense of urgency. "When we cross over, we will be friends forever."

After our conversation, I telephoned Stephen and gave him the good news. "My goodness! How wonderful! Gordon always was full of surprises!" He gave an embarrassed sounding laugh. "Did I tell you that last year I put Gordon's name on an AIDS memorial here in Wyoming?" "I don't think we should tell him that," I said. Stephen agreed.

After rediscovering Gordon, I began to stay more closely in touch with both Stephen and Gordon than I had over the many years since we had served together on the *Bennington*.

In the late 1990s, I went to San Francisco for a week, and Gordon and I spent most of a day together. From my hotel on 2nd Street, near the new Museum of Modern Art, we walked all over the city, and talked and talked and talked. We crossed Market Street and went to Union Square, and then to Columbus and Broadway, passing the City Lights Bookstore, no longer the tiny corner shop where I used to spend hours browsing. We went up Broadway to Montgomery to see the apartment house where Gordon had his conversation with God while supper overcooked. The neighborhood was much gentrified. The little Italian grocery store on the corner was gone. Beatniks, had there been any around, would not have felt comfortable there. We walked and talked all the way to North Beach where we had lunch at the Buena Vista Café, followed by Irish Coffee over which Gordon told me that, pleasant as life was on earth, he was getting tired and more and more looking forward to crossing permanently to the other side. "Most of the people I know are already there," he said, "and it is such a wonderful place to be." As always, because it was in the context of Gordon's intelligence and our long history of friendship, what he told me did not seem like a completely unbalanced fantasy. It was very real to him and, at least while I was in his presence, it almost became so for me.

"Most people," he said, "when I begin to tell them these things, just look at me as if I am crazy, so I shut up and change the subject. Of course, there are a few people scattered around the world who understand. Oh, Joel, it is so beautiful on the other side! There is so much love and peace and understanding. And the colors! Wait till you see the colors! They are so vivid!" "I hope, Gordon," I told him, "that they aren't too garish." He laughed. "You know," he said, "life on earth has been an experiment in negativity that has not turned out well. The experiment ended in the 1980s, and it is just winding down now. It is about to be over. Oh, don't worry. The world is not going to explode or anything like that. But we are being watched by beings from other galaxies. For the past twenty years I have been in communication with an alien who has told me so many things about where we came from, why we are here, and what is going to happen to us. They want to communicate with us, but they realize that we are not ready to hear from them, and it would only scare us to death. We are about to enter a new and wonderful phase in which many things will be explained to us."

One evening a few years after our meeting in San Francisco, the telephone rang about dinnertime, and John answered it. It was Gordon. "Is Joel okay?" he asked. "Yes. He's right here," said John, handing me the phone. Gordon had just had a very vivid vision of me in his apartment in San Francisco and assumed that I had crossed and was letting him know. When I assured that I was definitely alive and feeling fine, he seemed disappointed.

Gordon himself finally did cross to the other side, permanently as far as I can tell, in September of 2015. With Google search, I found his obituary online.

Gordon's vision of the afterlife did sound completely daft, but is it really much dafter than other visions put forth by many religions for thousands of years and believed by millions and millions of people? And few of those believers have had, as I have, so cheerful an eyewitness to describe what is in store for us. I can't help hoping that maybe Gordon was right.

22

LEARN THE ENGLISH OF TODAY!

—For C. L. S.

When I was discharged from the US Navy, urged to do so by my father, I applied to and was accepted into the graduate program in English at Stanford. I found a position as a dorm counselor at nearby Menlo College and eventually also taught a class in freshman English there. Someone once described Menlo, which did not become coeducational until 1971, as "a college for young men who were rich enough, but not smart enough, to get into Stanford." The dorm parking lot boasted mostly late model sports cars with a preponderance of Porsches, quite a few bearing surfboards. Among them I parked the brown and cream five-year-old Ford coupe I had purchased inexpensively for transportation. Once when I was about to get into my car, one of the students, who was about to get into his Porsche parked nearby, asked with a slight air of disbelief, "Gee, Mr. Fletcher. Is that your car?" I told him that it was. "Do you have any other cars?" "Afraid not," I said, obviously losing face with the young man.

I found my classes at Stanford mildly interesting. I was not particularly inspired by either of the stars of the English Department: poet Yvor Winters and novelist Wallace Stegner, neither a stimulating lecturer. Winters, in particular, seemed hardly aware of the students in his classroom and in a deadly monotone was prone to sweeping dogmatic judgments about who was worthy to be studied and who was not. He believed that only those whose writing sprang from a deep moral seriousness were worth considering. There was no place in his stultifying view of literature and life for wit, wonder, and delight.

He was also known to be vehemently homophobic. I had heard that he was extremely upset when his only son decided to study ballet. His disdain for Hart Crane, a poet I had ardently admired since I discovered him in my teens, seemed to be based on Crane's homosexuality. Lecturing about Crane, Winters implied that homosexual poets could never write truly great poetry because they were inevitably morally flawed.

The Anglo American poet Thom Gunn, Winters's most celebrated protégé, felt obliged, when he followed his life partner Mike Kitay to spend a year in Texas where Kitay was serving in the US Air Force, to pretend to Winters that he had gone because of a "fiancée." In a *Paris Review* interview many years later Gunn said: "He (Winters) would have been *appalled* at the idea I was queer."

Winter's strongly held view that homosexuality was a serious character defect set the tone for the department. My favorite class was one in Restoration theater taught by a young professor, Malcom Goldstein who, in spite of his best efforts, could not hide his camp attitudes and mannerisms, and gave the impression that he was trying too hard to fit in. He often praised Winters. Once he told our class, "I think Yvor is one of the great men in American letters today and undoubtedly the greatest among my own close personal friends." But I sensed that he was not comfortable in the exuberantly heterosexual climate of the Stanford English Department. If truth be told, neither was I.

The day after the election of John F. Kennedy in November of 1960, Robert Frost spoke and read his poetry at Stanford, an event I attended with some of my classmates. Frost began by saying of the election: "It was a triumph for Protestantism ... over itself. The Reformation is finally over. We've learned to live with the Catholic church.... The Archbishop of Canterbury has gone to see the Pope. I suppose that there is nothing left but the canonization of Martin Luther." Shortly thereafter, Frost was invited to read one of his poems at Kennedy's inauguration. He wrote a poem for the occasion, but blinded by the brilliant sun that clear January day, he recited one he knew by heart: "The Gift Outright," one of Kennedy's favorite poems.

I also looked forward to hearing Malcom Cowley as a guest lecturer in Wallace Stegner's Class in American Literature. His book about the "Lost Generation" of American writers and artists living in Paris in the 1920s and '30s had been my introduction to the possibilities of expatriate life, and I had read and reread it. Unfortunately, he proved to be a more stimulating writer than speaker and his lecture was unmemorable, a disappointment.

While I was on a summer visit home, one of the English instructors who had been hired to teach at Southwestern, at the last minute informed the dean who had hired him that he was not coming. In an act of shameless nepotism, my father proposed that I take the job to earn enough money to pay for finishing my studies at Stanford. I was persuaded and spent a pleasant enough year living rent-free in a cottage my parents owned in a lovely pecan grove outside the city limits, taking all my meals at home, and saving almost every cent of my salary.

When my contract ended that summer, I determined that I had saved enough for a trip to Europe before returning to my studies, I sailed for Europe on the liner *Nieuw Amsterdam* on June 2, 1962. I had told my family and friends that I would be there for a couple of months, but it was already in the back of my mind that, if I could find a way, I might stay longer. Somehow, the two months turned into more than twelve years.

As a midshipman on summer NROTC cruises, I had visited Paris, Lisbon, Stockholm, Copenhagen, and London. My brief stays in these fascinating cities had whetted my appetite for Europe. However, the idea of becoming an expatriate had been germinating in my mind for a long time.

France had loomed large in my life as a wondrous land since I was a small child. When I was about ten, , I had even taken lessons in French with an elderly Frenchman. In high school, I used to hang out with my friend Renée, whose uncle taught French at LSU. He had given her a bunch of old 78 rpm records of Edith Piaf, Charles Trenet, Jean Sablon, and other popular French singers. We would listen to them and fantasize about going to live in Paris on a dollar a day.

When I was fifteen, I spent the summer with my sister in Berkeley. One evening we went into San Francisco to see one of the most celebrated Americans in France: Josephine Baker, and her spectacular stage presence made a huge impression on me.

When I was a freshman at Tulane, I bought an LP of renowned *chanteuse* Yvette Guilbert, a painting by Toulouse-Lautrec of her wearing long black gloves on the jacket, and listened to it so often that I almost wore it out. I took three years of French at Tulane and in my third year won the French Government Prize for "son assiduité et ses succès dans l'étude de la Langue Française," though I suspected that the real reason I won the prize might have been that I had lent my Yvette Guilbert record to my French professor who was impressed that an undergraduate had such rarified tastes.

By the time I sailed for Europe in the summer of 1962, I was fertile ground for expatriation.

After I disembarked in Southampton, I stayed for a while in London, then went to Paris for a week. I had tickets for several operas at the Salzburg Festival in late August, which left ample time for a trip to Italy.

I took a night train from Paris to Rome. When I woke the next morning and groggily looked out the compartment window, I saw a landscape unlike any I had seen before. It was bathed in the golden light of summer. I could feel the change in the rhythms of the life that was passing by and sense the warmth of the sun.

I spent an exhausting but fascinating week in Rome, seeing all the sights, walking each day until my feet hurt. And then I went to bustling, dirty, picturesque Naples, where I took a ferry to the Island of Ischia.

I found a room for 600 lire a day, about eighty cents, in a *pensione* in what had been a convent in the ancient Castello Aragonese. The castle dated from the

Middle Ages and was perched on a huge volcanic rock connected to the island by a causeway. My room overlooked the island to the vineyards on the green slopes of Mount Epomeo, Ischia's extinct volcano. For the next two weeks I lived a blissfully simple life that consisted of hikes around the island, hours on the beach and in the surf, dishes of pasta, and glasses of wine. I was bearded and growing browner by the day, intoxicated by the sun and the gentle breeze off the sea. Even though I had not yet learned the expression, I was absorbing the concept of *dolce far niente*, the sweetness of doing nothing, the gift of enjoying life and its basic pleasures. My Calvinistic forbears would not have approved.

I had never given much thought to Italy. When I thought of Europe, I had always thought of France. But I was falling under Italy's spell. On my way to Salzburg, I spent a few days in Florence, and by then my newly blossoming Italophilia had begun to shove my Francophilia aside. After Salzburg, I returned to Florence and found a job teaching English at the American Language Center, also known as Istituto Americano, on the top floor of a building on the main square, Piazza della Repubblica. I rented an apartment near the Ponte Vecchio. It was in a modern building that had been built to replace one that had been destroyed during the war.

The apartment was small and narrow with a window at one end that looked out to a dark courtyard. The other inhabitants of the building seemed to be women who did a lot of entertaining. Men came and went at all hours of the day and night. The walls were so thin that I could hear the brunette next-door providing hospitality to her gentlemen callers. She evidently had a 45 rpm record player with only one record, a ballad sung by the pop diva Mina: "Renato, Renato, Renato." It played over and over and over again. I could hear the click-click, click-click each time the record finished and began again, and Mina's voice did not completely muffle the groans and moans of pleasure. A winter with a lot of snow, very unusual for Florence, often kept me at home in the coming months, and I must have heard that song and its accompaniment hundreds of times.

I enjoyed teaching at the Istituto Americano, which used a technique developed at the University of Michigan. "The Michigan Method" did not require the teacher to know Italian, in fact, teachers were discouraged from speaking with students in Italian to force them to understand English. The classes were usually small, from five to a dozen students, and most of the students were simpatici and eager to learn. I taught three or four classes every day, sometimes till late in the evening. The hourly pay was not generous, but in those days, Florence was an incredibly inexpensive place to live.

I found a few friends among the other American teachers at the Istituto. Three of them happened to be from Arkansas. Arthur was a budding art historian; John was an ex-Fulbright scholar of Italian descent who did not want to go home when his scholarship ended; and Carl, weary of teaching English literature at several American colleges and universities, had been persuaded by a painter friend to spend a year with him in Florence.

Carl was the one I had most in common with and we began a platonic friendship that has been a constant in both our lives.

The days, the weeks, the months went by very quickly, and soon we had been in Florence for a year. I was looking forward to the next one, but Carl had decided to return to the States to look for another job teaching at another college. I suggested that he apply to Southwestern for I knew that the English faculty often had a high turnover. It turned out that there had been several resignations and the dean was looking for replacements. So, Carl went to live in Lafayette, and I remained in Florence. He wrote that he was missing Florence more than he expected to and hoped one day to find a way to return.

Later that year, an opportunity arose for both of us to stay in Florence on a more promising basis. A small language school, a rival to the Istituto Americano, was put on the market by its owners, an American man and his Italian wife. The school, a modest establishment, was on the verge of failure, and the owners were fed up and eager to move to Los Angeles. They were not asking much, but they were not selling much: a list of their alleged current students, stacks of textbooks, an Olivetti electric typewriter, a mimeograph machine, several rooms full of used furniture, and a short lease on a rented apartment.

I wrote Carl about it, and he wrote back enthusiastically. We decided to buy the school. Looking back, I realize how naïve and foolhardy we were to dive blindly into such a risky venture. But it was the early 1960s, and many young Americans were doing crazy things that their parents, born during the sobering experience of the Great Depression, would never have dreamed of doing. Allen Ginsberg's *Howl* had become for some the defining poem of our generation and, even if most of us were not "angel headed hipsters burning the heavenly connection to the starry dynamo in the machinery of night," some of us were rebelling in quieter ways, turning our back on the comforts and rewards of conventional American life. Some were protesting the war in Vietnam; some experimenting with drugs; some getting involved in the struggle for civil rights for Blacks. "The times they were a changing." And armed with Frommer's *Europe on Five Dollars a Day*, young people had begun exploring the world. International travel was getting ever easier and, as my late friend, California novelist James D. Houston remarked: "See America last . . . if it does."

Carl had been offered a job teaching at the University of Maryland overseas program for the military for a larger salary than he had been paid in Lafayette and decided to take it for long enough to build up a comfortable financial cushion before returning to help run the school. While he was teaching soldiers on military bases in Iceland, Labrador, Newfoundland, and the Azores, I ran the school alone, keeping him posted with frequent letters.

The American School of Languages was located on the top floor of a building in the heart of downtown Florence. One, via de' Vecchietti (Street of Little Old Men) consisted of four classrooms and a one-bedroom apartment with access to a huge terrace above. I moved into the flat and began to plan for the first semester which began in early February. I had printed tasteful blue and beige posters that I hoped would stand out among the preponderance of red and yellow ones. They bore the new slogan we had devised for the school: "Imparate L'Inglese d'Oggi!" (Learn the English of Today!) I gave a generous tip, as I was advised to do to ensure prime placement, to the man who plastered them on the walls. I also took out ads in *La Nazione*, the Florentine daily newspaper, and had five thousand cards printed that, with the help of friends, took to bars and other businesses all over the city.

Two Italian friends helped me enormously with everything. Roberto, who had been one of my students at the other school, guided me through all the complex legalities that were a mystery to me, evaluated the financial situation that was left us, and kept our books. Simonetta did everything she could to help make the school a success, cheered me on through all of it. She became our gracious receptionist and our first teacher of Italian. I could not have done it without them, and they both became lifelong friends.

The list of students that I had been given by the previous owner was, as I should have suspected, inaccurate and probably largely fiction. Very few of them showed up for the new semester. But between students who had followed me from the other school, and the new ones brought in by our advertising, an encouraging number came to sign up for classes and pay the first *rata* (installment). It was an adventure, and instead of worrying, I was enjoying every minute of it. And gradually, our enrolment increased.

The school had an agreement to teach a small group of astronomers at the Observatory of Arcetri located on a hill just outside of Florence. The observatory was built in 1872, next to the Villa Il Gioiello where, condemned by the Catholic Church for heresy, Galileo spent his final years. I went on my motorbike to the observatory, and entered it through the circular library, the shelves of which were filled with the publications in identical bindings of the astronomers who worked there and had worked there. The names on the spines began with Galileo Galilei and ended with the names of my students. They were a delightful group and the conversation ranged over a variety of topics, going wherever they wanted it to go. Among them was a charming, witty, kindly Catholic priest, Father Tagliaferro, a specialist in sunspots. I once asked him how he became a priest. "By mistake," he answered.

The school slowly began to grow, and our students came from a cross-section of Florentine society. They included everyone from the director of Olivetti in Florence to the woman who gave out towels at the bathhouse beneath the train station.

In addition to the classes held at the school, we signed a contract with the Eli Lilly pharmaceutical factory in the suburb of Sesto Florentino to offer classes to their employees at the factory. One of our Lilly students was Dr. Di Napoli, who was from Napoli where he had studied English with a Neapolitan *professore*, and had an enormous English vocabulary, mispronounced and unintelligible. He had been told that he had a bright future at the company if he could learn to speak English that people could understand. He was desperate to do so and not only took the classes at the factory but came to the school three nights a week for private lessons. It was a struggle for him to unlearn all that he had learned, and in spite of his efforts, he made only limited progress.

One day the American director of Eli Lilly in Sesto called to tell me that finally they had been able to use Dr. Di Napoli's English skills. A Japanese executive was visiting the plant, and no one could understand his English except for Dr. Di Napoli, who would then translate it into Italian for his colleagues.

I needed help to keep the school clean and in order and found a maid whom I shared with a South African painter friend, Flo Shoul. Aurelia came twice a week to sweep, dust, polish, change my linen, and do the washing. She was a small woman with a hooked nose and a slight hump on her back. She came from the Florentine suburb of San Casciano, and a friend from there remembered her. He told me that during the Second World War, Aurelia was the only person to go out when bombs were falling because, she said, she was too ugly to be killed.

She kept the schoolrooms and my apartment fairly spic and span. She chattered while she worked, and listening to the narrative of her life, I learned a number of colorful Florentine expressions that were never used in polite company.

Aurelia told me that every weekend she took the train to a town on the Adriatic Coast to visit her uncle who, she claimed, had a title and was, in fact, a prince. Nothing about Aurelia suggested aristocratic connections, but I had heard that many Italian titles, those given by Mussolini, were not to be taken seriously. I knew one pretentious young man named Baroncelli who was able to purchase the title *barone* (baron) from a titled Sicilian family with the same last name and thus became the euphonious "Barone Baroncelli." So, I thought that maybe Aurelia's uncle really was a prince of one kind or another.

"Il mio zio, il principe" (my uncle, the prince) as she referred to him, was elderly, unmarried, and not in good health. Aurelia told me that she was the only one in the family who was kind to him. He had two very mean sisters who lived nearby but rarely came to see him.

Once after a weekend with her uncle, Aurelia told me that she had something very important to tell me, but that it was an enormous secret, and I could not even hint of it to anyone. "I must find a very discreet lawyer," she said, "un avvocato molto discreto." "Why?" I asked. "Because," she said in a whisper, "my uncle has decided to adopt me!" "Aurelia! That means you will become 'una principessa!'" She smiled.

There was, she confided, one condition that she had to agree to before he adopted her, and it had to do with his mean sisters. "After I inherit," she said, "I must hire a long black car with a uniformed chauffer and, wearing a new pair of white gloves, visit his sisters. During the visit, I must not take off my gloves nor sit down." She obviously was relishing the prospect of putting the mean sisters in their place.

After she had been working for me for some time, Aurelia began to act strangely. Instead of spending several hours cleaning, she would come early and stay the entire day. Since I paid her by the visit and not by the hour, I didn't really care, but it was disconcerting to have her there from nine in the morning until early evening, finding things that really did not need to be done. I called the friend I shared her with, and Flo reported the same bizarre behavior. "I can't get rid of her!" she said. Eventually Flo sent her Italian boyfriend, Aldo, to ask questions in the *quartiere* where Aurelia lived. He soon solved the mystery. To earn a little extra cash, Aurelia was renting out her room by the hour to the neighborhood whores and could not return home until their business was done.

In August, our lease on via de' Vecchieti expired, and the landlord demanded an enormous increase in rent. I began to look for another place for the school. It did not take long to find the perfect apartment on Piazza Santa Maria Novella, and for a lower rent that we had been paying. It was on the second floor, above a bar/café, with a balcony facing the façade of the beautiful Basilica of Santa Maria Novella, which contains many important Gothic and Renaissance masterworks of art.

Carl returned that summer to help run the school and found an elegant and comfortable small apartment near the Porta Romana, with a huge terrace overlooking the Giardino Torregiani, the largest private garden in Florence. I moved from via de' Vecchieti into a charming, but more modest flat in the via del Corso.

With Carl's added efforts, the school began to thrive. We began a course of lessons for the police force, *I carabinieri*, of the seaside town of Viareggio, an hour away from Florence by train. I taught the group of about a dozen. They proved to be very sweet-natured but not very bright. We met twice a week, and often on Thursday I had to repeat the lesson I had taught them on Tuesday because they had forgotten everything. Once I made them count, repeating after me, numbers from one to a hundred. By the time we got to a hundred, they were breathless, and several seemed to be on the verge of a nervous breakdown. It occurred to me that if someone wished to engage in a career in crime, Viareggio would probably be a very good place to begin.

More important and much more lucrative was a contract we signed with the NATO base in La Spezia, just up the coast from Viareggio, to provide English classes three times a week to students who came from the various NATO countries.

I began to spend the week at the Hotel Firenze in La Spezia, teaching at the NATO base on Monday, Wednesday, and Friday, taking the train to Viareggio on Tuesday and Thursday. My NATO students, unlike the policemen in Viareggio, were bright and a joy to teach. I taught from nine to noon and had the afternoons free. After my classes, I would usually take the short train trip up the coast to Vernazza, one of the Cinque Terre, five small villages on the coast then accessible only by train or footpath. I would have lunch on the terrace of a trattoria on a square overlooking the harbor, almost always a grilled, freshly caught fish and *un quarto* of dry white wine made from grapes of nearby vineyards. Vernazza had a small, rock-strewn beach, sheltered by cliffs. A large hole made by the sea in a boulder provided access. When I finished lunch, I would crawl through the opening, strip to my bathing suit and, somnolent from the wine and sun, swim and relax for an hour or two before taking the train back to La Spezia.

Several times, taking two days, I walked the entire Sentiero Azzurro (The Blue Path), that, with spectacular views of the Mediterranean, runs from the first village, Riomaggiore, to the last, Monterosso, a distance of about twenty-five miles. The first time I walked it from beginning to end, always eager to use my improving Italian, I stopped to ask a woman scrubbing a doorstep how far it was to the next village. "Non so. Mai stata." (Don't know. Never been.) She replied without looking up.

On Wednesday, November 3, 1966, I returned to Florence because the next day was a national holiday, and I had no classes for the rest of the week. That evening, I was invited to a banquet at the Grand Hotel Medici given by the American Chamber of Commerce in Florence for which we taught classes in commercial English. I was seated near a Mr. Paul Vogel, the representative of the Port of New Orleans in Milan, the speaker of the evening. After his talk, we watched a film he had brought with him about flood control on the Mississippi River.

It had been raining for days, and when the mayor of Florence, Piero Bargellini, arrived late, he began his speech by saying: "Don't bother about all this water. The city administration has ordered it especially as part of our campaign." The city had recently purchased a fleet of white garbage trucks with the slogan: "Per Una Firenze Pulita" (For a Clean Florence) emblazoned on them in bright green.

After the mayor's speech, someone else made a joke about the reviewing stand for the important politicians who were expected to attend the Liberation Day parade the next day. It had been set up facing a banner advertising the movie: *How to Steal A Million Dollars and Live Happily Ever After.*

It had been a convivial evening, and everyone left in a good mood. I had invited one of our teachers as my guest, and she gave me a ride back to Carl's apartment on the other side of the Arno. Since I was spending most of the week teaching on the coast, I had sublet my apartment and was staying weekends in Carl's guestroom.

We drove over the Ponte Santa Trinitá a little before midnight, and I noticed that the river was full and swift. And it was raining.

The next morning when I woke early and went out to buy some milk, it was still raining, though not very hard. But I could tell from the looks on people's faces that something was wrong. I walked down the street toward the Arno, and then I saw the water. Via San Agostino, about a hundred yards from the river and running parallel to it, was a torrent several feet deep. When I got back to Carl's flat, the lights were out. A few hours later, water from the Arno reached the doorway of his building and flooded the cellar. Since his apartment was on the top floor, it suffered no damage. Carl, fortunately, had parked his car on high ground and it also escaped damage. Later that day we drove it up to the Piazzale Michelangelo, overlooking the city. We saw an amazing sight. Several of the bridges were completely underwater. The first-floor windows of all the buildings along the river were no longer visible. Cars were being bounced around in the swift current and disappearing. And all day long it kept on raining.

We were not able to cross the river to check on the school until two days later, traversing total devastation. People were shoveling mud out of their shops, wheeling their belongings in wheelbarrows, standing in line for bread and milk. The morning paper came out on the Monday following the flood. It reported that more than six thousand shops had been lost, and at least twenty thousand automobiles. We passed the leather shop that belonged to one of our students. He was just opening it. Everything inside was ruined and, he told us, he had no flood insurance. "No one in Italy does."

The school was dry and unharmed, but Piazza Santa Maria Novella was ankle-deep in mud. Overturned cars and other detritus were scattered everywhere. Carl had been using my motorbike, and the night of the flood had left it tied up outside. I didn't even bother to look for it. I assumed it had been swept away, probably was somewhere between Florence and Pisa. But it hadn't. I found it on the steps of the Basilica. It was upright, a little damp and oily, but undamaged. A Christmas card in English was stuck in the spokes. "Season's Greeting and Best Wishes for a Happy New Year!" it said.

Vittorio's new motorboat in Portofino, 1964. Vittorio is standing partially out of the frame, top left, with his friend, a former racing car driver who sold him the boat.

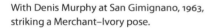

With Denis Murphy at San Gimignano, 1963, striking a Merchant–Ivory pose.

Denis and Joan Murphy in my room in Palazzo dei Rustici, posing for a silly photograph with pince-nez bought at the flea market, seconds before we learned of the assassination of John F. Kennedy, November 22, 1963.

Loretta Grellner (1925–2004), Charcoal drawing inscribed "Joel Fletcher in Palazzo dei Rustici, Florence, 1963."

Ambassador Jefferson Caffery, American diplomat. Orphan print.

Count Francesco Guicciardini in the "English Garden" behind Palazzo Guicciardini in Florence.

Count Francesco wearing a beret that had belonged to his late friend, the recently deceased Violet Trefusis.

Francesco's pool at Montopoli. "Just an excuse to get people to take their clothes off." Far left: Carl Selph. In front of me is Albert Boekhorst, then a Dutch student who became a distinguished professor at the University of Amsterdam and a lifelong friend. The other two in the photo are friends of Francesco whose names I have long ago forgotten.

Aboard the student ship, *Aurelia*. I am fourth from the left, back row, with the orientation staff. We organized a full program of lectures, classes, films, and theatrical events to keep the passengers busy during the seven-day crossing.

With the City University of New York graduate students in Paris, 1969 or 1970, in the days when I was almost always the tallest one in the room.

Thérèse Bonney as a war correspondent with her Rolliflex. Courtesy Bancroft Library, UC Berkeley.

Andre Ostier, photographer known for his portraits of celebrated artists and photographs of the prewar costume balls of Paris society in the 1930s, in the foyer of his apartment on the rue Bassano.

Mary Guggenheim in the Marais, Paris, circa 1969.

Mary Guggenheim on Hammersmith Bridge, 1972, while visiting me in London.

Mary Guggenheim with Voodoo doll in Anse La Butte, Louisiana, circa 1979, taken in the early nineteenth-century house of antiquarian Robert Smith.

Portrait of Édouard Roditi, oil on canvas, by Mary Guggenheim. Courtesy Estate of Mary Guggenheim.

Mary Guggenheim (1917–2001), *Two Girls Sleeping, One Only Pretending to Sleep*, oil on board, 1967. The "Two Girls Sleeping" are Mary's daughters, Montserrat and Maximilienne. According to Montserrat, this is the first painting that Mary did after moving to Paris in 1967. It was painted in the writer Edouard Roditi's apartment on the rue Grégoire-de-Tours where Mary was staying until she found her own apartment. Montserrat said that the painting was done one evening shortly after she and her sister had returned from boarding school. She woke and realized that her mother was painting her and, pleased by the attention, pretended to remain asleep until her mother had finished it. Courtesy of Estate of Mary Guggenheim.

In 1969, I helped to arrange a summer program in the United States for a group of students from the Lycée Carcado, an exclusive Catholic school for young women on the Boulevard Raspail in Paris. I invited Samia to go with me (back row, far left) when I went to pay a visit to these proper, conservatively dressed young women a month before they were to depart.

After I answered their questions about the exchange program, we were served homemade cookies and chatted informally. The beautiful Black girl holding the American flag, the daughter of an African tribal prince, was especially gracious and charming, and I was sorry to learn that because she had failed one of her exams, she was not allowed to go on the trip.

When these young women, who had appeared so demure, arrived to board the student ship *Aurelia*, they were almost unrecognizable, clad in hot pants and wearing lots of makeup. They were one of the wildest groups we transported during the years that I was the director of orientation on the summer sailings.

It was, after all, the era of "the summer of love" that had begun at Woodstock in 1967, and uninhibited behavior was rampant among the young passengers. It was not unusual for the CIEE to receive, several months after a crossing, letters from desperate young female passengers along the lines of: "I urgently need to have the last name and address of a German student named Rolf who was in cabin 347B on your such-and-such sailing from Le Havre to New York."

The Emira Samia, Hammersmith, circa 1970.

Peter Patout, pre-prison, at the Croissant d'Or, New Orleans.

Peter Gill, Nicholas Wright, and Colin Thatcher in the kitchen at 9 Lower Mall.

George Washington Goetschius and Peter Gill in the kitchen, 9 Lower Mall. It was in the kitchen at 9 Lower Mall that John Osborne read aloud his play, *Look Back in Anger*, written on a houseboat tied up nearby on the Thames, to George Goetschius, George Devine, and Tony Richardson. They produced it at the Royal Court Theatre and changed British theatrical history.

George Washington Goetschius in the kitchen of the downstairs flat at 9 Lower Mall. He is wearing a garment made for me from African fabric by Mary Guggenheim. She called it an *après-orgie* (after-orgy) though I never had occasion to wear it as such. Hanging on the wall behind George is the poster that Robert Rauschenberg signed for me in Paris a few years before.

Peter Gill reading in my flat, 9 Lower Mall, Hammersmith.

In the garden behind 9 Lower Mall with Nöel Greig (left) and Peter Gill. Greig was a budding playwright, director, actor, and a frequent visitor to the house. He went on to make a name for himself in radical gay theater in London, wrote more than fifty plays, many on the theme of gay liberation, and was a founder of the hugely successful Gay Sweatshop, the first fully professional gay theatrical company.

Simonetta on the Ponte Vecchio, Florence, 1963.

Eugenio with lamb at Casa Sant'Alessandro, spring 1974. I had rented the top floor of the farmhouse as a place to write. When I returned from a trip, I discovered that Simonetta and Eugenio had rented the bottom floor to a shepherd and his flock. We managed to coexist without too much difficulty, though it was a little noisy and smelly at times.

Simonetta and her daughter, Anna, at the Casa Sant'Alessandro, spring 1974.

In the Cagaloglu Hammam in Istanbul with my friend Timothy and the new owner who planned to turn it into a unisex sauna and kebab house.

My Uncle Claude Martin, most decorated soldier from Louisiana in the First World War, who persuaded my parents not to have me aborted.

On the porch at Whittington Hall, late 1930s. Left to right: Ellen, apart from the rest of us, and as usual, unsmiling. Then my father, my mother, my sister Flo holding the head of a dog; behind her my aunt Frances, holding my right hand; me with a hat and suit; my sister Lorraine, holding my left hand and smiling down at me.

Fannie Fletcher, circa 1980, by Philip Gould. Photo courtesy Philip Gould.

With John Copenhaver at the Café Sevigné on a buying trip to Paris.

John Alden Copenhaver on his horse at Big Spring Farm in southwestern Virginia, where he grew up.

23

RISO

In 1964, through friends at the US Department of Agriculture, my father wangled a research trip to study the production of rice in the Po Valley. He knew something about the growing of rice and was qualified to carry out such a study, but no doubt the real reason he accepted the assignment, probably fished for it, was that he wanted to visit his son in Italy and find out what the hell I was doing there.

There was a legitimate reason for the study. Italy was preparing to enter the Common Market and Italian rice farmers were trying very hard to perfect a long grain rice that would compete in European markets with the popular Louisiana and Texas long grains. The Italians had no trouble growing the short-grained rice that was fine in a risotto, but, because of irrigation water that was too cold and a growing season that was too short, they had not yet produced a long grain rice similar to the one that grows so well in the hot and humid American South. The purpose of the study was to determine how much progress they had made toward developing a long grain.

By the time my parents traveled to Italy, I had been living in Florence for the better part of a year, supporting myself by teaching English for a meager salary at the Istituto Americano. And I was living gloriously well, for in those days in Florence a meager salary went far. There were a number of decent *trattorie* where one could get a good three-course meal for the equivalent of fifty cents; a bottle of the best Antinori Chianti Riserva cost 600 lire, just under a dollar. After my first Florentine winter in a characterless, modern flat, I had rented for about eight dollars a month a room on the *piano nobile* of the fifteenth-century Palazzo dei Rustici where Leonardo da Vinci himself had spent some time in 1500 after he had he fled Milan because of the fall of his patrons, the Sforza family. The palazzo was the home of one of his pupils, the sculptor Giovan Francesco dei Rustici, and it was there that his famous master sought refuge. My room in Palazzo dei Rustici boasted a graceful marble fireplace topped by a fresco of Hercules, two arched alcoves that had windows facing the ochre façade of a Romanesque church, and a beautifully worn red brick floor that I kept swept and polished. Such was the grandeur of my dwelling that I was able to ignore the fact that there was no hot water nor any real source of heat . . . the fireplace was merely ornamental and probably had been for centuries. That winter I bought a series of old-fashioned and ineffective stoves at the flea market and was probably lucky to have escaped asphyxiation. However, even when it was cold and damp, sunlight often streamed into the two windowed alcoves, giving the illusion of warmth. And I solved the hot water problem by joining the Canottieri, a rowing club on the Arno just a few blocks away where I was able to take showers, shave, and maintain a reasonable level of personal hygiene.

The palazzo was a warren of rooms, large and small, rented out to foreigners: students, artists, and always a number of young Australians who were making their obligatory jaunt around the world before settling in down under. Next to my spacious room was a small one in which lived William, a skinny and reclusive young American, who, by living very frugally, had made the funds of a one-year fellowship stretch out to five. A weepy Australian girl, inappropriately named Gay, who also lived somewhere in the palazzo, was obsessed with him and would leave gifts of food and flowers with notes at his door. When she became too intense in her pursuit, William would disappear for a few weeks.

The grand *salone* next to my room was the studio of a Fulbright artist from California, John Hunter, who was working on series of huge paintings of Leda and the Swan. The working title he had given the series, which I believe he later wisely changed, was: "Take me to Your Leda."

Above me was a former Italian American Fulbright scholar from Arkansas who had decided to stay in Florence after his scholarship year was up and was also teaching at the Istituto Americano. An odd bird, his hobby was making life-sized Renaissance-style angels in papier-mâché, all of which had the face of his Italian lover, whom I often saw, coming and going, on the monumental stairway that went up to the piano nobile.

My life was far from luxurious, but it was comfortable and interesting. My teaching job provided me with a window onto Florentine life. My students, a number of whom became friends, included a young marchesa who lived in one of the ancient *palazzi* on Piazza Signoria, and her boyfriend, merely a count, who had a passion for comic books. I got to know bankers and shopkeepers, store clerks and housewives, some young, some middle-aged, some old—Florentines from all walks of life—who gave me glimpses into lives so very unlike my own.

My classes were over for the summer when I met my parents in Rome and accompanied them by train, after a stop in Florence, to the small city of Vercelli in the Piedmont, the heart of the Italian rice-growing region. I was serving as an unpaid guide and translator for my father; my mother was along for the ride.

The schedule of appointments and interviews with key people in the Italian rice industry had been arranged by someone in the US Department of Agriculture, and we were staying for several days in a fine old hotel in the center of Vercelli, using it as our base.

My father's first meeting in Vercelli was with the president of a rice milling machinery company in the boardroom at his factory. He was a short but not unattractive man in his late thirties. He was fluent in English, so my modest translating skills were not needed. We sat at a table with a few other executives from the company, and my father began to explain the reasons for his visit in a rather lengthy statement he had prepared. The president, Vittorio was his name, listened to my father with a very serious expression on his face, but soon began to look at me more often than he looked at my father, giving me brief, amiable smiles. When my father had finished speaking, Vittorio, instead of commenting on what my father had just told him, turned to me and asked, "How tall are you?"

"A little under six foot five," I said.

"Do you like going to the beach?" he enquired.

"Sometimes," I said.

"Maybe we can arrange a trip to the coast while you are here."

Vittorio had not much to say about my father's project, but as we were leaving, he offered enthusiastically to supply us with a car and driver for all our interviews while we were in Vercelli. "And you must be my guests for lunch at the hotel every day! I insist."

When we returned to the hotel, my father with obvious pride told my mother: "Joel really made a hit with the young company president." I kept my thoughts on the subject to myself.

Early the next morning Vittorio's handsome, uniformed driver picked us up at the hotel in an impressive black Mercedes limousine and whisked us off to the rice paddies that surround Vercelli. The landscape was vaguely familiar to me from the great Italian neorealist film of the 1940s, *Riso Amaro* (*Bitter Rice*), which had been filmed there. It was one of the few foreign films to make it to provincial Lafayette while I was in high school, and I remembered it well. Another Vittorio, Gassman, and sexy Silvana Mangano played the ill-fated lovers in the film.

None of the small army of *mondine*, the female rice field workers we saw in the fields, was as glamorous as Mangano, but my father was charmed and kept asking me to take photographs of them. We spent the better part of an hour watching the women wading in ankle-high water pulling weeds.

And then we were driven to an office of Ente Risi, the national association of Italian rice growers, where various officials told my father what they wanted him to hear about how the Italians were making great progress developing a long grain rice that would compete with the American long grain, something that many decades later still has not happened.

By 1 p.m. we were back at the hotel to have lunch with Vittorio. The food in the hotel was excellent. We ate, among other things, *panissa*, a dish made with rice and beans and accompanied by a lovely local red wine made from the *nebbiolo* grape.

Every time someone Vittorio knew passed by our table, and he seemed to know almost everyone in the dining room, he would ask me to stand up to demonstrate how tall I was. I must have been asked to stand at least a half dozen times in the course of the meal.

After my father's interviews with scientists, farmers, and bureaucrats in Vercelli were finished, we made a social visit to fulfill a promise my father had made before he left home. My parents had become friendly with an Italian priest who was assigned to the Bishopric of Lafayette. Monsignor Arlanti had grown up in a peasant family on a farm in the Piedmont, and he had told my father much about the region to prepare him for his trip. The monsignor's mother, sister, and brother still lived on the farm, and one afternoon Vittorio's driver took us to pay our respects. We found the family eagerly awaiting us, dressed in what must have been their Sunday best and standing behind a long table on the terrace of their stone farmhouse. The table was spread with a white cloth and crowded with all sorts of delicacies, most of them sugary. As soon as we got out of the limousine, the brother opened a bottle of Asti Spumante which he began pouring while making toast after toast: to my parents, to the absent monsignor, to God, to Italy, to America, to Louisiana. My usually abstemious father had several glasses and told them what a fine priest and man and friend was Monsignor Arlanti. I translated as best I could. They were very proud of their son/brother, the successful priest in America. Everyone was beaming. When it came time to leave, my father, in an expansive mood, kissed on both cheeks the elderly mother and then her daughter. The brother inclined his face to be similarly bussed, but my father simply shook his hand.

Back in Vittorio's Mercedes, speeding toward Vercelli, I said: "Daddy, you just made a *brutta figura*."

"I made a what?"

"A faux-pas."

"What do you mean?"

"Well, you kissed Monsignor Arlanti's mother and you kissed his sister, but you only shook the brother's hand. I'm sure he felt slighted."

"Hmmph," my father said, scowling. On the train trip up from Rome, he had been astonished to see men kissing each other goodbye at some of the stations on the way to Milan. I explained that this was an Italian custom and did not mean what it might have meant in America, that male family members and even friends often kissed each other when meeting or departing to express their affection. My father looked unconvinced and slightly disgusted. "I better never catch you kissing an Italian man," he muttered.

It was over the frequently interrupted lunches at the hotel each day that Vittorio's plan for our trip to the coast gradually took shape. At the end of our time in Vercelli, my parents and I would go to Milan where my father had further interviews. Then, when they were done at the end of the week, Vittorio's driver would pick me up and take me back to Vercelli while my parents spent the weekend resting at a comfortable hotel in Milan. From Vercelli, Vittorio and I would drive first to Genoa, and then on to Portofino where we would have lunch with his wife and two children. He was very eager, he said, for me to meet his family.

At first, everything went as planned. I was driven back to Vercelli and spent the night at the hotel. Next morning early, Vittorio came by to get me. He was driving a red Maserati convertible. Making polite conversation, we headed first for Genoa where, Vittorio informed me, we were picking up a friend who had just sold him a motorboat. The three of us would then drive to Portofino where Vittorio would take possession of the boat and we would spend the morning trying it out, then have lunch with his wife and two daughters who were staying in a hotel in nearby Rapallo.

There followed a blissful day. His friend, Marco, who had also sold him the Maserati, was an ex-race car driver turned car and boat salesman . . . a dashing fellow a bit older than Vittorio. We stopped only briefly at Marco's dealership. In his office was a trophy case filled with the booty of his years as a racer: several shelves of glitzy brass loving cups and statuettes on pedestals; in the middle of them, in a place of honor, was a US sailor's cap.

With the three of us crowded into the front and only seat of the Maserati, and Marco at the wheel, we took off down the winding and spectacular coast road to Portofino, a short, thrilling ride. We were in Portofino before noon and Marco gave Vittorio the keys to the new boat. It was a sleek twenty-foot motorboat, all gleaming wood and polished steel and brass.

Soon we were zipping out of the harbor and drinking inaugural champagne (so much more sensible than breaking a bottle of it on the prow), enjoying the sun, the wind, the speed, the blue sky, the gorgeous views of coastline. After an hour or so of aimlessly circling, revving and slowing and revving and slowing and performing various maneuvers that demonstrated the motorboat's speed, power, and agility, Vittorio announced we were going to have lunch at a restaurant in nearby Santa Margarita. "I'm looking forward to meeting your wife and family," said I. "Oh, that will be later," said Vittorio dismissively. "Perhaps they will join us for tea. We'll see."

Marco, Vittorio, and I had lunch outside on a terrace high up over the sea: beautifully roasted fish and a sublime white wine. After lunch, we got back on the boat and circled and revved and circled and drank more champagne. The afternoon went by very quickly. It was almost 5 p.m. when Vittorio said that it was time we headed back to Genoa, "So we won't be meeting your family for tea?" I asked. "No, we will drive back and have dinner together at their hotel tonight."

Soon we were back in the Maserati heading north. Marco was showing, it seemed to me, a little more reckless abandon than he had exhibited on the way down. He was driving very fast and passing every car in the way, curves or no curves. Suddenly, a large tourist bus loomed in front of us. Marco had a good shot at passing it, but an approaching car made him cut back too quickly and we sideswiped the bus. I pulled my elbow back just as the metal of the Maserati scraped the metal of the bus. Both vehicles came to a sudden halt. All the windows of the bus opened and a dozen or so heads, most of them blue-haired and American, poked out, screaming. I was pretty shaken, but Vittorio never lost his cool. We had hardly stopped scraping when he remarked in a rather off-hand way, "Non importa! Domani prendiamo l'Alfa Romeo." (Never mind! Tomorrow we'll take the Alfa Romeo.)

The damage, miraculously, turned out to be insignificant. There was not a scratch on the bus, and only a minor wound to the paint job on the Maserati.

Once back in Genoa, it was decided that instead of returning to Portofino for the meal with Vittorio's family, we would spend the night in Genoa so that Marco could have the blemished paint job repaired by the next morning.

"We will have to stay in a hotel here," Vittorio said, "but, of course, you will be my guest." He called to make a reservation. "Due stanze!" he repeated loudly, several times, making sure that both the hotel and I understood that we would not be sharing a room. We checked in to our separate rooms, agreeing to meet shortly in the lobby. "I want to take you somewhere nice for dinner," Vittorio told me.

The nice place he took me was a nightclub with an orchestra and quite a few young women sitting at the bar and at tables. After a mediocre meal, I found myself dancing with one of them. She was in her early twenties, had dark hair and eyes and the profile of Nefertiti. Her name was Lola.

Lola, without much success, tried hard to make conversation. "Ti piace la musica?" (Do you like music?) she asked me. "Si, mi piace la musica," I replied. "Ti piace Rita Pavone?" "Si, mi piace Rita Pavone." "Ti piace Gianni Morandi?" "Si, mi piace Gianni Morandi."

She went through the entire catalogue of 1960s Italian popular singers, and I assured her that I liked them all. Then we danced silently, cheek to cheek and several other body parts to several other body parts until the orchestra took a break.

When I returned to the table, Vittorio gave me a grave look. "Ti piace la Lola?" he asked. "Yes," I said, "I like Lola." "If you want to go to bed with her," he continued to stare gravely, "I will pay for it. Remember, tonight you are my guest." "Thank you, Vittorio," I said, "but it has been a long day and I am very tired. It is very generous of you, but I'm really not up to it."

When we got back to the hotel, Vittorio accompanied me to my room. He sat next to me on the bed. Neither of us spoke for what seemed a long time. Then suddenly, he bolted up, turned and shook my hand, and wished me pleasant dreams. "I'll see you at breakfast," he said, and disappeared quickly through the door.

The next day as we were driving back to Milan in the touched-up Maserati, Vittorio, with a very serious air, asked me: "Joel, why did you not want to go to bed with Lola last night?"

"I told you, Vittorio. I was very tired."

"I do not think that was the reason."

"What do you think *was* the reason?" I asked him.

"I think," he said, "that many of you American men are like a lot of Italian men."

"In what way?"

"When it comes to women, *é tutto teatro*! It's all theater!"

"You may be right," I said.

Vittorio rested his hand on my thigh. "You are going now with your parents to England?"

"Yes," I said.

"When are you coming back to Italy?"

"In about two weeks."

"Promise me something, Joel."

"What is that, Vittorio?"

"Call me when you come back. Come to see me." His hand gave my thigh a little squeeze. "I know how you must live in Florence," he said. "And that is no way to live in Italy. You should live the way I live. You need a job that gives you lots of money so you can have a nice villa, a nice car, maybe even a boat. You need to live the way I live. Perhaps I can help you do that."

"Sounds interesting," I said.

"Joel," he said, "do you promise you will call me as soon as you get back to Florence?" "I promise," I said, knowing that I never would.

24

DA NELLO

It was not the cheapest place to get a decent meal in Florence in the early 1960s. That would probably be da Frizzi, near the Piazza della Signoria, where the fixed price for a three-course meal (a quarter of a liter of wine or bottled water, a first course of pasta and a more substantial second course of meat, or a second course and dessert) was only 350 lire, a little more than half a dollar. A better three-course meal could be had da Nello where the *prezzo fisso* was 600 lire, about 80 cents.

Da Nello was on the Borgo Pinti, a narrow street with narrow sidewalks, that runs from near the historic center of Florence to Piazza Donatello, site of the English Cemetery where Elizabeth Barrett Browning, Walter Savage Landor, and other famous English (and some American) expatriates are entombed.

The trattoria had only one room, with a door that opened directly to the street. It was large enough to hold about a dozen tables. The kitchen was at the rear and a bar to the right as one entered. Nello, the proprietor, had a well-deserved nickname: "Il Crudo" (The Crude One). Unsmiling, wearing a filthy, bloodstained apron, he would plod through the diners on his way to the kitchen with a dripping side of beef on his shoulder. Gina, the only waitress, who, with her beak of a nose, looked like Dante in a fright wig, buzzed from table to table, bringing steaming plates of food, efficiently clearing the tables and resetting them. The menu offered five or six simple Tuscan dishes: roast pork, roast veal, roast chicken, boiled beef, perhaps a veal stew. The servings were just large enough, but not too large. Florentines show restraint in everything.

In my first years in Florence, I often had lunch da Nello and got to know by sight the regulars, occasionally conversed with some of them. Almost every day, at the same table for two against a wall, sat a plump, well-dressed couple of a certain age. The man, with unnaturally black hair and a goatee to match, always wore a tweed sport coat with a sweater and tie; his wife, a jacket and cloche hat, both made of faux leopard skin. One day she leaned toward me and said, "I know that you must be from a good family in America." "How can you tell?" I asked. "Whenever you cut your meat, you always switch the fork to your right hand before you take a bite."

A tiny, elderly woman with a haughty air, who held herself erectly, and ate slowly and deliberately, was always there when I went for lunch. Eventually, we began to recognize each other with a slight smile and a nod. Sometimes, when it was crowded, we shared a table. I learned that she was the Princess D'Annunzio, daughter-in-law of the famous poet, dramatist, and orator Prince Gabriele D'Annunzio, who became a national hero during the First World War. Considered a protofascist who had a great influence on the ideas of Mussolini, D'Annunzio was also a notorious womanizer. His most infamous love affair was with the celebrated actress, Eleonora Duse. Both have streets named after them in Florence and I suspect it is not mere coincidence that Via Gabriele D'Annunzio crosses Viale Eleonora Duse.

Once when I was sharing a table with Princess D'Annunzio, I mentioned that I was looking for a place to live. "There may soon be available an apartment with exactly the same floor plan as mine, next to my apartment," she told me. "The man who was keeping his mistress in the apartment recently died and I doubt that she will be able to afford it without him. If you would like to see what the apartment is like, I'll be glad to show you mine." So, I went one day to call on Principessa D'Annunzio in her apartment on Piazza Donatello. I suspected that she really wanted to rent a room to me in her own apartment but was too proud to say so directly. While she was showing me around, I spotted a large, framed photograph leaning against the wall under a stairway. It was of an elegant woman with a tiny waist. "What a beautiful woman!" I remarked. Principessa D'Annunzio frowned. "That was my mother-in-law," she said. "The vainest woman who ever lived. She attended her husband's funeral in her idea of mourning, a tight black sheath with a frilly white blouse. She finally had the decency to faint, but not until a robust young man was standing near enough to catch her in his arms. She often fainted when robust young men were standing near enough to catch her in their arms," she said with great disdain. Shortly after my visit, I read a biography of D'Annunzio that described his wife as saintly and kind, devoted to her husband in spite of his multiple infidelities. Her daughter-in-law had a very different opinion. I wondered where the truth lay.

Charming as she was, I would not have liked living in a room in the apartment of Princess D'Annunzio, and carefully steered the conversation away from that possibility. It did occur to me that living across from the English Cemetery and the tomb of the poet Walter Savage Landor, whose most famous poem begins "Past ruin'd Illion, Helen lives / Alcestis rises from the shades; Verse calls them forth; 'tis Verse that gives / Immortal youth to mortal maids," I would have been able to write to the English majors among my acquaintance: "Past ruin'd Walter Joel lives."

Da Nello

I often lunched at da Nello with my close friends Denis and Joan Murphy. Denis was British, a recent graduate of Magdalene College, Cambridge, and Joan was an American from Boston. We had become friends after Joan and I met while standing in line to buy cheese in a neighborhood *salumeria*. They lived in the top floor flat above the *salumeria* and we soon became the best of friends. Denis was teaching English at the British Institute, then located in the Palazzo Antinori on the chic via Tornabuoni. His part Portuguese ancestry gave him dark good looks unusual for an Englishman. Joan was a slender blonde who looked as if she might have stepped out of a Botticelli painting. They were a highly ornamental couple.

The British Institute was where most well-born Florentines went to learn English, and Denis and Joan had many friends among the fashionable and wealthy younger set who welcomed such beauty into their circle. A number of their well-off friends could not understand why Denis worked so hard and lived in a tiny walk-up flat. Hard work was for them an alien concept. The proper way, the only way, to live in Italy, they told him, was to have a job that provided a great deal of money and made few demands on one's time and energy. And how could one live happily in Italy without a comfortable villa, or at least a grand apartment? A number of them hinted that with their connections, Denis could easily find such a position.

To Denis, it sounded like a plan. So, he resigned from the British Institute, rented a charming *casa colonica* in the hills above Fiesole, bought a third-hand Alfa Romeo, and waited for his friends to find him a lucrative sinecure. When he told them what he had done, they seemed surprised and suddenly began to be hard to be in touch with. There followed a difficult autumn. Denis was forced to earn a living by driving all over Tuscany giving private English lessons, spending much of what he earned on gasoline for the thirsty Alfa Romeo. He soon realized that he should return to England where he would have better job prospects. They gave up the country house, and while putting together a plan to repatriate themselves, Denis and Joan moved in with me in my one large room in the Palazzo de Rustici.

One day toward the end of November, while we were having lunch at da Nello, Denis and Joan began bickering, as they often did during that stressful time. After we had finished our meal and paid for it, Denis suddenly bolted from the table and ran out the door. We had been talking about going to the nearby flea market, so Joan and I figured that was where he was headed and followed him there. Being careful not to let him see us, we watched him buy a pair of pince-nez at one of the stands. As soon as he left, we went to the same stand and each bought a pair. I led us on a short-cut back to Palazzo dei Rustici, so that when Denis arrived wearing his pince-nez, he found us sitting facing the door wearing our pince-nez. For a moment, through our glasses, he could not see us, and we could not see him, then we all had a good laugh and the silliness of the stunt dissolved the previous tension between them. Right after I took a photograph of them wearing their ancient spectacles, my upstairs neighbor, an American ex-Fulbright scholar, knocked on the door and came in. "I'm off to look for a second-hand chest," he told us. "I really need one badly, and I hope I can find something that doesn't cost too much." He described in detail what he was looking for and where he was going to look for it.

"Good luck," I told him.

He turned to leave, and then paused and said, "Oh, by the way, I just heard that President Kennedy has been shot."

We were stunned. As was everyone I knew in Florence, except for my neighbor who was so preoccupied with his furniture. In the next few days, everywhere I went I was greeted with warm expressions of sympathy for the tragic loss. But gradually, as the days passed, I sensed that the Florentines' sympathy seemed to wane, replaced by an attitude of, "Kennedy was too good for you Americans, you didn't deserve him, and you let him be killed." I realized it was a hybrid of the anti-Americanism, consisting of a mixture of envy and disdain, that I experienced in one form or another during the many years I lived in Europe.

Denis and Joan left on the train for England a short time later. And it did not take him long to find a job in the administration of his former college. Their marriage did not last, but Denis went on to have a long and distinguished career, winning much renown for his fundraising skills, eventually becoming senior bursar of Magdalene College.

A few years ago, when my partner John and I visited Denis in Cambridge, he invited us to have dinner with the Dons in the Magdalene College Dining Hall. We sat under a striking Wyndham Lewis portrait of T. S. Eliot and had a very delicious meal in mostly delightful company. I was seated between Denis and Dr. Richard Luckett, keeper of the Samuel Pepys Library who, though insouciantly inebriated, made amusing conversation. John had less luck. His dining companion was borderline rude and only wanted to talk condescendingly about his own achievement, which had to do with an obscure but shatteringly important invention he had made in a chemistry laboratory. After dinner, when we moved to another room for port, I sat next to the man and wormed out of him the startling information that, in spite of his Masterpiece Theatre accent, he was actually from Port Arthur, Texas.

But it had been a wonderful evening, a very long way from da Nello on the Borgo Pinti.

25

LORETTA

I think we both realized at the same time that we were too old to be doing what we had just set out to do. The night before, over dinner and wine, we had decided it would be a great adventure. We were in the middle of a gorgeous Italian spring and the idea of hitchhiking the short distance from Florence to Pisa, the countryside in glorious bloom under the bluest of Tuscan skies, was irresistible. But now that we were actually standing by the side of the road with our thumbs out, we were having second thoughts.

I was on the far side of my twenties; Loretta was in her mid-thirties and looking very uncomfortable. She was a gifted artist on sabbatical from Chicago where she taught at the Art Institute and had been sent to me by my old New Orleans friend, Nick Polites, who was living in Chicago trying to forge some kind of career in advertising. Loretta, he had written, was spending a year in Florence after a painful breakup with a wild, hard-living, hard-drinking girl named Megan, known for driving recklessly and breaking hearts and who was eventually to die in a car crash in Los Angeles.

Loretta, reserved, quiet, and soft-spoken, was the exact opposite. She was living in the Pensione Bartolini on the Arno that was the inspiration for the Pensione Bertolini in Forester's novel *A Room with a View*. It had a long tradition of hosting artists, writers, and college professors. A collage by Beatnik poet Gregory Corso, who had been a recent guest, was framed and hanging in the entrance hall. Among the other guests in the pensione that year were novelist Robert Ferro and his lover, Michael Grumley, both members of The Violet Quill, a group of gay writers in New York in the 1980s.

I did not meet them that year, but years later discovered Loretta as a character named Loretta in Ferro's novel *The Blue Nile*. It is very unflattering and untruthful depiction, describing her as a mysterious and promiscuous lodger whose door was always left open. The novel's Loretta was no doubt the projection of Ferro's own fantasies. She, however, fared better in the novel than my dear friend Count Francesco Guicciardini, the kindest, gentlest, most civilized of men. In the novel, thinly disguised, he is portrayed as a sadomasochist with a dungeon beneath his Renaissance palazzo where he tortures and is tortured by young men. Nothing could have been more removed from the truth.

I don't remember who eventually picked us up and drove us to Pisa. I do remember that when we began to hitch back, we admitted to each other that it had not been a genial idea and that we were never going to do such a thing again.

We had not been standing long by the side of the road when a Porsche roared up and stopped for us. The driver was a handsome and taciturn man with curly, dirty blond hair. He hardly spoke a word on the drive back to Florence and we were too embarrassed to volunteer much about ourselves.

About a week later, Loretta and I were invited to have tea at the Castello di Vincigliata on a hill near Fiesole. The castle had been built in the medieval style in the middle of the nineteenth century on the site of a genuine medieval castle that had long before fallen into ruin. Early in the twentieth century, Gertrude Stein and Alice B. Toklas had spent one summer there. Ms. Stein wrote that one morning she discovered their French maid, whom they had brought with them, sitting on the steps reading the Florentine paper, *La Nazione*. "I didn't know that you understood Italian," Stein commented. "I don't," replied the maid, "but all the *important* words are in French."

Loretta and I had been invited by a Mrs. Graetz whose husband had recently purchased the castle. He had owned a shipping company in Israel and when it was nationalized, he was given an enormous sum of money as compensation. The entire family dabbled in the arts, so they decided to move to their castle in Italy and pursue their interests.

When they were settled, the Graetzs joined an association of people who lived in restored castles: La Vita Moderna nei Vecchi Castelli (Modern Life in Ancient Castles) though, as someone pointed out, that since their castle only pretended to be ancient, a more suitable organization might have been "Ancient Life in Modern Castles." Once, when the organization held a meeting at Vincigliata, the president of the association, a nobleman who lived in a castle near Milan, arrived late and discovered one of the perils of such a life. Seeing the guests standing in what appeared to be an open *loggia*, he rushed toward them, only to collide with the plate glass with which the Graetzs had enclosed it and was taken to the hospital and given many stitches.

It was through a close friend of mine, Flo Shoul, a Jewish South African painter, that I met Mrs. Graetz. Flo was with us when went to the castle that afternoon, and were shown into a drawing room where Mrs. Graetz, a portly woman well into middle age, was awaiting us. As she was pouring our tea, the man who had given us a lift in his Porsche entered the room. "This is my son Reuven," said Mrs.

Graetz. He stared at us and we stared back at him, but our previous encounter was not mentioned.

Loretta and I continued to hang out and make little excursions together, but our hitchhiking days were over forever. At the end of her sabbatical year, Loretta returned to Chicago. Nick mentioned her in a few of his letters, but eventually we completely lost touch.

A quarter of a century later, I was in Madison, Wisconsin, to arrange an art exhibition. While there, I looked up a friend I had not seen since high school. Sarah, for a time, had been my "girlfriend" and I recall taking her to the Jefferson Theater in Lafayette, and watching a movie with Rock Hudson and Doris Day while we unenthusiastically held hands. It was not until many years later that I realized that while I was indulging in fantasies about Rock Hudson, her dreams were about Doris Day. She had married one of our classmates. They had moved away and had a couple of children. Later, I heard that they had divorced, and she was living with another woman in Madison, working as a choir director for a Methodist church. I looked them up while I was in Madison, and we had a meal together.

"I met someone who knows you," she told me. A few years before, she and her friend were invited to dinner at the home of a woman she had never met. On the way, she stopped to buy a bottle of wine for her hostess and decided on a good Chianti. "When I gave it to her, she remarked that she had visited Chianti years before with her friend Joel Fletcher." It was, of course, Loretta, who had left Chicago and was living in a small town near Madison. Sarah remembered the name of the town, and I was able to find her telephone number.

I phoned, and she suggested that we meet at the restaurant at Taliesin, the Frank Lloyd Wright compound not far from where she was living. A few nights later, we did, and had a wonderful evening remembering our carefree days in Florence. "I have something for you," she told me and handed me a cardboard tube. In it was a large charcoal drawing she had done of me while I was sitting at a table in Palazzo dei Rustici, the charming Renaissance slum where I was living the year that she spent in Florence. I was delighted!

In the years to come, we kept loosely in touch, exchanging Christmas cards, but not much else. She died of cancer in 2004. The beautiful drawing she did of me is framed and on my bedroom wall. It bothers me only a little that no one ever recognizes that it is an accurate depiction of a much younger me.

26

MR. AMBASSADOR

The most distinguished person ever born in Lafayette, Louisiana, was Ambassador Jefferson Caffery. Today most people there know him as a parkway, but there are still a few who remember the man. After a highly eventful and successful career as a diplomat, he spent the last few decades of his life partly in Rome at the Grand Hotel, partly in Lafayette at the Sheraton Town House Motel on Pinhook Road. At the latter, he always took two rooms, separated by a carport. One room was for Mrs. Caffery, the other was for the ambassador and his valet/chauffeur, Stefan.

Caffery, born to a prominent family in Lafayette in 1886, was a member of the first class at the newly founded Southwestern Louisiana Industrial Institute before he transferred to Tulane from which he graduated in 1906. He studied law privately with his father and was admitted to the Louisiana Bar in 1909, but by that time he had already decided, after a trip to Europe in 1908, to join the Foreign Service. He took the examination in January of 1911 and did brilliantly. His first posting was to the United States Legation at Caracas. It was the beginning of a forty-four-year career in which he witnessed and participated in some of the most important events in twentieth-century history.

In the 1930s, he served as ambassador to Cuba, where he narrowly survived an assassination attempt. He then became the United States ambassador to Brazil, a post he held throughout the Second World War. In 1944, because of his skill and experience, he was given the plum post of ambassador to France in the crucial postwar years. His last posting was as ambassador to Egypt, where he remained until his retirement in 1955.

While serving as ambassador to France, Caffery became friendly with the then apostolic nuncio, Giuseppe Roncalli. When Roncalli became Pope John XXIII, he invited Caffery, who was by then living in Rome, to help him plan the Ecumenical Conference. "Since I can no longer come to see you," the new Pope told Caffery, "you must come to see me." (When the Pope visited prisoners in the Regina Coeli

Prison in Rome, he is said to have told them: "Because you cannot come to see me, I have come to see you.")

I first met the ambassador shortly after I got out of the navy and was visiting at home in Lafayette. I went with my parents and the Cafferys to spend the night at the still private Hodges Gardens in central Louisiana as guests of Mr. and Mrs. A. J. Hodges. Mr. Hodges had made a fortune in gas, oil, and timber, and he and his wife had created a seven-hundred-acre botanical garden, now a state park, where they lived in a vast hotel-like house on a manmade island in the middle of a manmade two-hundred-acre lake.

I drove us from Lafayette and, following instructions I had been given, parked near a pier on the lake where I found and pushed a button. Doors on the island opened and an automated ferry emerged. We boarded it, pushed another button, and the ferry began its return journey. It deposited us in a tunnel that led to a room with an enormous glass case filled with what seemed every porcelain bird ever produced by the Boehm factory, a collection put together by Mrs. Hodges. Soft light classical music was playing in the background. The Hodges loved music and had it piped into all the rooms in the house from a central "music room." It was inescapable.

We were shown by a servant to our rooms, which were large and comfortable. Next to my king-sized bed was a keypad with buttons to open and close the curtains and turn the lights up and down. There were also buttons to increase and decrease the volume of the music, but it never completely disappeared. When turned down to the lowest volume, the ghost of it remained, half-heard from the hallway.

That evening, after fruit juice cocktails in a living room that resembled the lobby of an upscale Holiday Inn, dinner was served in the adjoining dining room on a very long table made, apparently, of ebony. The place settings were of gold with gold goblets and gold flatware.

On the plates of gold, we were served pork chops and collard greens, and the golden goblets were filled with buttermilk. We patted our lips with heavy damask napkins and made polite conversation with background music by André Kostelanetz, Leroy Anderson, and, finally, Tchaikovsky. Conversation became more difficult when dessert was served to the blast of cannons of the "1812 Overture."

After dessert we moved back into the living room, where we took our places, each one alone on a huge sofa, for the evening's entertainment: an LP of speeches by a former vice president of General Motors who spoke for more than an hour of the wonderful opportunities offered the world by American capitalism. At one point, I glanced over at Ambassador Caffery, who, with head cocked to one side, seemed to be listening with great interest. Then I noticed that his eyes were closed. It was a technique he had no doubt perfected at many excruciatingly boring official dinners.

The next time I dined with the Cafferys was in their suite at the Grand Hotel in Rome on my first trip to Italy in the summer of 1962. The meal was served at a beautifully appointed table by white-jacketed waiters who appeared and disappeared swiftly and quietly, bringing or removing plates and silverware.

When we had finished the main course, suddenly a small plate, a knife, and a fork were placed in front of me. As a server entered carrying an artfully arranged bowl of fruit, it dawned on me that for the first time in my life I was going to have to perform on a piece of fruit an act that heretofore I had only witnessed with awe. While eating in Italian *trattorie*, I had been fascinated by the way Italians ate fruit with a knife and fork. Apples, oranges, and bananas were all elegantly peeled, sliced, and consumed with a flourish I had never before witnessed. I had always eaten apples by picking them up and biting into them, oranges by clumsily peeling them with my two hands, and bananas the way that monkeys eat bananas. Observing the brio with which Italians dispatched fruit, I was impressed and a little intimidated.

I quickly sized-up the situation. The bowl, in addition to a bunch of grapes, contained two apples, two pears, two oranges, and *three* bananas. Obviously, I thought, someone is going to take a banana, so I will take one and do whatever the other banana-taker does.

But no sooner was the banana on my plate than the waiter turned on his heel and left the room. "Go ahead, Joel," Mrs. Caffery said, "the Ambassador and I never eat fruit."

I am sure that my performance was not a model of grace and skill, but at least I managed to get the damn thing peeled and eaten without having it fly off my plate.

The evening went by very quickly and pleasantly as Ambassador Caffery was an impressive raconteur and had interesting stories to tell. My favorite was about his time in Japan as a young diplomat where he had gone to administer US aid after the earthquake that almost destroyed Tokyo and Yokohama in 1923.

He described a ceremony at the Imperial Court in which then French ambassador Paul Claudel presented a citation to Emperor Yoshihito who had been getting increasingly gaga. The ceremony took place in the ornate throne room of the Imperial Palace with the court in full regalia and the entire diplomatic corps wearing their formal morning coats. Paul Claudel appeared on the long carpet leading to the imperial throne with the citation, a rolled-up parchment tied with a blue ribbon. He gravely made his way toward the emperor, and when he reached the throne, bowed deeply, handed the citation to the emperor, and bowed again. When he came up from the second bow, Claudel found the emperor peering at him through the rolled-up parchment as if it were a telescope. The emperor was gently escorted from the room and never again seen in public.

Ambassador Caffery also told the story of how, as American ambassador to Egypt, he had rescued King Farouk and got him safely out of the country when he was overthrown by the Egyptian Revolution of 1952, managing to get him aboard his yacht and away from danger to eventual exile in Italy.

Whenever Ambassador Caffery heard that Farouk was in Rome, he avoided restaurants and other public places where they might meet because the hugely corpulent and eternally grateful Farouk would always enfold Caffery in a bear-hug and attempt to kiss him, and the prospect made the somewhat aloof and very proper diplomat shudder with revulsion. "I was only doing my duty," Caffery said. "I certainly did not care about that dreadful man!"

In the fifteen-or-so years that I knew Ambassador Caffery, I heard most of his stories more than once, and I always enjoyed rehearing them. They were vivid episodes of personal history intertwined with some of the most significant events of the twentieth century. Eventually, I learned to play him like a juke box. I knew all the right cues. "Mr. Ambassador," I would say, "weren't you in Tokyo just after the 1923 earthquake?" And then he would always tell the wonderful tale of the emperor's last public appearance.

Caffery's most significant posting was his five-year ambassadorship to France at the end of the Second World War when he was a witness to and a participant in one of the most fascinating periods in modern history. It is an era well described by Antony Beevor and Artemis Cooper in their richly detailed book, *Paris After the Liberation*, in which they characterize Caffery as "Courageous and generous . . . a discreet homosexual, although his lover, one of his own staff, was slightly less careful to preserve the secrecy of their relationship."

John Kirchick, in his widely praised *Secret City: The Hidden History of Gay Washington*, wrote: "the early twentieth-century U.S. Foreign Service was a uniquely attractive institution for gay men, affording them a measure of freedom and a literal world of possibilities unavailable at home. First and foremost, it offered a respectable career path for confirmed bachelors, long tours overseas obviating uncomfortable questions about the lack of a wife and family."

Caffery was in his early forties when he married Gertrude McCarthy, the heiress of a Chicago meatpacking family. They married in Rio de Janeiro after he had been made US ambassador to Brazil, when a wealthy wife would have been a real asset to his rising career.

His faithful valet, Stefan Bajc, shared the ambassador's motel room on their visits to Lafayette. Stefan was dark-haired with pale skin. Whenever I saw him, he played the role of valet/chauffeur to perfection. Once in Rome, wearing his uniform and cap, he silently drove us in the ambassador's huge and ancient black limousine (a Packard, as I recall) to Ostia Antica and stood guard at the car while the ambassador, unopened *Baedeker* in hand, and I strode through the ruins of the Roman port.

When Caffery died in Lafayette in 1974, the year after Mrs. Caffery, he left Stefan a quarter of a million dollars. Philip Dur, one of Caffery's protégés in the diplomatic corps and his biographer, told me that Bajc protested that it was too much, took only half that amount, and returned to his native Yugoslavia to be married. The last I heard of him, he was living again in Rome.

Whatever their marital arrangements were while they were alive, ambassador and Mrs. Caffery are now buried side by side, together for eternity in the cemetery of St. John's Cathedral in Lafayette.

27

COUNT FRANCESCO

Count Francesco Guicciardini, whose ancestor of the same name in the sixteenth century wrote the first history of Florence and the first history of Italy, had a very good address:

Il Conte Francesco Guicciardini
Palazzo Guicciardini
Via Guicciardini
Firenze

Palazzo Guicciardini, really a series of palazzi in Florence that extend from the Palazzo Pitti to the Ponte Vecchio, was built on land that has belonged to the Guicciardini family since the thirteenth century.

Count Francesco was an unpretentious and sweetly charming man who wore his heritage very lightly. The first time he showed me around the palazzo, he pointed out two paintings that hung in simple gold frames in the anteroom of the library and said: "These are our Caravaggios. They tell me they are very good ones." He paused and considered them. "I don't know . . . *I* like them."

When I got to know Francesco in the early 1960s, he was in his mid-fifties and lived in a modernized and comfortable flat on the ground floor of the palazzo. His mother, who had been one of the great beauties of Florence, lived in grander quarters above on the piano nobile, the same floor that included a handsome library and a number of formal sitting rooms that must have been much used on official occasions when Francesco's ancestors helped the Medici govern Florence. The impressive library had bookcases that ran from a polished red brick floor to the ceiling high above. The room was bisected by three arches held up by slender columns of pietra serena, the gray stone typical of Tuscany, and from the ceiling hung an enormous Flemish brass chandelier.

Oddly, the library housed the largest collection in Italy of books on Quakerism. One of Francesco's ancestors in the nineteenth century had gone to England and become a Quaker. *Lo zio quacquero*, as he was known in the family, had brought back with him a huge number of volumes about his new religion.

At one time the library had held the priceless archive of the Guicciardini, family papers going back to the beginning of the Renaissance, but in the 1930s Francesco's uncle, Count Paolo, got tired of scholars with dirty feet tracking through the palazzo to study the archive and moved the collection to a ground floor suite of rooms with a separate entrance behind the palazzo. There rows of sturdy shelves are marked with labels that bear the names of all the great families of Florence: Medici, Strozzi, Machiavelli, Alberti, Antinori, Bardi, Ghiberti, Vespucci, among them. The two things I remember most about my visit to the archive with Francesco was a shelf labeled: "Vari Cardinali" (Miscellaneous Cardinals) and a letter from that scourge of earthly pleasures, Savonarola, to the monks of the Convent of San Marco that began with a most un-Savonarola-like greeting: "I miei carissimi, dolcissimi fratellini" (My dearest, sweetest little brothers).

Francesco's mother, La Contessa Guicciardini, then in her seventies, was still very striking. In a silver frame on Francesco's baby grand piano was a photograph of her as a haughty young woman with a single long strand of pearls around her neck. It showed what a stunner she had once been. She had come from Naples, from a family more ancient and noble than the Guicciardini whose titles only went back to the Renaissance. Like many southern Italians, she was of a superstitious nature and clung to her superstitions, even as she lived among the more pragmatic Florentines.

Francesco was fond of telling a story about when he was a young boy and he and his mother were spending the season at Bagni di Lucca, then a fashionable resort in the Tuscan Hills outside of Florence. One day they were having lunch on the terrace of the hotel when a carriage from Naples arrived, and from it descended a Neapolitan nobleman who was widely considered to be *un malòcchio*, an "evil eye," who brings misfortune wherever he goes. When La Contessa recognized him, she was beside herself. *Malòcchi*, according to tradition, always bring tragedy to the people they encounter. However, one must be very polite to them, or the ensuing disaster will be even worse. So, La Contessa invited the *malòcchio*, whose family she had known in Naples, to join them for dinner. He did, and Francesco said his mother was at her most charming and gracious throughout the meal. But when they retired to their room, she forbade Francesco to undress. And, still wearing a tiara and necklace, she lay down on top of her bed, her eyes open, waiting.

Shortly after midnight, an earthquake shook the hotel. La Contessa grabbed Francesco and dashed to the exit. When the other guests, clad in pajamas and robes began to emerge from the hotel a short time later, they found La Contessa, every diamond in place, standing at a distance, holding Francesco firmly by the hand. "How did you know?" someone asked her. "I knew," she replied.

Francesco enjoyed entertaining an international circle of friends at lunch in the elegant dining room on the piano nobile where, under the gaze of ancestral portraits, simple but excellent food was served on ancient armorial china bearing the *stemma* of the Guicciardini: three hunting horns on a shield. Francesco sat at one end of a long table that seated eight comfortably, his mother at the other end. The guests who sat between them were usually an interesting mix of nationalities, professions, and of diverse social backgrounds. Francesco was anything but a snob.

The first time I was among the invited, after an aperitivo in one of the sitting rooms, we moved into the dining room where we were joined by La Contessa. She strode regally into the room, took her seat, and before acknowledging the presence of the guests, turned to Francesco and enquired in a world-weary voice: "Che lingua si parla oggi?" "We're speaking English today, mother," Francesco replied cheerily.

When the handsome, white-jacketed manservant arrived with platters heaped with food, Francesco would always say: "Maria's not a fancy cook, but we think her veal stew is rather good." Maria's *stufato di vitello* was excellent, and often the main course at Francesco's lunches.

While the manservant poured wine into the crystal goblets, Francesco would say: "I hope you like this wine. It's certainly not a great wine, but it comes from our vineyards at San Gimignano, and we find it quite pleasant." It was, of course, a very good wine that went perfectly with Maria's unpretentious but tasty stew.

Francesco owned a weekend and summer retreat in the tiny town of Montopoli val d'Arno, about thirty miles west of Florence. It was a low, long villa with ochre walls that filled an entire block and revealed very little of itself to the street, which was named via Francesco Guicciardini. On the other side of the house was a balcony with an iron railing and red brick floor that ran the length of the house and overlooked a valley that could have been painted by Leonardo da Vinci. Indeed, the town of Vinci, where the great artist was born, is only about fifteen miles distant from Montopoli.

When the weather was agreeable, Francesco would invite friends, many of them young and attractive men, for lunch or to spend the night, or the weekend. The villa boasted a small swimming pool. "It's really just an excuse to get people to take off their clothes," said Francesco, and he almost always had his Brownie camera, snapping away. During the cold and dreary winter months, the same friends would go to have tea in Francesco's apartment, sit around a coffee table, and leaf through the pages of albums containing the photographic bounty of the summer.

Francesco also led an active social life in loftier circles than those who appeared around his tiny swimming pool in summer and his coffee table in winter. He often mentioned his friend Marcella, also a countess, who was exceedingly proud of her jewels. After a dinner party at which they had both been guests, he told me that someone complimented her on her diamond necklace. "I'm glad you like it," she said, "but tonight I am only wearing *half* of it!" He also told me about another dinner party when Marcella was seated next to a white Russian émigré, quite a few of whom had settled in Florence after the Revolution. He admired a brooch she was wearing. Pleased, she told him, "It really is lovely, isn't it? It's made from lapis lazuli." "I know," he replied, "in St. Petersburg we had a staircase made of it."

Francesco was a close friend of Violet Trefusis, daughter of Mrs. Alice Keppel, a former mistress of King Edward the VII of England, who had retired to Florence and lived the rest of her life in the lovely Villa dell'Ombrellino, once the home of Galileo, on a hill overlooking the Arno in the very posh neighborhood of Bellosguardo. Francesco told me that every spring, Mrs. Keppel would summon her gardeners to the terrace of the villa and instruct them in fractured Italian, the only two words of the language that she learned in the many years she had lived there: "Bisogna begonias," by which she meant: "There must be begonias."

After Mrs. Keppel passed away, her daughter Violet continued to live in the villa, and in the 1960s, in her sixties, she split her time between Florence and La Tour de Saint Loup, an ancient tower northeast of Paris that had been a gift from one of her lovers, the wealthy sewing machine heiress, Winnaretta Singer.

As a young woman Violet had been at the center of a scandal even more notorious than her mother's affair with the King of England. In the 1920s, she and English writer Vita Sackville-West left their respective husbands and eloped to France. They eventually returned to their spouses but remained devoted to each other till the end of their lives, and their story was recast in a number of works of fiction over the next decades, including novels by Virginia Woolf and Nancy Mitford.

In 1973, Sackville-West's son, Nigel, published *Portrait of a Marriage*, a book that described his mother's affair with Trefusis and his father's many affairs with men. Shortly after it appeared, an anonymous bit of verse began circulating among the Anglo-Florentine community in Florence. Francesco, who recited it to me, attributed it to Sir Harold Acton, another prominent Anglo-Florentine. It began:

With your mother confessed as a Lesbian,
And your father declared as a queer,
The question we feel we must ask you,
Is how you contrived to be here?

Acton was also said to be the author of a facetious "social note" shortly after it became known that Trefusis and Sackville-West had eloped: "Miss Violet Trefusis has recently left the Isle of Man for the Island of Lesbos."

One early summer day, Francesco invited me to accompany him to have coffee with Acton, who lived in the magnificent Villa La Pietra just outside of Florence.

In his youth, Acton had been one of the celebrated "Bright Young Things" in Oxford and London, the partial inspiration for the character of Anthony Blanche in Evelyn Waugh's *Brideshead Revisited*.

Born in Florence of Anglo-American parentage, and educated at Eton and Oxford, Acton had always felt a deep affinity for China. In 1932 he had gone to live in the city that was then named Peking, lecturing on English literature at the National University. He completely immersed himself in the Chinese way of life and might have remained there had he not been chased out by the beginning of the Second World War in 1939. He served in the Royal Air Force during the war and then returned to Florence and embarked on a career as a writer, producing several novels, books of poetry, works of history, biography, and autobiography. Among his most notable works, which I had read before I met him, were *The Memoirs of an Aesthete*, *The Last Medici*, and *The Bourbons of Naples*, all of which I had greatly enjoyed.

Francesco drove his modest gray Fiat sedan through the magnificent gates of La Pietra and parked in front of the impressive *portone*. The huge door was opened by a servant wearing the obligatory white jacket. He showed us into a handsomely furnished sitting room. A few minutes later, we heard the loud patter of steps rapidly descending the marble stairway in the entrance hall. Sir Harold appeared, a bald, dapper man who looked vaguely oriental, as if he had been physically changed by his years in China. As he entered the room, he held his hand over his mouth to conceal a burp and explained: "I had dinner last night with Violet Trefusis and one never knows what one is eating at a place like that."

The servant soon appeared with a tray of coffee, and as we sat and sipped, Sir Harold told us about a letter he had just received from a man who wanted to build an amphitheater and asked if he could send someone to make a copy of Acton's amphitheater. "You would think," he said with an air of indignation, "that anyone who could afford to build an amphitheater, could also afford an architect to come up with his own design."

He also mentioned that he was plotting to get back from America his collection of rare Chinese porcelain that he had put together during his years in Peking. He had been forced to leave it behind, but an American professor from a midwestern university had later managed get it out of China and sent it to the university for safekeeping. In order to save the collection, Acton had reluctantly agreed, but now, he wanted it back!

It was a beautiful, sunny day and Sir Harold, gracious and charming and witty, was soon showing us around his beautiful garden, including the amphitheater.

When we returned to the villa, he told us that he was soon to leave with a group of friends to spend a few weeks on the island of Ischia in the Bay of Naples. He looked at me with a twinkle in his eyes and said, "Why don't you come with us? I think you would find it amusing!" I was flattered, but not tempted. And in any case, I was leaving the next day for a much less glamorous destination: my annual summer trip back to Louisiana.

28

THE SECOND ACT OF PARSIFAL?

When I lived in Florence, I had a beautiful and intelligent Siamese cat I named Parsifal. Someone told me that cats responded to Ps and Ss, as in "pussy," so I decided that Parsifal would be an excellent name for my pet.

Parsifal seemed to be fond enough of me, and I was fond enough of him. He slept with me on my bed, and twice, while I was napping, he quietly chewed an almost perfectly round hole, just over my heart, in the sweater I was wearing.

Parsifal and I shared a small *attico* apartment on via del Corso in the heart of Florence. It was on the fifth floor of an ancient building, and the stairs up to it grew increasingly vertical as one ascended. The front windows looked into the windows of a hotel across the street where tourists without inhibitions sometimes presented unexpected and lascivious *tableaux vivants*. The bathroom window on the back of the apartment provided a spectacular view of Brunelleschi's Duomo.

We spent a number of happy years there, but then came the terrible flood of November 4, 1966. The modest English language school that my friend Carl and I had bought to give us an excuse to live in Florence, along with much of the city, was dealt an almost fatal blow. It occurred just a week before our students were supposed to pay the second installment of their tuition and very few of them did; many we never saw again. The branches we had in Viareggio and La Spezia, and courses we taught at the Eli Lily factory in nearby Sesto Fiorentino, continued to bring a steady stream of revenue, but it was barely enough to meet our expenses. We struggled on, but the next autumn, when I was offered a job in Paris with the Council on International Educational Exchange, Carl told me to accept it, and I did. Carl was able to support himself with the school for the next few years, but then gradually went into the export business with another partner, and our little language school disappeared into the ether.

As attached as I was to Parsifal, I decided that it would be better to find him a new home in Florence rather than try to take him to Paris. I told all my friends, and an American art historian named Stella Rudolph, whom I knew slightly, said she would be delighted to have him.

So, the day before I took the night train from Florence to Paris, Stella came to fetch him, and I patted him goodbye and wished them both well.

About a year after I went to live in Paris, I returned to Florence for a visit. Shortly after my arrival, I ran into Stella in the street. "How is Parsifal getting along?" I asked her. "Oh, dear," she said. "When I got him home, he went crazy and dashed around breaking things. I just couldn't cope with him. He was destroying my apartment. So, I took him out to the street and gave him to the first person I saw who would take him."

I was, of course, very upset and angry. But there was nothing I could do. I never laid eyes on Stella again.

A few years after I moved to Paris, I heard from an Israeli friend in Geneva, who had for a time shared the apartment on via del Corso with me and Parsifal, that late one night he had been listening to a radio interview from Paris with a contemporary French composer. At one point, the interviewer remarked: "You must have a great love for Richard Wagner." "On the contrary," the composer replied, "I actually detest Wagner!" "Then why," asked the interviewer, "do you have a Siamese cat named Parsifal?" "The cat already was named that when it was given to me," answered the composer.

A few years ago, I was reading the *Later Diaries* of American composer Ned Rorem and came across a passage in which he mentioned going to lunch in Paris at the apartment of fellow composer Henri Sauget. He wrote: "New also is the blue-eyed cat, Parsifal, the replacement of the forty-pound Angora that five years ago lunched with us."

Could there have been another Siamese cat in Europe named Parsifal? Perhaps. Perhaps not. But if I were the kind of person who believes in the mystical power of cats, I would suspect that somehow Parsifal arranged to follow me to Paris.

29

PARIS, FINALLY

I arrived in Paris early on an October morning in 1967, on Il Palatino, the overnight train from Florence, to begin my job as field representative of the Council on International Educational Exchange.

I became aware of the CIEE, and they became aware of me, when I found a position on the orientation staff of the council's student ship, Aurelia, as a way of getting free passage to the United States and back. The first summer I had organized the language program during the crossing. But the past summer I had been made the director of the entire orientation program. It had gone very well, and I was offered a full-time job with the Paris office, maintaining contacts with the many study abroad programs in Europe of the hundred or so American colleges and universities that made up CIEE's membership.

The job description was appealing. During the autumn, winter, and early spring months, I was to spend my time traveling around Europe, meeting with the program directors of the various academic programs to determine their needs and concerns, then write reports about them that were sent to the New York and Paris offices of the CIEE. During the late spring and summer months, I was to direct the orientation program on the Aurelia for the American students going to Europe, and the European students going to the States. Occasionally I would be in charge of organizing conferences for the program directors.

The salary was not large, but my expense account was generous, and, in those days, Americans were expected to eat in good restaurants and stay in fine hotels, still affordable compared to those in the United States. Since I was on the road for two or three weeks of every month, most of my living expenses were covered by the council.

The council had about thirty employees in Paris, half were American, the other half a mixture of nationalities. It was located on an upper floor of the American Legion Building on rue Pierre Charron, near the Champs-Élysées.

The director was a dapper American bon vivant named Jack Egle, who had settled in Paris after the Second World War and whose first wife had been the daughter of Maurice Thorez, leader of the French Communist Party, which placed him under a permanent cloud of suspicion in official government circles. Jack made no secret of his love for the more glamorous aspects of expatriate life in Paris, the celebrated restaurants, the nightclubs, the beautiful women, wine, and cigars. His two sports were golf and poker, and among his poker-playing chums was the novelist James Jones. Jack must have fancied himself a latter-day Scott Fitzgerald.

I soon learned never to take the elevator with Jack in the morning because whoever he was riding with always got stuck with whatever project that was going through his mind.

I was fortunate to have a highly efficient secretary named Annick who kept me well organized. She always knew exactly where I was supposed to be and what I was supposed to be doing and made sure that I knew about it. She probably made me seem better at my job than I actually was, and I was very grateful to her.

Being on the road so much of the time prevented me from developing much of a social life in Paris. Whenever I was invited somewhere, I was usually going to be away on a trip. As a result, I spent much of my time alone, and as golden autumn turned to gray winter, I was often lonely. I started to spend a great deal of time at the Cinémathèque Française, then located in the Palais de Chaillot, very near my first apartment. Often, on weekends, I would attend the 2 o'clock screening, the 4 o'clock screening, go home for a bite, and thus miss the 6 o'clock screening, but would return for the 8 and 10 o'clock screenings. A ticket cost less than three francs, and I eventually made friends with the Czech woman who sold tickets and let all her friends in for free.

The films that were shown at the *cinémathèque* ranged from the classic to the obscure. Most had been collected by the legendary and eccentric co-founder Henri Langlois, who started in the 1930s to look for and rescue films that were at risk of disappearing forever. His collection began with ten films that he stored in his bathtub. It eventually grew to more than sixty thousand.

Langlois, portly, messy-looking with unruly hair, and always a cigarette in hand, was often in the lobby between showings, in intense conversation with his Rubenesque mistress, Mary Meerson, and Lotte Eisner, the cinémathèque's archivist and the leading authority on German Expressionist cinema, whom I later to came to know.

The films were shown in their original language but often with strange subtitles. Perhaps a Russian film with Hungarian titles or a German film with Lithuanian subtitles. American films were shown with French subtitles that were not always reliable translations. In one scene of the 1947 film *Body and Soul*, with John Garfield playing a prizefighter as "the body" and Lilli Palmer, his girlfriend, as "the soul," they are standing in a doorway gazing into each other's eyes while Miss Palmer recites William Blake's "The Tyger." The subtitle translated "fearful symmetry" as "Quel cimetière effrayant" (What a dreadful cemetery).

I happened to be away from Paris and missed witnessing an historic event that occurred at the cinémathèque in January of 1968. André Malraux, de Gaulle's Minister of Culture and a well-known public intellectual, fired Langlois, who was idolized by the young filmmakers, known as *la nouvelle vague* (new wave), who had changed the face of French film in the mid-twentieth century. A protest was organized at the cinémathèque by many of the most famous of them, including Jean-Luc Godard, François Truffaut, Alain Renais, Eric Rohmer, and others, and some of their actors. The protest was a foreshadowing of the tumult to come. Malraux reinstalled Langlois in April, but that did not stop the momentum of the movement that resulted in the great social upheaval that came to be known as "The Events of May."

That winter, a wiry, attractive man who had been sitting next to me at the cinémathèque, spoke to me as we were leaving after the film. Jean-Jacques, the scion of a foie-gras manufacturing family from Luchon, a spa town near the Spanish border, became my first romantic attachment in Paris. He was in his last year at the Sorbonne, though I gathered, since he was older than most students, it had taken him some time to get there.

One evening in early May, Jean-Jacques and I had tickets for a performance at the Odéon Théâtre of the Paul Taylor Dance Company. He called me that afternoon and said, "Something is going on at the Odéon. Can you meet me there right now to see what's happening?" Soon we were sitting in the seats that we were supposed to have sat in that evening. Something was, indeed, going on at the Odéon and all over the Latin Quarter. It was the beginning of the "Les Événements de Mai," a period of social unrest in France that led to some permanent changes in French society.

The theater was filled with a raucous crowd of students, cheering the speeches of those among them who ventured on to the stage. The crowd quieted down when the figure of celebrated French actor, Jean-Louis Barrault, director of the Odéon, appeared front and center. He had no trouble commanding attention and all eyes were on him as he opened wide his arms and proclaimed: "Bienvenue!" Barrault's welcoming the students to the august halls of the national theater was one of the defining moments of the uprising. In August, when the rioting suddenly stopped because so many of the French had prepaid vacations by the sea that they had no intention of giving up, and the Gaullists came back into power, Barrault was fired.

I was living in the staid, conservative 16th arrondissement, far from the all the violent action on the Left Bank. The only overt political action I witnessed on my street, Avenue d'Eylau, was a tiny, ancient woman putting Gaullist leaflets on

the windshields of parked cars. But the rioting was soon making international headlines. A few days after my evening at the Odéon, I had a worried telephone call from my mother. "You were in Florence and there was a flood! You moved to Paris and now there's a revolution! Everywhere you go son, there's a disaster."
"I'm coming home for Christmas, Mama," I told her.

It was actually an exhilarating time to be in Paris. Parisians were, on the whole, being much nicer than usual to each other. Because of the gas shortage, people were hitchhiking and being given rides by total strangers all over the city. The excitement in the air was palpable.

This historic event, however, marked the end of my romance with Jean-Jacques, who was living at the Sorbonne, marching in demonstrations, throwing paving stones at *les flics*, writing tracts, producing posters on mimeograph machines, and no doubt participating in the orgiastic behavior, rumors of which had begun to leak out. He was completely caught up in the camaraderie of his fellow students and it was no time to be having an affair with a boring American who surely could not understand the significance of their rebellion.

I had liberated from a wall one of the iconic, handmade posters: a caricature of de Gaulle with the inscription "Le Chien-lit, c'est lui!" (He is the dog's bed), an expression he had used to describe the students at the beginning of the riots. Jean-Jacques convinced me that I, as a foreigner, had no right to this historic document, and I surrendered it to him, a gesture that did not save our relationship. I still regret having done so.

The first of the council's summer sailings of the *Aurelia* was scheduled from Le Havre in late May and because of the unrest, it was rescheduled from Barcelona. It was not one of the sailings that I was assigned to, and I was asked to drive four members of our Paris staff to Spain to help with the embarkation. We set out in a rented Renault sedan, large enough to accommodate the five of us, plus two canisters filled with gasoline because so many gas stations had closed. We made it safely there in spite of the fact that Michelle, a silly secretary in the back seat, refused to stop smoking, the ashes from her cigarette falling onto the gas-filled *bidons* at her feet.

When I returned to Paris, I was sent to Brussels to maintain communications with our office in New York. I was lodged in a pleasant hotel not far from the Grand Place, and each morning I had to drive to a dreary suburb to a dreary office to collect the New York mail. Back at the hotel I would read it and then fax a summary to the Paris office, the fax machine being the only reliable means for the rest of the world to communicate with France, then almost completely crippled by strikes.

Apart from the beautiful and truly grand Grand Place, I found Brussels not very interesting. I was not tempted to be a flâneur, one who wanders idly through streets exploring, as I often was in Paris. I was also beginning to get bored with the delicious but too rich food. One evening after dinner, I decided I would try to see a little of the nightlife. I had never been a bar bunny. And I especially disliked the bitchy, snobby atmosphere of the few gay bars I had occasionally gone to in Paris. I don't remember how I found the name of the bar in Brussels. It was dark and not very crowded. I sat at the bar and ordered a drink. Soon a guy came up and sat next to me, engaged me in conversation. He was dark and good looking, if not a brilliant conversationalist. After I finished my drink, he asked if he could buy me another one. "Sure," I said. He nodded at the bartender. "A drink for my friend," he said. While his attention was on the bartender, another man I had noticed staring at us, walked up and whispered in my ear, "Be careful," and walked away. I had only taken a few sips of the drink when I began to feel woozy. I immediately realized that the drink had been spiked. I bolted from the bar, quickly found a taxi, and went back to my hotel. I barely made it to my bed when, fully clothed, I passed out. The next morning when I woke with a headache, I realized how lucky I had been. Had the guy who whispered the warning been my guardian angel in disguise?

Later that year, the council was planning a conference for the directors of all the study abroad programs of their member institutions, which they did every two or three years. This one was to be in Palma de Mallorca, the inaugural event in a brand-new convention center. Jack flew to Palma to oversee the planning but focused on golfing and let the inexperienced staff of the Palacio de Congresos make all the arrangements. When he arrived back in Paris, his savvy assistant realized that the reservations for the directors had been made at hotels all over the island and that it would be practically impossible for many of them to arrive on time for the morning sessions. I was asked to go to Palma to try to straighten things out, which I was more than happy to do.

Annick made a reservation for me at the Gran Hotel Mediterraneo, a vast and splendid nineteenth-century hotel. I had a suite of rooms that was larger than my Paris apartment with a terrace that looked over the city.

After dinner at the hotel, I went for a drink at the bar. There was a very large blonde sitting on the stool next to mine, chatting animatedly with a few friends. I was soon included in the conversation, and it slowly dawned on me that the enormous woman was Anita Ekberg, whose much skinnier self I had watched with fascination as she romped in the Trevi Fountain with Marcello Mastroianni in Fellini's masterpiece *La Dolce Vita*.

The next morning, I drove my rental car to the *palacio* and met the administrator, a Madam Serrat, who was seated behind a large, uncluttered desk, a shawl draped around her shoulders, a wary, wide-eyed look on her face. Since I spoke no Spanish, and she spoke no English, we conversed in French. I explained the problem. She shrugged and said she didn't think it was much of a problem. I pointed out that as the first event at the new center, it was very important that it go smoothly and that if we could not be accommodated, we would have to relocate the conference elsewhere. She saw my point, and after I spent several days gently nagging and insisting, we managed to consolidate the reservations at a few nearby hotels. By this time, I had figured out that the palacio had been built by a very rich man to provide employment for his relatives, not all of whom seemed enthusiastic about their jobs.

At our last meeting, I asked Mme. Serrat if she could do a few other things that needed to be done. She looked alarmed. "Je ne sais pas, Monsieur Fletcher," she said. "La semaine prochaine sera très chargée à cause de d'événements imprévus" (I don't know, Mr. Fletcher. Next week will be very busy due to unforeseen events). When I got back to Paris, I had a sign made of her astute observation and put it on the wall behind my desk.

It was a Friday afternoon. I was to fly back to Paris that evening and then fly to Madrid on Monday for a meeting with the head of the Fulbright Commission in Spain. When I called Jack to report my success, he said, why don't you just stay there over the weekend and fly from Palma to Madrid on Monday? I took no persuading.

Although it was late winter, the weather on Mallorca was beautiful and springlike. I drove all over the island, admiring the views. I stopped at the village of Valldemossa to visit the convent that had been the love nest of Chopin and George Sand one winter in the 1830s and saw the piano on which Chopin is said to have composed his preludes. From a road on the hill above his house, I glimpsed the poet Robert Graves working in his garden. I was not getting rich working for the council, but the job certainly had its perks.

The student ship *Aurelia*, on which I spent a good part of each summer, was an excellent way for students and other travelers on a budget to cross the Atlantic, even if it was not a luxury liner. The quarters were cramped, the food was decent enough, but the coffee was shockingly bad for an Italian ship. The Italian management believed Americans did not appreciate good coffee and thought they could get away with serving them watered down bilge. As director of the orientation program, I had a comfortable private cabin with bath, and I had all my meals at the captain's table, where the food was both abundant and delicious, and the coffee was strong and tasted like coffee.

The *Aurelia*, a poky ship, took seven days to cross the ocean, but the days and nights were filled with interesting cultural and educational events. University professors and other specialists in their fields were given free passage in return for lectures and classes, most of them designed to prepare the students for their time abroad. And going to Europe seemed much more significant when one spent a week getting there, as opposed to hoping on a jet plane and arriving in a matter of hours. The years I spent aboard the *Aurelia* were the last for student ships. Cheap charter flights soon killed them off completely.

Some of the crossings were especially memorable. In the summer of 1968, The Living Theater, the avant-garde theater group that since 1963 had been alarming audiences all over Europe with their explosive "Happenings," returned to the United States on the *Aurelia*, adding a wild element to the voyage. One night they presented a "Happening" in the ship's Riviera Lounge where on most evenings the ship's orchestra played dance music that the young crowd must have found dated. That evening the entertainment was anything but passé. It unrolled in a series of noisy and unruly scenes that culminated in the total nudity of the founders of the group, Judith Malina and Julien Beck, both of whom were long past the date when some might have found the sight appealing. The audience was perhaps shocked but certainly not surprised.

On another crossing, Eleanor Dulles, sister of former Secretary of State John Foster Dulles, an economist and author who herself had held several important government positions, was one of the staff giving lectures on the ship. Halfway across the ocean, we encountered a fierce storm and there were very few people that night in the Riviera Lounge. I still had my sea legs from my years on an aircraft carrier in the Pacific, and the orchestra, evidently accustomed to a pitching deck, played on undeterred, but there were not more than a dozen of us. Dr. Dulles, a short, rather dumpy woman with thick glasses, wearing a tweedy suit appropriate for a distinguished academic in her later years, was with us. Suddenly she and a tall, handsome Swiss exchange student in his twenties were waltzing around and around and around the rolling floor.

Once when we were loading passengers in Southampton, the young CIEE employee who was taking tickets came to find me and told me that a "hippy type" was trying to buy passage for his American girlfriend and wanted to pay with a personal check. She was unsure if she should take it. She handed me the check. It was signed: "Mick Jagger." "Take it," I told her.

After a few years in the employ of the council, I was offered a job by one of its member institutions, City University of New York. I would be doing essentially the same thing for CUNY as I had for the CIEE, but with less travel and double the salary. I accepted the offer.

I became the assistant to a diminutive dean from Queen's College who, I had been told off the record, had been given the job in Paris to get him away from the campus because of his controversial behavior during the student protests in 1968. As academics often do, he had a very high opinion of himself and was not particularly easy to work with, but we got along well enough. I felt sorry for his French wife, a head taller than he, who was evidently unaware that her husband often sneaked off to frolic with whores in Montmartre.

Every Monday, the dean and I met for lunch at a bistro on the rue Marbeuf to review the plans for the week. We always split a bottle of white wine over the first course, a bottle of red wine over the second course, and ended the meal with an

Armagnac, a Cognac, or both. I would somehow manage to make it back with the notes I had made to my apartment in the Marais and was functional again by Tuesday.

I was in frequent contact with my opposite number on the staff of Queens College in New York, a lanky young man of Irish descent who was somewhat slapdash in his work. Once he sent me the wrong arrival date for a group of twenty students who were coming to France for a year abroad. Before they went to their homestays in various cities in France, they were to spend a week in Paris. They were to arrive the last week in August, when Paris was always crowded with tourists, the hotels full, so I had made their reservations far in advance. Two days before I was expecting them, I received an apologetic telephone call from New York. They were going to be there the next day, and I had to scramble to find hotel rooms for them. By late evening of the day they arrived at Le Bourget Airport, I had succeeded in placing them all except for one smelly young man from Brooklyn with a backpack and thick glasses, who was becoming even smellier as we trudged up the Boulevard St. Michel in the sultry heat, going into hotel after hotel, all of them with no vacancy. About 10 p.m., I was almost resigned to the unpleasant prospect of taking him home to sleep on my sofa. We went into one last hotel. The desk clerk again informed us that the hotel was *complet*. A few minutes later, we were standing in front of the hotel while I was trying to figure out what to do next, when suddenly there was a loud "splat!" on the sidewalk near us, followed by screams. Someone had jumped from a window on the top floor of the hotel that we had just left. Stunned, we looked at the broken body, and were about to move away, when the desk clerk came out of the hotel, running towards us. "Attendez! Attendez!" he shouted. "I believe we may have a room."

Working for CUNY, I was spending more time in Paris than I had when I was scooting all over Europe visiting study abroad programs, and I had been able to make and keep up with a number of friends. I had been given by an American friend in Florence the name and telephone number of Nestor Almendros, who had been his classmate at Middlebury College. Nestor and I occasionally went out for a meal together, but he primarily became a phone friend. We were both early risers and my day often began with a cup of coffee and a chat with Nestor.

Nestor was born in Spain but, when he was eighteen, had gone to live in Cuba where his passionately anti-Franco father was in exile. Nestor was living and teaching in the United States when Castro came to power in Cuba in 1953. Excited by the promise of the revolution, he returned and began to play an important role in the Cuban film industry, producing several documentaries for Castro. They were not well received, and he soon realized how oppressive the regime was turning out to be. He resigned from his position and tried to leave the country, not an easy thing to do. He told me that for several months he was cut off from all his friends and family, had little money, was living alone, before he managed to get out of Cuba with nothing but the clothes he was wearing and a fifty-dollar bill shoved up his rear end. He had fallen in love with a Cuban man who had earlier escaped to New York and Nestor decided to go there to try to find him. He had no address for him but began a fruitless search among other Cuban exiles he knew. No luck. One day when he was in a crowded subway car, the car stopped in a station, and the doors opened. There was his beloved. They exchanged a look and Nestor tried to get out of the car to embrace him. Before he was able to fight his way through the jam of passengers, the door slammed shut, the subway car sped off, and Nestor never saw the man again.

He left New York and went to Cinecittà in Rome where, he said, he lived for a couple of years on oatmeal, studying to be a cinematographer. By the time we became friends in Paris, he was well established and collaborating with a number of major French directors, including Eric Rohmer, François Truffaut, and Barbet Schroeder. One of the perks of being his friend was getting free tickets to his films' premieres in Paris.

After we both left Paris, Nestor went to work in Hollywood and won an Oscar for his first film, *Days of Heaven*, directed by Terence Malik. He also had Oscar nominations for his cinematography of *Kramer vs. Kramer*, *The Blue Lagoon*, and *Sophie's Choice*.

We lost touch for many years, but in 1990, I sent a Christmas card to his Paris address, having heard that he had kept the apartment. In reply, he sent me a postcard remembering the good times we had in Paris and said he hoped we would meet again.

It was not to happen. In 1992, Nestor died of AIDS-related lymphoma, one of the multitudes of gifted gay men who untimely were taken away from the world. Nestor and I had only been friends, not lovers, but I sometimes wonder how the plague missed me as it took some, too many, of the men I had slept with. Once again, it was perhaps proof of a vigilant guardian angel.

I had two Brazilian artist friends in Paris. One was named Mozart, the other Rossini. Rossini Perez was by far the more serious and successful artist. He was considered a major Brazilian printmaker of the twentieth century. He had frequent exhibitions in prestigious galleries, and his work was in the collections of museums around the world, including the Museum of Modern Art in New York. He was one of the artists commissioned to provide artworks for Brasilia, the city that was founded in 1960 to be the new capital of the country.

Rossini and his American lover had built a wonderful rabbit warren of a studio on the ground floor of a building on Place de la Bastille, on the site that the new Paris Opera now occupies. He gave wonderful parties, attended mostly by Brazilian expatriates, many very beautiful, of all genders and persuasions. There was always a relaxed, almost dreamlike atmosphere, no doubt created by the constant bossa nova beat in the background and delicious Brazilian food loaded with hash.

Mozart Pela, on the other hand, was something of a slacker. He looked perpetually weary, produced little, though probably more than one painting a year, as claimed by our mutual friend Edouard Roditi. He had a passion for mass-produced ceramic vases of the 1940s and 1950s, considered tacky by most people, and by prowling through flea markets, had amassed a large collection of them for very little money.

Mozart lived in an HLM, low cost, subsidized housing, in an unfashionable neighborhood. One evening he invited me to dinner to repay me for the several parties at my apartment to which he had been invited. When I arrived at the address, a sinister looking brick apartment house, barely illuminated by a distant streetlight, I found a tiny woman at the front door. It was Lotte Eisner, the German film critic and historian I had often seen in the lobby of the cinémathèque. She told me that she had rung the bell, but had received no answer. I rang it again. No response. We waited a little longer and then sat down on the stoop. We eventually decided that chronically fatigued Mozart was probably in his apartment too exhausted to fix dinner and therefore not answering the bell. I asked Lotte if I could invite her for a meal, if we could find a place to eat. We soon did. A modest, brightly lit neighborhood brasserie where we had excellent omelets and a few glasses of wine. We talked about many things, including the cinémathèque and its recent programming. When we finished, I walked her to her *métro* station, and she asked me if I were free the next Sunday afternoon at teatime. I was, I told her, and she gave me her address in Neuilly, a wealthy residential neighborhood on the western outskirts of Paris.

When I left my apartment on that Sunday, it occurred to me that I ought to bring Lotte flowers, or some other little offering. The Marais, where I lived, was bustling with open shops and lots of people in the streets, and I could have easily have found a florist. But I decided that I didn't want to lug a bouquet on the métro on the long ride to Neuilly. I would just find something there.

When I exited the Pont de Neuilly métro station, I found everything closed tight, not a person in sight. The shops were shuttered, and the streets were empty. The *haute bourgeoisie* of the neighborhood were all in their expensive bourgeois dwellings, enjoying a quiet Sunday afternoon. Under a bright sun, it looked like a surreal De Chirico cityscape, devoid of any human figures.

I made my way to Lotte's street and started down it. A couple, holding hands, were walking at some distance in front of me, but otherwise the street was completely deserted. Suddenly the couple stopped and disappeared into a doorway of what turned out to be a fruit and vegetable store, perhaps the only open store in all of Neuilly. In the window was a display of pineapples. A pineapple would make a fine gift for Lotte, I thought, and entered the store. I stood behind the couple and saw that they too were buying a pineapple. Soon, I was back out in the street, holding my pineapple. They were in front of me, holding their pineapple.

They stopped at a door in the next block and rang a bell. It was the address Lotte had given me. I also rang the bell and went in. They were waiting for the lift in the lobby. "Are you going to Lotte's?" I asked. "Yes," they said. The couple turned out to be the German filmmaker, Werner Herzog, and his wife, Martje.

Lotte graciously accepted our pineapples and served us tea. We spent the next few hours talking about movies, of course. Herzog had made his first feature film, which I had not seen, but Lotte evidently considered him a serious talent.

We had a lovely time together and I hoped I would see them again. But I never did. It was early spring of 1970, and though I did not yet know it, I would soon be leaving Paris.

In the coming years, I read about Herzog's career as it developed and saw many of his films. Lotte was the narrator of his 1971 documentary, *Fata Morgana*, about desert mirages, mostly those in Sahara. In 1974, Herzog learned that Lotte had fallen ill and would probably not survive. He became convinced that if he walked for her from Munich to Paris that she would live. He set out in November of 1974 with a new pair of boots and a duffel bag with a few essentials. It took him three weeks of walking through snow and ice to reach Paris. Lotte, miraculously, recovered. In 1978, Herzog published *Vom Gehen im Eis* (*Of Walking in Ice*) the diary he kept on his trek.

Sometime before my afternoon in Neuilly, I had received my contract from CUNY for a second year in Paris. I signed it, returned it, and was looking forward to the next year, even if I had a rather irritating boss. But that spring. New York City declared bankruptcy and I soon received another letter from CUNY telling me that, unfortunately, they did not have the money to pay my salary.

Instead of being upset, I remember that I felt strangely exhilarated by the news and went to the Café Les Deux Magots on Boulevard Saint Germain to have a drink and ponder it. From Deux Magots, I went to the CIEE office to let my former colleagues, with whom I was still friendly, know what had happened.

"Well," said Jack, "We're getting ready to open an office in London to arrange student exchanges between England and the US. How you like to go to London for us?"

So, I was unemployed for only a few hours before the next phase of my lucky life began. My guardian angel must have had something to with it.

30

THÉRÈSE BONNEY AND THE REPUDIATION OF CHIC

Paris, summer, 1968. In my tiny apartment on the rue de Sevigné, Thérèse Bonney, wearing combat boots and a voluminous dun-colored cape that made her look like a tank commander, sat on the sofa next to a man she had earlier refused to meet. Her only visible nod to ornament was an aboriginal chastity belt that she wore as a necklace. Even seated, she cut a daunting figure and had a style that was all her own.

The man next to Thérèse was the American scholar and writer George Wickes who was in Paris researching a book about Americans living in Paris in the 1930s. He wanted to interview Thérèse, but she had said no to his request. When he mentioned his disappointment, I suggested that I invite her to lunch with him and a few other friends where he could meet her informally and exercise his not inconsiderable charm. It worked. They got along beautifully. They had a lot to talk about since he knew so much about the period through which she had lived. George got his interview a few days later.

Thérèse was then living in a large apartment on the Boulevard de la Tour Maubourg, not far from Les Invalides. She was fearing eviction because the apartment was coveted by a Gaullist minister who was pulling strings to get it.

The apartment housed her large collection of paintings, tapestries, and furniture that she had acquired over her many years as a resident of Paris and as a friend and champion of many of the most important artists and designers of the early twentieth century in France. She worked at a desk designed for her by Pierre Chareau. On a wall hung what she told me was the first tapestry made by Lurçat. There were paintings of her by Georges Rouault and Robert Delaunay; there were, as I recall, about twenty Raoul Dufy watercolors in her spacious bathroom, and over the dining room table was a larger-than-life-size portrait of her by Dufy. The portrait had three chins. Thérèse told me that when he finished it, it had two. "Duffy" (she pronounced his name as if he were an Irishman), she said she told him, "I don't have a double chin! And he reached up and added a third one!" Mary Guggenheim, who introduced me to Thérèse, told me that she and Dufy had been lovers for many years, and perhaps they were. When she went off to photograph the Second World War, she carried a small Dufy painting in her knapsack.

She was born Mabel Teresa Bonney in Syracuse, New York, the daughter of an electrician and a bookkeeper/bank clerk, but grew up in Oakland, California. She studied languages at the University of California at Berkeley, where Mabel Teresa soon became Thérèse. After graduation, she went on for a master's degree at Radcliffe. She considered a career in teaching but decided she would prefer a more adventurous option. While she was pursuing doctoral studies at Columbia University, she found a job as private secretary to Jacques Copeau, director of the *Théâtre du Vieux Colombier*, then touring in the United States. About the same time, she and her older sister, Louise, opened the first bookshop devoted to French theater in New York City.

Most reference works give the date of her arrival in France as 1919, but she told me that she first arrived in Paris, where she was to spend most of the rest of her life, on the day after the Armistice ending World War I was signed. That would have been November 12, 1918. By 1919 she was the representative in Paris of the American Association of Colleges, helping to choose the French students who would be part of an exchange program to encourage good relations between the United States and its Allies. Soon she was also working for the National Catholic War Council, an organization recognized by the US War Department to do welfare work overseas. And by April of 1919, Thérèse was finishing up her doctoral studies at the Sorbonne. She received her doctorate in 1921, and by so doing, became the youngest person, the fourth woman, and the tenth American to receive this distinction. The event was trumpeted in the French press, and Thérèse became an overnight celebrity in Paris. "I was like Pocahontas to them," she said.

It was about this time that she gave up her plan to become a teacher and started translating American plays for the French theater and French plays for the American stage. She also began writing a column for the French newspaper *Le Figaro*. And this led to her opening the first illustrated press service in Europe run by an American. At first, she hired photographers to take photographs for the Bonney Service, but becoming dissatisfied with some of the results, she bought a Rolliflex and learned to take photographs herself. This was the beginning of her remarkable career as a photographer.

In addition to literature in general, and the theater in particular, Thérèse was deeply interested in the visual arts and design and was an eyewitness to the birth of "modernism" in France. She was in Paris for the groundbreaking 1925

Paris Exposition Internationale des Arts Décoratifs et Industriale Modernes, which gave birth to the movement known today as art deco, and took some of her earliest photographs of this epochal event. In the years following, Thérèse became one of the principal documenters of the growth and development of art deco. She also photographed the 1931 Exposition Internationale Coloniale and the 1937 Exposition Internationale des Arts et Techniques dans la Vie Moderne. In the 1920s and 1930s, Paris was in the vanguard of modern design, and Thérèse was at the heart of it, a witness to it all. And she became a major conduit to the United States of what was happening in art and design in France.

She was one of the organizers of the first art deco exhibition in the United States, held at Lord & Taylor's in 1928. She also brought important French art and the dealers who sold it to America. There is a 1934 photograph of Bonney on the liner *Île-de-France* with Ambrose Vollard and Etiennne Bignou, two leading Parisian art dealers, on their way to New York. She also arranged trips to America for prominent fashion and textile designers. She had taken it as her mission to introduce to her country all that she loved about the country she had adopted.

A Frenchman once told me that I spoke French like a Swede who had lived for many years in Languedoc. He was probably just trying to be funny, but I took it as a compliment since so many of the Americans I knew spoke the language with flat and ugly accents. I would not describe Thérèse's accent as flat and ugly. But it was very American.

Though she spoke French fluently and correctly, she made absolutely no attempt to sound as if it were her native tongue. As I got to know her better, I came to realize that her unmistakably American accent was, in a strange way, an indication of her integrity. That she was an American living in France was an important part of her identity. But she was first and foremost an American, so why should she try to sound like something she was not?

One spring evening in the late 60s, I took Thérèse to the opening of an exhibition of paintings by our mutual friend, Mary Guggenheim. The exhibition was in a handsome gallery on the right bank, a suitable venue for Mary's work, but the crowd in attendance was less than chic. There were many pairs of jeans and quite a few scruffy-looking bohemian friends and acquaintances of the artist. Thérèse was shocked. It was a far cry from the fashionable *vernissages* she had attended in the Paris of celebrated fashion designers Chanel, Schiaparelli, and Vionnet, all of whom had made clothes for her. The next morning my telephone rang early. It was Thérèse: "Mr. Fletcher, darling," she said, "the goo is gone!" It took me a moment to realize that she was talking about the absence of *goût—g-o-û-t*, the French word for "taste."

Thérèse's career as an unofficial ambassador for French culture to the world came to an end with the outbreak of World War II. This cataclysmic event transformed her into an intrepid war photographer and an agent for the Office of Strategic Services.

Her first experience as a war photographer came about accidentally when she happened to be in Finland in 1939 and produced an amazing photographic record of the Russian invasion of that country. She then returned to France and covered the Nazi invasion and the Battle of France, and, working with the Red Cross, also helped, under fire, to care for refugees at the Belgian border.

In 1940 she returned to the United States where the Library of Congress mounted an exhibition of her photographs of the victims of war. The title of the exhibition was *To Whom Wars Are Done*. The Museum of Modern Art in New York also mounted an exhibition of some of these photographs titled *War Comes to the People*. In 1943, she turned her photographs of displaced children into a book, *Europe's Children*, which was the inspiration in 1948 for *The Search*, the first movie starring Montgomery Clift.

Thérèse was always a little vague about what she had done while serving in the OSS (forerunner of the CIA), and I regret not asking more questions about it. She did once mention that she had been involved in a plot, that came to nothing, to smuggle General de Gaulle back into France during the German occupation.

After the war, Thérèse did not resume her work in documenting art and design. "After what I had seen, it just seemed too trivial, too unimportant," she told me. Instead, she became involved in various humanitarian projects. She focused her attention on Ammerschwihr, a village in the Alsaçe region of France that had been almost completely destroyed during the war, raising money to feed and clothe its inhabitants and to rebuild their ruined homes.

Thérèse was particularly close to the fashion designer Madeleine Vionnet who between the wars had developed an international reputation for the simple elegance of her clothes, counting such glamorous women as Marlene Dietrich, Katharine Hepburn, Greta Garbo, and Joan Crawford among her clients. Some years after the war, when Thérèse learned that the City of Paris was giving a medal to Coco Chanel, whom she (and almost everyone else) considered a Nazi collaborator, Thérèse was so infuriated that she did not rest until she had successfully lobbied for Vionnet to be given an even more important honor.

She lectured and wrote several books, including an official map and guide to Paris illustrated by Dufy. When our friendship began, she was actively lobbying Washington to extend Medicare benefits to US citizens living abroad.

Eventually, the thing she most dreaded occurred: eviction from her elegant apartment. After a battle that had lasted for years, the government minister was finally able to acquire the apartment for himself.

Faced, at her advanced age, with having to find a new place to live, Thérèse first came up with a plan to move to Florence where she had become friends with a family that owned a pensione on Piazza Santo Spirito. She had often stayed there and remembered a spacious room with a balcony overlooking the square that she thought would be suitable. She told me that she would rent a truck in which I could drive her and her collection of art, furniture, and other belongings over the Alps to Italy. I did not think this a very good idea and, fortunately, she found another apartment in Paris. It was on the rue Cognac Jay, in the same arrondissement where she had lived for so many years.

After I left Paris to live in London in 1970, I never saw Thérèse again, though we continued to correspond by mail. The last letter I had from her was written in 1973 from her new apartment where she had settled in and was again leading an active life. She mentions that she is "getting ready for a big Pow Wow." It was, she wrote, to be "a nostalgic commemoration of the Battle of the Colmar Pocket, the only Franco-American Battle of World War II."

She continued to lobby for an extension of Medicare and began to study for a degree in gerontology at the Sorbonne. She also worked on an autobiography which, alas, was never finished. She tried to persuade the University of California at Berkeley, her alma mater, to provide her a house where she could live with her art collection and conduct "salon-seminars" for students. The university was not interested.

Thérèse died of heart failure in January of 1978 at the American Hospital in Paris (where, someone once remarked, "All the best people go to die and usually do"). She left most of her collection, including photographs, paintings, and furniture to the Bancroft Library of the University of California in Berkeley. The Cooper-Hewitt National Design Museum also received about four thousand vintage photographic prints.

I was fortunate to have as a friend this remarkable woman, a living link with the fabled Paris of the 1920s and '30s, and I cherish the memories of the times we spent together.

31

M. DE LAFAYETTE CHEZ LES LAFAYETTES

It is curious that my great-grandmother, Mary Leopard Fletcher, whose grandfather was anything but a hero during the American Revolutionary War—according to a family story, to avoid fighting in the American Revolution, he moved from Pennsylvania to South Carolina where he changed his name from Lippert to Leopard—should have named her first-born and only surviving son after one of the greatest heroes of the Revolution: the Marquis de Lafayette. My grandfather, Joel Lafayette Fletcher Sr., was born in Grant Parish in 1868. The name has come down through my father to me. By coincidence, in 1920, my father, Joel Lafayette Fletcher Jr., accepted a teaching job in Lafayette in southern Louisiana, where fifteen years later I was born.

In the 1960s, when I was living in Paris, my middle name was often remarked upon. Once my secretary made a restaurant reservation for me under the name of "Monsieur de Lafayette," and I got an excellent table even though the *patron* seemed surprised to greet a tall American instead of a French aristocrat.

One of my friends in Paris, the photographer André Ostier, knew descendants of the Marquis de Lafayette: the Count and Countess de Chambrun, who were living in the Chateau La Grange east of Paris where the Marquis lived from 1802 until his death in 1834. He thought it would be amusing to take someone whose name was Lafayette, from a town named Lafayette, to meet the French Lafayettes.

Count René de Chambrun, from a family that was both ancient and wealthy—the family business was the Baccarat crystal factory—was descended from Virginie de Lafayette, the Marquis's daughter. In 1935 he married Josée Laval, only child of Pierre Laval who, as Vichy Prime Minister of France, was to become infamous as a collaborator with the Nazis. The year of his marriage, de Chambrun purchased the family chateau, La Grange, from his cousin Louis de Lasteyrie, who was granted a life tenancy. When Louis finally died in 1955, de Chambrun and his wife moved in and began its restoration.

The Comte de Chambrun's mother, from a wealthy Ohio family, was closely related to the Roosevelts, and early in the Second World War, when France was about to fall to the Germans, he was sent by the then Prime Minister of France, Paul Reynaud, to Washington on an unsuccessful attempt to persuade his cousin, Franklin Delano Roosevelt, to join the Allies in the fight.

Before and during the Second World War, de Chambrun was very close to his father-in-law, Pierre Laval; close as well to General Pétain, the Vichy Head of State, an old family friend who was his godfather. In fact, "Bunny," as de Chambrun was called by family and friends, often served to smooth over tensions between the president and the prime minister during the Vichy years.

It is remarkable, given his close involvement with the collaborationist regime, that de Chambrun escaped reprisals after the Liberation. No doubt his American connections protected him. He is also said to have enabled a number of prominent French Jews, including René Clair, Golo Mann, and Franz Werfel, to escape to the United States.

When the war ended, Pierre Laval was tried for treason, found guilty, and executed by a firing squad on October 15, 1945. For the rest of their lives, de Chambrun and his wife devoted much of their energies to whitewashing the role Laval had played as a collaborator. De Chambrun wrote three books on the subject.

On the way to La Grange, my friend André told me that the de Chambruns, because of their relationship with Laval, had long been held in low esteem by most of the American community in Paris, and that they returned the hostility. I wondered how I was going to be received.

We drove to La Grange on a lovely day in early spring. There were six guests invited by the de Chambruns for tea, including Maurice Escande, the recently retired director of the Comédie Française, and a beautiful blonde actress named Miriam Colombey who had just returned from a tour of Japan where, with characteristic Gallic wit, she had been given the nickname "Colombey-les-Deux-Pagodes" (a play on the name of de Gaulle's hometown of Colombey-les-Deux-Églises).

Count René, before we went in to tea, showed us around the château and its amazing collection of artifacts and papers from Lafayette. After the death of the Marquis, his descendants, who considered him something of a renegade, tossed all of his papers and many of his belongings into the attic of the château, which fortunately was cool and dry and insect free, and there they remained for over a century in a perfect state of preservation. When de Chambrun and his wife acquired the château, they began its restoration and the cataloguing of Lafayette's papers, displaying some of the most important. At that point, the only writer they had allowed access to the archive was André Maurois who was doing research for his book on the Marquis's wife, *Adrienne ou la vie de Mme de La Fayette*, published in 1960.

As the count led us through the rooms and hallways pointing out many treasures, his narrative was generously sprinkled with anti-American remarks. At one point, he paused before a door and said: "This is where we keep our *second* copy of the Declaration of Independence. The Americans think we have only one. Someone from that library in Washington was here recently trying to persuade me to lend them things for an exhibition ... which, of course, I refused to do ... and I almost opened this door by mistake and revealed our secret." At this point, he looked at me and said: "Vous êtes Anglais, n'est-ce pas, monsieur?" "Non," I said to him, "Je suis Americain de Lafayette en Louisiane." He showed a measure of integrity by continuing to say rude things about Americans even after he knew that I was one.

After the tour, we were shown into an ornate room where we were introduced to La Comtesse, a horse-faced woman with what seemed a permanent scowl, and, seated at a large round table, were served a fairly lavish tea. As I recall there was a white-jacketed footman behind each chair, but perhaps my memory is embellishing.

André had earlier mentioned to me that there had been a rumor going around Paris during the Occupation that the reason Marcel Carné was able to make his classic film, *Les Enfants du Paradis*, was that its star, Arletty, was having an affair with Josée Laval. Many years later I went to hear Olivier Bernier, a biographer of Lafayette, talk about a book he had written about Paris in the 1930s. Afterwards, while he was signing my copy of his book, I told him André's story about Josée and Arletty. He jumped out of his chair and exclaimed: "I hope that it is true! I hope that it is true!" He told me that when he was researching Lafayette, the de Chambruns had not let him examine their archive, but that fortunately he had found copies of much that it contained elsewhere.

A few weeks after my afternoon at La Grange I saw the powerful Maurice Ophüls film about the Nazi Occupation of Paris: *Le Chagrin et la Pitié*. The film contains the information that when the Nazis ordered all the Jewish men in Paris sent to concentration camps, Pierre Laval was the one who extended the order to include women and children. The de Chambruns in attempting to rehabilitate his reputation certainly had their work cut out.

Josée died in 1992. "Bunny" lived on until 2002. By that time, he seems to have softened his views of Americans and American institutions for his obituary mentioned his generosity in allowing scholars access to his archives of both Lafayette and Laval, and in helping Cornell University obtain and publish the papers of Lafayette. I imagine that with the passing of time and the fading of memories, Americans in Paris and elsewhere became more accepting of the de Chambruns, and they must have grown more kindly disposed toward Americans.

The Count and Countess de Chambrun are buried near the tomb of the Marquis de Lafayette in the Picpus Cemetery in Paris. Although hours for the cemetery are posted on its gate, it is difficult to find it open, and then access is granted only after a tip is given to the *gardien*. I lucked out one All Saint's Day a few years ago and saw their graves on my way to pay respects to the Marquis.

It is said that the only place that the American flag flew in Paris during the Occupation was over Lafayette's grave. The walls of the Picpus Cemetery are very high and the Nazis did not know it was there. It still flies there today.

32

EATING PARIS

"It would be ignoble to live in Paris for the food alone," wrote Henry James, and he was undoubtedly right. Fortunately, I was able to live in Paris without ignoble motives and very much enjoy the culinary delights of the city, in so far as I was able to afford them.

Paris in the late 1960s, like everywhere in Europe, was much more affordable than it was to become. Every month, my friend Stella and I would budget one hundred francs, about twenty dollars, to eat in a Michelin starred restaurant. By being careful with our choices and having one of the least expensive wines on the menu, we were able to eat well in an august establishment. But there were so many other good, less expensive, unstarred restaurants, brasseries, and cafés where one could get excellent meals.

My office was in Pershing Hall, a handsome eighteenth-century building just off the Champs-Élysées that in the 1920s was transformed into a memorial and headquarters for the American Legion, its façade ornamented with the sculpted heads of a sailor, a soldier, and an aviator. A number of American organizations rented space there. Nearby there were several modest restaurants with fixed-price lunches and fast service that catered to the office workers in the neighborhood. When I was really pressed for time, I would cross the street to *La Belle Ferronière*, an elegant café, where I would stand at the bar and eat *un jambon-beurre*, my favorite French sandwich, consisting of a crusty baguette with thin slices of ham, a dab of Dijon mustard, and a generous lathering of sweet French butter. Accompanied by a gulped-down *espresso*, I was fortified for the afternoon.

For a time, I started fixing a "steak tartare" at my desk. There were several elegant food shops on the nearby rue Marbeuf. I would go into the butcher shop and buy 250 grams of their finest steak and have the butcher grind it for me. Then I would go to the shop that sold dairy products a few doors down and buy one egg. In the bottom drawer of my filing cabinet, I kept brandy, mustard, Worcestershire

Sauce, salt and pepper, a fork to mash it all together, and a plate to prepare it on. I found it delicious, but after once suffering severe post-prandial gastrointestinal distress, I gave up the practice, much to the relief of my secretary who thought the sight of me preparing and consuming raw meat bizarre and disgusting.

My colleagues and I sometimes went for lunch to the Cantine Rachmaninoff in the cellar of the Russian Conservatory on the Quai de New York, a short walk from our office. In theory, one was supposed to be either a student or professor of Russian music to eat there, but no ever asked. The lunch crowd at the Cantine Rachmaninoff was not much different from those seen at other neighborhood bistros and cafes, consisting predominantly of office workers scarfing down the inexpensive and excellent bortsch, beef stroganoff, *blinis*, and *pirojkis*.

The conservatory was also not far from my first apartment in Paris, and occasionally I would go there for dinner. In the evening, the Cantine was an altogether different scene. Then it was taken over by elderly White Russians, the remnants of those who had emigrated to Paris after the October Revolution in 1917 and were still hanging on. Many musicians, artists, and writers fled Russia after the Revolution and settled in Paris. Rachmaninoff was one of them. He became the first honorary president of the conservatory when it was founded in 1923, and later it was named after him. Prince Yusupov, who had married the niece of the Tsar and murdered the mad monk Rasputin, had been a regular at the Cantine until his death the year before I went to live in Paris. Dinner there was like walking into a movie by Sergei Eisenstein with ancient, aristocratic faces, wrinkled and full of character, molded by the hard times they had seen. The air was thick with cigarette and cigar smoke and waitresses were busy snatching carafes of vodka from the floor to ceiling freezer that was filled with them.

My favorite place for a Saturday night meal in Paris was the venerable La Coupole in Montparnasse. On Saturday night La Coupole was at its most glamorous, its least touristy, as lively as it had been in the roaring twenties when it opened. The crowd was often sprinkled with faces recognizable from the movies. And there were always single women of a certain age, dressed to the nines, savoring a succulent meal before disappearing into the cellar to dance with handsome gigolos at so many francs a dance.

I always ordered the same thing at La Coupole: the pepper steak and the butterscotch sundae, both of which I dearly loved. It was also the only restaurant in Paris, or anywhere else in the world for that matter, where I once got into a brawl.

An old family friend from Louisiana, who had been born with the charming and distinguished name, Laurence Montague, had unfortunately, unhappily, and briefly been married to a man named Ziegler and became known ever after by the harsher and more Teutonic: Lottie Ziegler. But Lottie was French to the core, from a creole family near New Orleans. She had studied in her youth at the Sorbonne, and taught French at the college in Lafayette. She dressed with a decidedly French elegance and flair, albeit by way of Neiman Marcus.

Lottie, well into her sixties, went to Europe almost every summer, always by ocean liner since she had a deadly fear of flying. In the summer of 1969, she had gone first to Italy to visit our mutual friend, Carl Selph, and then planned to come to Paris. Since she did not want to fly, she asked me about trains. I recommended Il Palatino that left Florence in the evening and arrived in Paris at a reasonable time the next morning.

On the Saturday morning she was to arrive, I went to the Gare de Lyon to meet her. When I arrived at the station, I was startled to see a large sign announcing a train wreck. The Palatino had crashed into another train near the Italian/French border and been derailed. Ominously, the sign advised: "Survivors will be brought in on another train arriving at 2 p.m." I went back to my apartment and telephoned the American Hospital to ask if I could have admitted a friend who might have been injured in a train wreck. "Of course, you can," I was told and also told where I should go and what I should do. I was back at the station a little before 2, hoping that Lottie had survived and not been too badly injured. The train of survivors arrived more-or-less on time and passengers began to emerge. I soon spotted Lottie, chic as always, a porter carrying her luggage on a cart behind her. She seemed to be having an animated conversation with the people around her. I ran to her. "Lottie, I'm so glad you are here! Are you okay?" "What an adventure I've had!" she said gaily. She had been in the last car of the train which had been flung off the track and down an embankment. A flying suitcase had narrowly missed her head. When the car stopped falling, she and other passengers had to be helped out of the train and carried up to the track where they had sat on their luggage for hours waiting to be picked up by the rescue train. "I met some of the most wonderful people, and we had such a good time!" She seemed to be fine, but I mentioned that I had called the American Hospital and they were ready to admit her if need be. "Don't be ridiculous," she said, "I don't need to go to a hospital, but I do need a drink. Take me to the Café Flore." So, by taxi we went to the Café Flore, near the Left Bank Hotel where Lottie always stayed, and had a drink while she told me all the exciting details of the train wreck. "I remembered that you told me that the train bed was a little rough around Modena, and when we derailed, I thought that must be what you meant so I wasn't scared at all."

Another woman friend was arriving in Paris from London that afternoon and I had planned for us all to go out to dinner that evening. Samia was to arrive at Orly airport at five, then she and Lottie were to come to my apartment for a drink at seven. I had made a reservation at La Coupole for 8:30 p.m. I was looking forward to an interesting evening and a good meal with my two smart, engaging friends.

By late afternoon, the blue skies that had been above us all day had been replaced by dark clouds, and a hard rain had begun to fall. It was still raining when Lottie punctually arrived by taxi at my door. We chatted while we waited for Samia, and we waited, and we waited. A little before eight, I called La Couple to say we were going to be late. Finally, at about 8:30, there was a phone call from Samia. Her plane had been struck by lightning while landing, and everyone was trapped in the plane for several hours. But not to worry, she said. She would take a taxi directly to my flat. We did not worry, but another two hours went by before Samia rang the bell. The taxi had left the airport in a blinding rain and halfway into the city had run off the road and into a ditch. Finally, Samia had been picked up by another taxi, and showed up at my door a little before 10 p.m., damp and frazzled, but being brave about it all. It was after 11 p.m. when we finally got to La Coupole, and instead of the table I had reserved in a fashionable section with a view of the terrace, we were given what was available, a table far in the rear, just in front of the entrance to the men's room. We were all on edge after a train wreck, a plane struck by lightning, and a taxi crash, and getting very hungry. While we were perusing the menus, sipping our aperitifs, and trying to relax and make small talk, I noticed a portly man with a ginger beard and a lighted cigar, weaving his way toward us on his way to the men's room. Unfortunately, I glanced up at him as he was passing our table and for a moment, we locked eyes. He stopped and continued to stare at me, and then did something he never should have done. He reached over and tweaked my moustache. The stresses and strains of the day had already put me near the breaking point. I lost control, rose, and gave him a mighty shove. Then he shoved me back. I think I gave him one more shove before two waiters arrived, grabbed us, and pulled us apart. I politely asked the waiter who was holding my arms to release me, and I sat back down. The man with the ginger beard continued unsteadily to the men's room. I apologized to Lotte and Samia who were looking alarmed. We had just ordered when suddenly ginger beard emerged from the men's room. As he passed by, he once again paused, then flicked the ash from his cigar on the table. Once again, I was filled with uncontrollable fury and rose to attack. But then I saw the look in the ladies' eyes, which had changed from anxiety to sheer horror, and suddenly I was struck by the absurdity of it all. Instead of continuing the combat, I sat back down and began to laugh. By the time the food arrived, we were starving, and it tasted very good. The evening was memorable, but not in the way I had planned.

The most expensive meal I had in Paris in the 1960s did not end well. It was at Lasserre, then one of the top-rated restaurants in France with three Michelin stars. A pretentious English friend who lived in New York, and came to Paris once a year on business with a generous expense account, claimed that he only ate in three-star restaurants and several times invited me to join him at one, his company unwittingly paying the bill. He was eager to dine at Lasserre which he had heard about. He had been flirting with the drug scene in New York and had been told that Lasserre was the best place to smoke pot in Paris because if the fumes got too thick, one could summon the waiter and ask him to open the retractable roof. A doubtful assertion, but the kind of smart remark he liked making as proof of his sophistication.

Unlikely as it might seem, the founder of the restaurant, René Lasserre, had a cousin in Lafayette who was a family friend. When he heard that I was going to Europe, "Rock" Lasserre gave me one of his cards and told me that if I ever dined at his cousin's restaurant to give it to the maître d'. I had carried the card in my wallet for a number of years, and it was smudged and dogeared, but when we arrived at Lasserre, I did as I had been told. René was not there that evening, but we did get a complimentary Armagnac at the end of the meal. It was probably that final jigger of strong alcohol that triggered the disaster. Since he was not paying for the meal, my host encouraged me to order extravagantly, and I was glad to oblige. My memory of the details of the meal are hazy, but I do remember a succession of excessively rich dishes, including a veal dish with a thick and heavenly cream sauce and lots of truffles. We also drank at least a bottle of wine apiece, followed by the Armagnac. Understandably, I was feeling shaky when I rose at the end of the meal, and we said our goodbyes. I managed to get a taxi back to my apartment. I made it up the stairs and into the bathroom where I threw up, and then flushed almost 1,000 francs of the finest French food and wine into the sewers of Paris.

At the beginning of my second year in Paris, I became the tenant one of the legends of twentieth-century French cuisine and was given access to a celebrated kitchen.

When I moved to Paris in the autumn of 1967, I had found a convenient, comfortable, and unspeakably dreary apartment in the chic Trocadero neighborhood. Avenue d'Eylau, in the 16th arrondissement, was considered a good address, and it was a short bus ride to my office on rue Pierre Charron, but the apartment itself was one of the most depressing places I have ever lived. The walls were painted a sickly green that suggested arsenic poisoning. My landlady had found oil cloth of the same hue, enlivened with a design of pink and yellow plumes, from which she had made drapes and covered all the furniture. After a year in this dismal flat, when my lease was about to expire, I began to look for more agreeable place to live. One day I saw an ad in the *International Herald Tribune* for a room and bath in a large apartment on Avenue Victor Hugo, an even better address than Avenue d'Eylau. I answered it and soon found myself being interviewed by Louisette Bertholle, who recently had become slightly famous for having co-authored *Mastering the Art of French Cooking* with Julia Child and Simone Beck. The room and bath she advertised, she had created within her large apartment for her mother, and which, since her mother had passed away, had begun to rent out.

In 1968, Julia Child had not yet emerged as the culinary superstar she was soon to become, but I was aware of her and had a copy of the English edition of the cookbook, given me by my friend Samia who considered it her bible. In the course of my interview, Mme. Bertholle told me about the cookbook and the cooking school the three women had run in Paris. She had particular praise for Julia Child. "Recently we went to *Taillevent* and ordered salmon and only Julia's palate was sensitive enough to detect that it was slightly off." She told me several other interesting stories about Julia and Simca Beck and the fun they had had with their school and how pleased they were that their book was proving to be a success. She complained, however, that since she had become a celebrated cook none of her friends ever invited her over for a meal. "They just take me to restaurants," she sadly said.

Mme. Bertholle, who evidently decided that I would make a suitable tenant, eventually got around to telling me about the room that was beautifully furnished with eighteenth-century antiques. I was, she told me, to make myself at home in the apartment and feel free to use the spacious and well-equipped kitchen that for a time had been the site of L'École des Trois Gourmandes. And then she said: "Julia will vacuum your room twice a week and change your sheets and towels once a week, and empty your trash." I had a sudden vision of Ms. Child arriving with a Hoover, but it turned out, of course, that she was actually referring to Julia, the Portuguese maid.

For the next eight months, until I found a lovely apartment in the Marais, I lived happily *chez* Mme. Bertholle. I did not take advantage of the magnificently equipped kitchen. I was too intimidated by the formidable *batterie de cuisine* and only occasionally made pasta or some other simple dish. I am embarrassed to admit that I mostly went into the kitchen to boil a couple of eggs and make instant coffee before going to the office each day. Freeze-dried coffee had just come on the market and an amazing number of people were persuaded that it was a delicacy instead of an abomination.

Louisette and her new husband, le Comte de Nalèche, were usually away at their country place in Loire, but at the end of each month they would spend a few nights in Paris. When she came to town, I would deliver my rent check and we would have a drink and a pleasant chat in the *Salon*. I heard about her childhood, part of which she had spent in Savannah, Georgia, as the daughter of a French diplomat. She told me how she had been mistreated by her first husband who had run off with a woman younger than their daughter. She also described her good fortune in meeting the elderly count who became her second husband and was kind to her.

Once while we were having our monthly tête-à-tête, she informed me that she had decided to write a cookbook of American food for the French and asked me for some typical Louisiana recipes. When she was next in Paris, I gave her a number of recipes for classic Louisiana dishes that a friend had kindly sent me. She approved of the gumbo recipe but greeted the one for shrimp étouffée with a cry of horror because it called for sautéing the shrimp for twenty minutes. "Much, much too long," she exclaimed. "They will be leather! Five minutes is enough, seven minutes at most."

When I returned to Louisiana some years later and began to make shrimp étouffées, I followed her advice and never sautéed the shrimp for more than five or six minutes. She was right of course.

33

THE OTHER MS. GUGGENHEIM

Before I left Florence to live in Paris, Robert Wolf, an acerbic art historian, and his companion, the equally acerbic Australian painter, Ronald Millen, who were known collectively as "I Lupi," the Italian plural of "wolf," gave me the names of two of their friends whom they said I should look up.

One was Édouard Roditi, who wrote short stories and art criticism, but was principally known as a poet and translator. The other was Mary Guggenheim, also a translator, as well as a novelist, playwright, painter, sculptor, and former ballerina. She was often confused with the more famous, but much less talented, Peggy, to whom she was extremely distantly, if at all, related. Many people assumed that she must be a close relation; she never corrected this assumption.

When I eventually did look up Mary and Édouard, I regretted that I had not done so earlier because being included in their circle of friends greatly enriched my life in Paris.

Édouard, whose parents were Sephardic Jews from Istanbul, held American citizenship. His parents had become naturalized American citizens before he was born in Paris. He was educated at Balliol College at Oxford, was closely associated with the Surrealist movement, and the first to translate the writings of its founder, André Breton, into English. He worked with Office of War Information in New York during the Second World War and was one of the translators at the Nuremberg war crime trials.

Édouard entertained frequently in his walk-up apartment on the rue Grégoire-de-Tours, not far from Boulevard Saint-Germain. On weekends, he held a kind of open house. The menu for lunch or dinner was always the same: a cous-cous prepared and served by a rotating cast of young Moroccan men. The guest list varied widely because in addition to his many friends in Paris, it often included friends-of-friends from abroad who were just passing through.

Édouard was a witty conversationalist, but the first half hour of a visit to his house was always a boring monologue about how much money he had recently made, or not made, and how much sex he had had, or not had. During this phase of the meal, I pretended to listen while I looked at the walls which were hung with a variety of interesting pictures. Occasionally, I would tune in to the most interesting bits, like the time he told of his seduction, when he was very young, by the Spanish poet Federico Garcia Lorca.

Édouard was away on an extended trip when I first tried to get in touch, and Mary and her two daughters were living in his apartment while she looked for one of their own. She suggested that we meet at Le Procope, the oldest café in Paris. Founded in 1686, frequented by Voltaire, Rousseau, Diderot, Benjamin Franklin, and other literary and historical figures, today it is still known for its history and ambience, if not so much for its food. It proved an auspicious meeting place to begin our friendship.

Not long before, Mary had moved permanently to Paris from Los Angeles, leaving a husband, but taking her two teenage daughters, Maximilienne and Montserrat. The latter had acquired her name because Mary was visiting Montserrat in Spain when she discovered she was pregnant. The sisters were lovely and smart young women, who inherited much of their mother's flair for life, but with less of her eccentricity. When Montserrat became nubile in Paris, her boyfriend was a handsome young blond, the grandson of the notorious Putzi Hanfstaengl, Harvard graduate and a one-time confidant of Adolph Hitler, who later defected and worked for Franklin Roosevelt and became engaged to writer Djuna Barnes. It seemed for a time that Mary's daughter was destined to become Montserrat Guggenheim Hanfstaengl; though she later married someone with a less unwieldy last name.

Mary was born in Saint Louis, Missouri, into a prominent and wealthy family. The first years of her education were in a convent school in Saint Louis, and then she went to study at an exclusive school in Lausanne, Switzerland, where Indira Gandhi was among her classmates. She was granted early admission to the University of Chicago and was awarded a bachelor of arts degree when she was only eighteen. For the next few years, she studied painting, sculpture, writing, and ballet, eventually deciding to concentrate on ballet. She studied in Chicago with Bernice Holmes and then, as the protégée of Bronislava Nijinska, sister of the celebrated dancer Vaslav Nijinsky, she danced for three years with the Ballets Russes de Monte Carlo.

When the Second World War broke out broke out, Mary went to work as a translator for the Office of War Information in New York City, where she first met Roditi, and at the end of the war was sent to San Francisco as a translator for the United Nations Charter Conference. She had worked alongside many writers during the war and was inspired by them to write prolifically during the 1940s and 1950s, though her work was not published, and then not very much of it, until later in her life.

When I knew her in Paris in the late 1960s, Mary was still writing, but focusing more on painting and sculpting, and was having exhibitions and getting commissions. Her style could be described as late post-Impressionist, very much influenced by painters like Bonnard and Vuillard, whose works she adored.

Mary painted two portraits of me. She put the finishing touches to the first one just after she had had a huge row with one of her other friends and she painted her seething anger into my expression. It was a very scary picture. The second one was less charged, and I quite liked it. It was included in an exhibition of her work at a tony right bank gallery, the *vernissage* of which I attended. Of the thirty or so paintings on view, mine was by far the least expensive. Most of the canvases were 3,000 to 4,000 francs; Portrait de M. Fletcher was only 500 . . . about 100 dollars. My feelings were a little hurt until Montserrat explained that her mother had given it a low price because she thought I might like to buy it.

Our mutual friends, Jean Nicholas, a banker, and Gino Harsh, an expatriate musician, were also at the opening and while considering my portrait the three of us came up with a plan. I would buy the painting, but we would have a little fun doing so.

The next day, I gave 500 francs and taxi fare to one of my colleagues, Jeanne Trabant, a former model who, fiftyish, still retained an aura of glamour. Following my instructions, Jeanne swept into the gallery with her Hermès scarf and sunglasses and told the gallery owner that she wanted to buy "le portrait de M. Fletcher," but that she had to take it with her because she was leaving that evening for Istanbul. The gallery owner explained that the show was to continue for another few weeks and he would have to get permission from the artist to take the painting out of the exhibit. He telephoned Mary. She was not at home, but Montserrat picked up and told him that she was sure that her mother would be happy to sell anything at any time. So, Jeanne paid the 500 francs and went off in a taxi, presumably bound for Istanbul.

That evening the portrait was sitting on a table in my living room when Mary telephoned and excitedly told me that my portrait had been bought by a mysterious woman who was taking it that very evening to Istanbul. "That's very strange," I told her. "The last time there was a portrait of me in an exhibition, the very same thing happened." She gasped.

Jean, Gino, and I had not yet worked out all the details, but we planned to write a letter to send to a friend of theirs in Turkey, a letter that he would then forward to Mary. It was to begin: "Dear Madame Guggenheim, I am writing to thank you for your discretion in not exhibiting the portrait of the prince under his real name . . ."

Alas, the plot got no further because a few days later when I answered a knock at my door, there was Mary who saw the portrait sitting on the table behind me. When I confessed what we had planned, she was visibly disappointed. "Couldn't we do it anyway?" she asked.

Mary was a devotee of the many flea markets in Paris and furnished her life and created her wardrobe with her finds at the *puces*. She claimed to have worked out a formula by which she could tell exactly how many days after a cold snap the belongings of those unfortunates who had perished during it would appear for sale at the fleas of d'Aligre, Montreuil, Porte de Vanves, and the most celebrated of all, Saint Ouen at the Porte de Clignancourt. She would get up before dawn and, equipped with a flashlight and an umbrella in case of rain, she would make the rounds to get the best bargains. She was particularly expert at finding cast-off *haute couture* and wore almost exclusively Dior, Chanel, Schiaparelli, and other famous names. She would have been a real fashion plate had not all her gowns been faded, hopelessly tattered, and badly stained. People often stopped in the street to stare at the bizarre apparition she presented, but she did not mind being a spectacle. She seemed, rather, to enjoy it. Once after she had been to a Miró exhibition, she proudly told me, "More people were looking at me than at the paintings."

When Mary came to visit me in Lafayette in the late 1970s, she was writing yet another of her soon-to-be-unpublished novels. Every morning, my mother's new maid, Mary Jane, would find Mary in one of her spectacular-for-all-the-wrong-reasons gowns at the kitchen table typing away on my portable Olivetti. Mary Jane was from Carencro, a rural village on the outskirts of Lafayette, and as yet knew little of the world beyond it. Every day that she laid her eyes on Mary, they grew wider. On the day after Mary had flown back to Paris, I gave Mary Jane a ride back to Carencro. As soon as we were in the car, she asked: "Tell me, do all the girls in Miss Mary's hometown dress the way she does?" "Not all of them," I told her.

Mary did many things well, but in the kitchen she was a disaster, sometimes spectacularly so. She often invited me to dinner and thus I was a witness to many of her culinary mishaps. Two I remember vividly. On one occasion, she tried to prepare salted cod from a recipe Édouard Roditi had given her. The recipe was for twelve persons, and Mary altered it to serve four. She reduced all amounts, including the time the cod was supposed to soak in milk to make it edible. The result was a white lump that only a cow would have enjoyed licking. And once for my birthday dinner, having cooked dried lentils without letting them soak first, she served me what appeared to be a plate of gravel.

On the evenings that I was invited to dine chez Mary, I became accustomed to dashing out just before the Paris food stores closed at 8 p.m. to buy something to replace whatever we were supposed to have been eating. Usually it was the makings of *pasta alla carbonara* that I could assemble and cook in less than half an hour.

Mary's infamy as a cook is a footnote in the history of French literature. When she was a young woman living in New York, she was asked, because she was fluent in French, to show visiting writer Simone de Beauvoir around the city. At the time Mary was involved in an on-again, off-again affair with Nelson Algren in Chicago. As Mlle. de Beauvoir was preparing to leave New York to spend a few days in Chicago, Mary gave her Algren's phone number, telling her: "He's a writer, too. You'll have lots to talk about." Mary once showed me a letter she had received from Algren shortly afterwards in which he had written: "Who is this Simone de Boudoir you sent me?" It took Mary fifteen years to get around to reading *The Mandarins*, de Beauvoir's 1954 novel inspired by her romance with Algren. Only then did Mary realize that her generous gesture had led to a famous love affair, and she was furious!

A few years ago, I came across a volume of de Beauvoir's letters to her most celebrated lover, Jean-Paul Sartre, and turned to the index to see if any of the letters mentioned Mary. One did. In it de Beauvoir describes how this madwoman who had been her guide to New York City insisted that she come to her apartment for dinner. Miss Guggenheim, wrote de Beauvoir, spent an hour in the kitchen making a *zabaglione* that proved to be inedible.

After I moved from Paris to London, I kept in touch with both Édouard and Mary, and both came to visit me in Hammersmith. In the 1970s, Mary and her daughters moved back to San Francisco. During the last ten years of her life she developed dementia and was lovingly looked after by Montserrat and Maximilienne. She continued to paint prolifically until just before she died in 2001. The next year, at a San Francisco art space, her daughters arranged a retrospective of her work that I was able to attend. Seeing a large body of her work all together, I realized that she was actually a much better painter than I gave her credit for when we were living in Paris. I bought a small painting of Montserrat and Maximilienne asleep in Edouard Roditi's apartment in Paris. Montserrat said it was the first painting Mary had done in Paris when they moved there, just about the time we met.

34

LUNCH AT THE
HÔTEL DU PARC ROYAL

One bright spring day in Paris, in the family-style dining room of the modest Hôtel Du Parc Royal on the corner of rue du Parc Royal and rue Payenne (around the corner from where the Musée Picasso is today), I was having lunch with three friends: Jean, Gino, and Marilyn. Jean was a French banker, infinitely kind and cultivated; Gino, Jean's lover, a brilliant but volatile American musician who had come to Paris to study piano with Nadia Boulanger years before; and Marilyn (aka Superdyke), a smart, wealthy, peripatetic lesbian from Omaha who was sometimes good company, sometimes tedious, often potty-mouthed.

Shortly after we were seated at a large, round table, Gino and Marilyn began an obscene conversation about a certain sex act of which, it seemed, they had both had a lot of experience. We were in the liberated sixties, but my gentlemanly southern sensibility was not yet quite used to hearing educated women using foul language. I remembered how shocked I had been the first time, not long before, that I heard one of my female colleagues loudly exclaim in the office we shared: "Oh, f**k!"

I looked around the table and saw that there was another person seated with us: an elderly, but still beautiful woman. She had elegant bearing, neatly coiffed white hair, and her sagging jowls were held firmly in place by a blue silk ribbon wrapped around her thin neck. Just as I was thinking to myself that I hoped she didn't understand English, she turned to me and said with a clear and lovely English accent: "May I have the vinegar, please?"

"Are you English?" I unnecessarily enquired.

"Yes," she replied, "but I have been in Paris for a very long time. I came over to dance at the Folies Bergère at the turn of the last century." She smiled. "You can't imagine how wonderful life was in Paris then! It was so marvelous, and I had many extraordinary adventures. My life was really a dream." Her pretty blue eyes sparkled at the memory.

"But then," she said, her voice darkening, "The First World War came along and that changed everything. The life I had known was suddenly over. I was completely broke, I didn't have a sou. I was desperate and I had to do something!" She paused. "So, I went to Rio de Janeiro." A slight smile appeared on her lips. "I met a man there who gave me some good advice: If you want to get back to Europe, he told me, don't let them buy you anything but champagne." She smiled again. "I developed quite a taste for it. A gentleman I knew used to send me a case of it every now and then."

"Not only was I a dancer," she continued, "but I was also a model. I modeled for both Degas and Boldini. Degas . . . *ce salaud*! (that bastard!)" I stopped worrying about her understanding the dirty talk that was going on at the table. She no doubt had heard it all. "I still have some of the drawings that Boldini did of me," she said. "Perhaps someday I will show them to you."

Alas, I never saw her again. But a few years later, in the last room of a Degas retrospective at the Metropolitan Museum of Art in New York, were some large and loose charcoal sketches he had done in old age of dancers. Could the lovely lady from the Hôtel du Parc Royal have been among them?

35

THE EMIRA

The Emira Samia al Jazairi, a descendant of Abd al-Qadir, the great nineteenth-century national hero of Algeria, was like the girl with the curl in the middle of her forehead: when she was good, she was very, very good; when she was not, she could be terrifying. The Arab blood of her paternal line made for a very volatile mix with the Irish blood of her maternal line. Her mother was related to the Jameson's of Irish Whisky fame.

While Samia was still a teenager living with her family in Paris, she fled to London to escape a marriage that had been arranged for her by her diplomat father. Her first years in England were difficult. For a time, she worked as a char-woman to have enough money to eat. But she was young, smart, and beautiful, and she eventually met and married the Cambridge-educated harpsichordist Colin Tilney, by whom she had a smart and beautiful daughter. The marriage did not last, but it did introduce Samia into a circle of cultivated and sophisticated men and women.

When Algeria won its independence from France, its revolutionary government, cognizant of its historical traditions, offered Samia her a title and land if she would return to the country. Her brother did accept their offer, but Samia preferred to remain in England with her friends and her modest Victorian terrace house in Islington.

I met Samia when I was living in Paris working for the Council on International Educational Exchange, a large consortium of American colleges and universities with study abroad programs. Samia was working for a small consortium of western American universities, arranging orientation programs and home stays for their students. She stopped by the offices of CIEE one day, and I was asked to show her around. I found her fascinating, and we instantly became friends.

I was impressed by her energy and her style. She often flew back and forth across the English Channel with a pair of crystal goblets in her purse. She would order a split of champagne on the flight over the Channel but refused to drink it out of the plastic glasses in which it was served. The second goblet was for the passenger who happened to be in the seat next to hers. She made many new friends that way.

Samia lived her life with great intensity. When she was charming, her charm was intense. When she was in a state, so was her fury. When I visited her at her house on Baalbek Road in London, I never knew which Samia was going to open the door. Fortunately, the charming Samia was more often in evidence than the terrifying one.

She delighted in giving memorable dinner parties at which she cooked her heart out. The food was always rich, delicious, and plentiful. At the end of the meal she would put on the table a box of dinner mints in which the mints had been replaced with anti-acid tablets. At that point, many of her guests needed them. Instead of after dinner drinks, she thoughtfully offered them Alka-Seltzer.

When she came to Paris, we had lunch or dinner together, and I learned a lot about her life. She had recently been liberated from a marriage that had been even more disastrous than her first, which had not ended well. The second one left her with two young red-haired sons and bruises from an abusive spouse. She also told me about the stormy marriage of her parents, both of whom she described as monsters. Her father, she said, had been an important diplomat and a friend of de Gaulle. The General, she claimed, often came to dinner and sometimes helped her mother with the washing up. (I had a hard time imagining the savior of France wearing an apron, standing in front of a sink, up to his elbows in soap suds, but maybe it was true.)

Samia was very seductive, and, at some point, we began to have what passed as an affair, but it soon fizzled out, confirming for me what I already knew, that I was not bisexual.

I was in the relationship with Samia when my parents came to visit me in Paris and the four of us had dinner together at one of my favorite spots: Brasserie Flo on Avenue Victor Hugo. As soon I introduced Samia, there was an almost electric spark between her and my father, and the remainder of the meal became a spirited conversation between the two of them. My mother and I sat on the sidelines and listened, unable to get a word in. We soon stopped trying. I had been a little worried about what my parents and Samia would think of each other, and I was pleased that my father and Samia were getting along so well, but Mother's nose was definitely out of joint. She did not like that woman.

Samia soon after embarked on her third unsuccessful marriage. This one was to an English banker named Nigel, younger than she, and about the time I moved to London, her new husband was sent to work at a bank in Pittsburgh for a couple of years. She often wrote me long and affectionate letters from Pennsylvania, describing their life. It sounded quite pleasant, but by the time they returned to

London, the marriage was over. During my last months in London, we saw each other fairly frequently. One day she telephoned to tell me that she had run into Nigel in the street, and he pretended that he had no idea who she was.

When her brother and his wife were visiting from Algeria, she brought them to my flat in Hammersmith for dinner. The wife, Samia told me, was a national heroine for her part in the Algerian struggle for independence, and her character was depicted in Gilo Pontecorvo's film *The Battle of Algiers*, which I remembered seeing. Her sister-in-law was one of the women terrorists planting bombs in cafés, blowing them up and killing people. I was a little apprehensive about our dinner together, but they were pleasant and amiable, and the former terrorist told me how much she liked my spaghetti, asked for the recipe.

Samia also invited me to meet her mother and stepfather, who were living in a flat in the Barbican Estates. I was curious to meet her mother, about whom she had told me a great deal ... none of it good ... but I was also eager to have a close look at the Barbican complex, considered an outstanding example of the brutalist style of architecture that flourished in Britain in the 1950s and after.

Ever since I had known her, Samia had complained about her mother and described her as a rich, spoiled, uncaring person. "She sends us very expensive gifts for Christmas and birthdays, and when she is in London, she telephones us from Claridge's, where she always stays, but she never has time to come to see us," Samia had told me more than once.

After Samia's father died, her mother had married a retired American military officer from Texas where they had lived for years until recently moving back to England.

Contrary to my expectations, I found Samia's mother to be witty, warm, elegant, and charming. We had an immediate rapport. Her stepfather looked the part of a retired army officer from Texas, seated and silent with a glass of whisky in his hand.

In the elevator going down after the visit, Samia looked sullen and asked accusingly: "You liked my mother, didn't you?" I confessed that I had. She was not pleased. "People always like my mother. She is very good at first impressions. No one ever realizes what a witch she is." I quickly changed the subject.

When Samia came to visit me in Louisiana a few years later, my mother, by then a widow, remembered her well and was not happy to see her.

Samia had developed what only can be described as a bread-making fetish and was constantly baking loaves and rolls for friends and people she was trying to impress. I believe that it was part of an attempt to project herself as a great nurturer.

I was not surprised, upon her arrival at Lafayette Municipal Airport, that she ordered me to go straight to a supermarket where she could buy flour and other items required to make bread. Her suitcase was hardly stowed in the guest room when she invaded the kitchen and began to sift and knead and roll in a great cloud of all-purpose flour while my mother looked on in astonishment from a doorway.

Perhaps it was the fault of the jet lag, but the rolls she made that day were hard as stone and inedible. Mother could not help smiling when she picked one up and tapped its granite-like surface. "Perhaps," she whispered to me, "we could paint them in bright colors and hang them on the Christmas tree." After Samia flew away, I heard Mother on the phone telling someone: "Joel's friend Samia spent a month with us last weekend."

Samia continued to burn her candle on both ends and "did not last the night." She was a restless over-achiever, consumed with a huge, restless energy, always going to bed long after midnight and rising before dawn. She was barely fifty when a stroke took her away. However, given that she slept only a few hours each night, her conscious time on this earth was probably the equivalent of someone much older.

36

STEALING ANGELS

The first Patout I met was Félix Patout, who had been the lover of Raymond Abner, an Egyptian artist friend of mine. For many years Raymond lived in an ancient house in a large garden behind l'Obervatoire de Paris where, when the weather was pleasant on Saturday afternoons, he held a kind of outdoor *salon* among the lilac bushes. These informal gatherings were attended by his many friends in the artistic community of Paris who knew if they dropped by, they would be welcomed. They were not the French superstars of art, but sometimes were related to them. I remember meeting the widow of the painter Yves Klein and the father of celebrated actor Jean-Paul Belmondo. And it was at one of Raymond's Saturday afternoons that he introduced me to Félix.

Félix had gone to study art in Paris as a young man and had remained in Europe. Raymond told me that he was actually paid a stipend to stay away because his flamboyance alarmed his bourgeois family. Félix must have been in his sixties when we met, and his behavior could still be described as flamboyant. He seemed unashamedly sex-obsessed. During the few conversations I had with him, he never looked me in the eye, but instead stared fixedly at my crotch, making me very uncomfortable.

Since Félix had family money, he did not have to make a living, and had plenty of time for both cruising and creating art. I suspect he spent more time on the former than the latter. I have seen only one of his creations: a small and charming bronze of a seated figure that belonged to Raymond.

The more I learned about Félix's upbringing from Raymond, and later from one of his cousins, the more I realized that the poor guy probably never had a chance to become a well-adjusted adult.

Félix was from a wealthy sugar family from southern Louisiana. M. A. Patout & Sons, founded in 1825, is the oldest family run sugar company in the United States, and one of the largest. Their main holdings are located around the company town of Patoutville, but many of the family live in the larger and more-sophisticated town of New Iberia, about sixteen miles away. It was in New Iberia that Félix grew up in one of the imposing Victorian houses on Main Street.

Félix's father, Henry Patout, played semi-professional baseball and, traveling with his team, was often away from home. The dominant person in Félix's life was his mother, Levie Fourmy Patout, one of New Iberia's numerous grandes dames. Félix was about the same age as the kidnapped Lindbergh child, and his mother lived in such fear that a similar fate would befall Félix, that for a number of years she sent him to school dressed as a little girl.

When Félix was a teenager, every summer his mother would announce to all her friends that she and her son were going off on their annual jaunt to Europe. When the day for their departure arrived, she would dismiss the servants and close all the shutters. For the next several weeks, she and Félix would remain quietly indoors while she studied a guidebook to whichever European city they were supposed to be visiting: Paris, London, Rome, Vienna. When sufficient time for a trip to Europe and back had elapsed, she would fling open the shutters, welcome back the servants, and telephone her friends to vividly describe all the sights she had read about in a guidebook.

When I returned to live in Louisiana in 1975, I met more Patouts. Some of them were gay, but probably not enough to justify the family motto, a play on their name that someone who thought he was being witty, suggested: "Pas Tous, Mais Presque" (Not All, But Almost). Peter Patout was one of them. He is open about all aspects of his life which is one of the reasons he is loved by so many.

If not all Patouts were born with the gay gene, I suspect all of them do have the cooking gene. Peter, once a New Orleans antique dealer and now a very successful real estate agent specializing in historic properties, is no exception. He is famous for lavish dinner parties cooked up in his miniscule kitchen on Bourbon Street where he has held forth, with one significant interruption, for many years.

The interruption occurred in the late 1990s when Peter, together with more than twenty other New Orleans antique dealers and collectors, unwisely bought from a skillful con man and his associates some objects that had been stolen from several New Orleans cemeteries: benches, urns, and marble angels. Objects that are found, not only in southern cemeteries, but also in southern gardens.

When the thieves, who were stealing for drug money, were apprehended, they faced life sentences because of previous convictions. Then the head of the gang had a stroke of genius. It occurred to him that if he could implicate the people who had bought from him in the crime, he and his accomplices might be able to get off with lighter sentences. So, he persuaded the investigating police that the collectors and dealers to whom they had sold the stolen goods had actually commissioned them to steal and had told them what they wanted and where to steal it. It was a preposterous lie, but it made a much better news story than a gang of drug addicts being caught and sent to jail. The thieves' allegations soon caught fire in the local press and spread quickly to the national and international news as well. Many citizens of New Orleans, where cemeteries loom large as the sacred resting places of their ancestors, were horrified and incensed.

Peter, who had recently been featured in a number of upscale lifestyle magazines, suddenly found himself the subject of a growing scandal in the media where every lurid rumor about the case was reported as fact. To protest his innocence, he gave a press conference in front of the New Orleans tomb where several of his ancestors are buried. Among other things, he pointed out that the statue of an angel the police had confiscated from his house was made of plaster of Paris and thus could never have come from a cemetery where it would have soon melted away. Perhaps because he made the police look dumb, they soon made him the principal focus of their investigation. The NOPD, who had a long history of being portrayed in the press as corrupt, relished the chance to be seen as "good guys" getting to the bottom of a heinous crime.

Of the many dealers and collectors who had bought from the gang, only three were indicted, and of the three, only Peter was convicted. That the scion of a prominent plantation family was involved in a shocking crime was too juicy a story for the press to ignore, and the press convicted Peter long before the jury did. In the end, he was the sacrificial lamb demanded by public outrage and spent eighteen months in the Dixon Correctional Facility in Jackson, Louisiana, before his sentence was vacated on appeal, and he was released after having spent much more time in prison for the crime than any of the actual thieves.

Peter has said that one thing that helped him get through the difficulties of prison life was the thought of the hardships his ancestors must have faced in the nineteenth century when they left a comfortable bourgeois life in France to carve their sugar plantations out of the fertile but harsh bayou land of southern Louisiana. "I have the same blood as they had," he told himself, "and if they could survive that, I can survive this."

Peter has the gift of always being able to find the silver lining of any grim situation. When, immediately after sentencing, he was thrown into the brutal New Orleans City Jail, he was comforted to learn that the sheriff in charge of the jail took pride in his recipe for cheese grits that prisoners were served. It was a small thing for Peter to look forward to at breakfast each day. His first cell mate, a Cuban named Adonis, shared Peter's love of good food, and with imagination and culinary know-how, they were able to transform leftovers and condiments smuggled from the dining hall back to their cell into quasi-gourmet treats.

Peter was eventually transferred to the prison farm at Jackson, where he was assigned to the gardening detail. He enjoyed the work outside in the orchard and in the flower gardens of a nearby historic home. Now, when he refers to his time in prison, he often begins by saying, "When I was away at horticultural school…"

Shortly after his release from prison, Peter was visiting with one of his customers from a wealthy and prominent family in northern Louisiana. The customer lived in a crenellated castle near Monroe. In the 1930s, her grandmother had gone to Scotland, had seen castles, and decided that she needed one, too. "Now, tell me, Peter," she enquired, "which Louisiana prison were you in?" "I was at Jackson," he told her. "What a pity!" she replied. "If you had been in Angola, you could have met my cousin."

His many friends are happy that Peter, his joie de vivre unquenched and himself not much the worse for wear, is once again inviting them to memorable dinner parties in the French Quarter, where the food is prepared with innate skill and verve and served on his elegant white-and-gold Vieux Paris china.

On Mardi Gras day Peter holds an open house for all his friends (and their friends) in the courtyard of his Bourbon Street home. It is always a crowded but relaxed and festive occasion, providing some respite from the madness of the Quarter streets on the most frenzied day of the carnival season.

Once Peter invited to his Mardi Gras party two elderly retired nuns who had taught him in the Catholic elementary school in Jeanerette on the Bayou Teche. Not wanting to crimp anyone's style and put a damper on the party, they requested that Peter not tell anyone that they were retired nuns. "We've seen it all, anyway," one of them told Peter. "Nothing can shock us anymore." Peter respected their wishes, but not surprisingly, several other former pupils were there and blew their cover. "So much for Sister Incognito," Peter told them.

When I get homesick for the food in the Louisiana I left for Virginia, I sometimes make Peter's red beans and rice. It is truly delicious.

Here is the recipe:

1 lb. of dried red beans
1 medium onion, peeled and chopped
½ bell pepper, roughly chopped
1 bunch of green onions, roughly chopped
3 cloves of garlic, peeled and roughly chopped
3 stalks of celery, roughly chopped
1 stick of butter
2 bay leaves
1 teaspoon salt
¼ teaspoon Cayenne pepper 2 dashes of Tabasco
1 teaspoon red wine vinegar
1 lb. good quality smoked sausage, preferably andouille, chopped into bite-sized pieces

10 ounces sliced and cubed country ham
Enough beef or chicken stock to completely cover the other ingredients

Soak beans overnight in cold water. Rinse and drain, picking through the beans for any dirt or stones. In a deep pot, place beans and the other ingredients. Bring to a boil, then simmer over a low flame for 1½ hours. Check after 1 hour to make sure there is enough liquid. Add more stock or water, if needed.

For the rice:
2 cups of long grain rice
4 cups of water
2 teaspoons salt
2 bay leaves

When the red beans and rice are almost done, boil rice in a covered pot of water with salt and bay leaves for twenty minutes or until tender. Serve the red beans over the rice. Serves eight.

37

9 LOWER MALL

—For R. H., a welcome and reliable witness

In the early 1970s, I went to London on secondment from a federation of American Universities to the British Ministry of Education as head of a program to arrange educational exchanges between the United States and Great Britain. In theory, I was working for Margaret Thatcher, then education minister, but I met her only once, briefly, at a reception, and am quite sure that she was not aware of my existence. I was supposed to meet her a second time and have my photo taken with her, but that event was sabotaged by Idi Amin. I was taking part in an educational fair at the Earl's Court Exhibition Centre and from my stand on the balcony was dispensing information and brochures about our exchange programs. We were told that on the last afternoon Mrs. Thatcher would visit the fair and be photographed with each of the exhibitors. However, earlier that day Idi Amin, "the butcher of Uganda," did something very naughty and she had to attend an emergency cabinet meeting instead. In her place, she sent her deputy, Lord Belstead, a tall and rather gawky bachelor baron, who later, when Thatcher was prime minister, became leader of the House of Lords. My stand happened to be just outside the entrance to the men's lavatory and Lord Belstead and I were photographed shaking hands and grinning inanely at each other, under a sign that proclaimed "Gentlemen." It looked like a publicity still for *Monty Python's Flying Circus*.

My first task on arriving in London was to find a place to live. I spent a few weeks in a beyond-dreary rented room in an apartment in Chelsea that I had found through an acquaintance in Paris. I was very eager to find someplace cheerier. And soon I did.

When I had worked for the CIEE in Paris, one of my duties was to act as coordinator of the orientation program on crossings of the student ship *Aurelia*, chartered each summer to take students back and forth across the Atlantic. I had met many interesting people on these crossings and became close friends with a number of them. One of the most remarkable was a little person named Martha Friedlander, whose full-time job was head of social work at Roosevelt Hospital in Manhattan. We made an odd pair, to say the least, since I was six-foot-five and Marty was just a hair over four-feet. Whenever she visited me and we went out on the town, she insisted on holding my hand as we walked down the street. In London, I could sense people trying hard not to stare at us, but in Paris, uninhibited Parisians would often stop and gawk. In any case, we always strolled on unabashed.

Shortly after I arrived in London, Marty turned up and got in touch. She told me that she was staying with friends in Hammersmith and asked if I would I be free to have tea with them the following Sunday. I was happy to have an invitation in a city where I knew almost no one.

The address she gave me was 9 Lower Mall in Hammersmith. It was a charming brick house overlooking the Thames with a balcony to which clung a climbing rose. I later learned that it had been built in 1714 to accommodate a German mistress of King George I. In the nineteenth century, the celebrated Victorian photographer Alvin Langdon Coburn had lived there.

The friends turned out to be her former professor at the Columbia University School of Social Work, George Washington Goetschius, and his lover, the playwright Donald Howarth.

We had tea in a lovely room on the second floor, with windows looking out over the rose-cloaked balcony to the river. When I left, Donald took my phone number and said he hoped they would see me again. I told him I would very much like that.

The very next day, I had a phone call from Donald. "I understand that you are looking for a place to live," he said. I told him that I was. "Well, he said, "George left today to visit his parents in Long Island and, though he doesn't know it, I am leaving at the end of the week to go to South Africa. I am going to put on a production of *Othello*. The authorities won't let me cast a Black actor in the title role, so I have rewritten the play with Othello off stage. I plan to be gone for several years and I was wondering if you would like to sublet my flat while I'm gone?"

And that is how I came to live at 9 Lower Mall. When George returned from Long Island, he was surprised to find me in Donald's flat, but he didn't hold it against me, and we became friends. I also got to be friendly with Peter Gill, the theater director and playwright who lived on the top floor of the house. In spite of the fact that George, Peter, and most of my other new English friends just assumed that I was working for the CIA (or perhaps because of it . . . an illicit thrill), they accepted me into their lives and for a little over two years, I greatly enjoyed living there. Years later, it occurred to me that I probably was working for the CIA, but no one had ever told me. I was not then aware that the student body of Langley High School in McLean, Virginia, the first American school to sign up for one of our exchange programs, included the children of many CIA agents whose headquarters was nearby.

9 Lower Mall turned out to be a magical place to live. There were always engaging people around to talk to, free theater tickets, and lots of parties that in good weather usually spilled out onto the sidewalk in front of the house, next to the river. Passersby often wandered up and joined the festivities.

In addition to the parties at the house, we spent considerable time next door at the Blue Anchor Pub. There may have been more glasses from the Blue Anchor at 9 Lower Mall than there were in the pub itself, having been snitched and brought home by several generations of people who lived there.

George told many stories about what life had been like in the house in the years before I arrived. He had moved from New York to London in 1954 to work as a consultant to the London Council on Social Service. He soon met the theater and film director Tony Richardson. They became lovers, and George moved into Tony's flat in the house in Hammersmith. The house then belonged to George Devine, also a theater director, and his wife, Sophie, a costume designer.

When Goetschius became a member of the household, Devine and Richardson were making plans for a new theater company. Goetschius took an active part in these discussions and became involved in the project. The result was the founding the next year of The English Stage Company at the Royal Court Theatre on Sloane Square, an event that was to radically change the history of British theater.

John Osborne wrote his ground-breaking play, *Look Back in Anger*, while living on a houseboat tied up in nearby Chiswick and read it aloud for the first time, seated at the kitchen table at 9 Lower Mall, to Devine, Richardson, and Goetschius. They were enormously impressed and decided to stage it at the Royal Court. The play was a huge success and marked the beginning of what came to be known as "kitchen sink theatre," plays dealing with the gritty, everyday life in postwar England in a realistic manner, as opposed to the genteel drawing-room dramas that had long been the hallmark of the British stage.

The house in the mid-1950s had been the center of a lively group of friends who were involved in theater. In addition to John Osborne, the group included his wife, the actress Mary Ure, and the directors Bill Gaskill, Karel Reisz, and Lindsay Anderson. Many other luminaries of the British stage were often around. When Laurence Olivier eloped with Joan Plowright, pursued by reporters and photographers, they sought refuge with the Devines until the press discovered them, forcing them to escape by climbing over the garden wall.

Although the Royal Court was an important part of the London theatrical scene in the fifties, and George and Sophie Devine were themselves minor celebrities, money was often in short supply. One Sunday morning when George

Goetschius went out early to get the newspapers, he found Sophie fully dressed, properly made-up, wearing a hat and holding a pair of gloves, seated in the front hall. "What on earth are you doing sitting there, dressed like that, at this hour?" George asked. "The milkman is coming and I haven't enough money to pay the bill," Sophie replied. At that moment, the milkman appeared at the door and Sophie sprang into action. In her best upper-class accent, she began to explain, while slowly putting on one glove, that she had not been able to get to the bank the day before." The milkman, totally intimidated by the accent and the aristocratic gesture with the glove, abjectly backed out. "Oh, Mrs. Devine, that is quite all right, quite all right." As soon as he was gone, Sophie took off her finery, scrubbed her face, and went back to bed.

By the end of the decade, the relationship between Richardson and Goetschius had begun to unravel. One night when Tony had stayed out late and forgotten to take his key, as he was entering the house through a window, he was interrupted by a policeman. Tony protested that he lived there and that George, who was sleeping upstairs, could identify him. They woke George who said, "No, officer. I've never seen this man before in my life." Tony was hauled off to jail where George let him stay for what was left of the night.

In 1959, Tony ran off to live with Vanessa Redgrave, whom he eventually married. A few months later, Donald Howarth took Richardson's place, and, in spite of difficulties caused by separations and George's recurring illnesses, they were together until the end of George's life.

After George and Sophie Devine had both died, Goetschius and Howarth bought the house from their daughter, Harriet. When I moved in, in summer of 1970, it still had the air of a theatrical boardinghouse.

Part of that was because the house had come with a sitting tenant who had been there since the days of the Devines. Ralph, in the third-floor flat, was an aging transvestite who worked as a costume maker at Sadler's Wells Opera. Sometimes he wore at home costumes that he had filched from the theater, the most memorable being an ensemble in purple silk, complete with a towering, powdered wig from a production of *The Queen of Spades*. But he was always in one kind of drag or another. The butchest outfit I ever saw him in was a gaudily flowered muumuu.

Whenever the doorbell rang . . . there was only one for all four apartments . . . Ralph would rush down to open the door. I had learned to warn friends who were coming to visit for the first time that they might be greeted by an outrageous apparition and, more often than not, they were.

One day I received a letter from my mother telling me that Diette McKeithen, mother of the then governor of Louisiana, and an old friend and former classmate of hers at the now defunct Mississippi Synodical College for Young Ladies in Holly Springs, Mississippi, was going to be spending some time in London. She would be traveling with a group of Methodist women who were planning to visit every church in the British Isles where John Wesley had preached. "Diette said she would love to see you," Mother wrote, "so I gave her your address. She said that when she got to London she would just hop in a taxi and hope to find you home."

I never heard from Mrs. McKeithen, and my mother never heard from her again. It was not hard to figure out why. The sight of Ralph, wearing God-knows-what, greeting her at the door must have been extremely unnerving to someone on a tour of Methodist chapels.

Ralph provided an entertaining spectacle around the house, but, unfortunately, there was a darker side to his tenancy. He was often drunk and, on several occasions, being careless with cigarettes, almost burned the place down. He also brought home unsavory characters who threatened the calm with rowdy and noisy behavior. George and Donald had been trying to get rid of him for years but had not been able to do so because sitting tenants in England are given strong protections. When I arrived on the scene, George was able to persuade the local council, who had the final say on tenants' rights, that I was his American cousin. As a "family member," I took precedence over a sitting tenant. The ruse worked. Ralph and all his gowns went elsewhere, and I moved into his old flat.

The downstairs flat, which was much larger with more space than I needed, was taken over by Nicholas Wright, who had immigrated from South Africa and was at the beginning of a very successful career as a playwright and director. He rented out several of the rooms to friends, some almost as colorful as Ralph, but not nearly as dangerous.

And the festivities continued. Once there was a joyous excursion by taxi to the Black Cap Pub in Camden Town to see Rex Jameson as Mrs. Shufflewick, an extraordinary drag performer who created a cockney persona with large handbags and hats heavy with artificial flowers and wax fruit. She projected a lower-class attempt at gentility laced with profanity and bawdy jokes. She was often completely soused and sometimes almost fell off the stage, only to be caught and pushed back on by her loyal fans. Peter and Nicholas had her act down pat and could perform it almost better than she could, especially when she lapsed into alcoholic incoherence. At one point, Nicholas booked her for a season Upstairs at the Royal Court, the small, experimental theater that had been a rehearsal room until it was transformed into a seventy-seat space and where some of the most successful Royal Court productions had their start.

After finishing work on a BBC series of dramatizations of James Joyce's *Dubliners*, Peter Gill had saved enough money out of his budget to give a party for all those involved in the production: roughly a hundred people. One of his actors, Colin Thatcher (no relation to Margaret), and I were asked to prepare the food. We went to Soho and bought fresh mushrooms and onions, an enormous hunk of Parmigiano cheese, and a huge bag of rice, enough to make risotto for the expected hundred guests.

Since no one had a pot large enough or a stove large enough to accommodate a risotto for one hundred, we had multiple pots cooking in three kitchens on three floors that evening, and rushed up and down the stairs, trying to keep the risotto from scorching.

The guests started arriving shortly after nine. Of the one hundred invited, only about forty showed up, and most had already eaten. Among the few who graciously ate our dinner were the American actress Betsy Blair and her then husband, Czech movie director Karel Reisz. I gave them generous portions, but they scarcely made a dent in the heaps of food. When the party ended, there were large platters of cold risotto everywhere. The fish in the Thames outside our door were very well fed that night.

Every April, the Oxford-Cambridge Boat Race passes in front of the house, about halfway to the finish line. On the day of the race, Lower Mall becomes impossibly mobbed with onlookers, some of them unruly. It is not a pleasant place to be. So, it was a house tradition that on Boat Race Day a communal meal was served at the big table in the downstairs kitchen. It was timed to coincide with the beginning and, hopefully, the end of the race. We were about to eat the pudding when we heard the loud cheering outside as the hulls passed our front door. We could hear more cheering in the distance as the hulls crossed the finish line in Chiswick, a few miles away. "Well," said Peter, putting down his napkin, "shall we all go down and kiss the cox of the winning crew?"

The Stonewall riot in Greenwich Village in June of 1969 was the event that marked the beginning of the gay liberation movement in the United States. The Gay Liberation Front in England was founded the next year, and one of the founders was a student at the London School of Economics where George Goetschius was a lecturer. It was probably through George that we were kept informed of its activities. I remember how amazed we all were when we learned that the GLF was organizing a dance at the Hammersmith Town Hall on nearby King Street, a short walk from the house. Peter declared, "We must go," and so we did, in a group. I suspect we all were feeling a bit uneasy about going to a gay event in a building that housed our local government. Homosexual acts between consenting adults had only been legalized in Great Britain three years before, and a strong backlash had been building since. We did not know what to expect. But it was just a large, noisy party in a brightly lit hall with people of all description, a few in drag, dancing to a loud rock band, and having a very good time.

I did have one surprise that evening. The last time I had made a visit to Louisiana, I was introduced to a young married couple from New Iberia who were planning to spend a year studying in London. I gave them my telephone number and told them to get in touch. They did, and we had lunch together shortly after they arrived. By chance, they found a flat in Putney, just across the river from Hammersmith. "Good," I told them. "We'll get to see each other often." But it didn't happen. I liked the wife very much. She was pretty, smart, and gracious. I found her husband, David, a little strange. He had red hair and wore a gold earring. Each time we met he was wearing a spiffy pork pie hat, a suit with a gaudy vest, a wild tie, and a Rotary pin in his lapel. Some months after they had moved across the river, the wife called me in tears. She and David were separating. Unreconcilable differences. So, I was not completely shocked to see David, wearing, instead of his pork pie, a broad-brimmed straw hat with ribbons, à la Katharine Hepburn, on stage, waving his arms and wildly gyrating to the rock music. I remarked to my friends that David's closet must have been equipped with an ejector seat.

On the way home after the dance, I reflected on the strangeness of going to a gay event that appeared to be sanctioned by the local government, something that not long before would have been unimaginable. The old order of things was changing in the Western world. And I had a feeling that a sea change was coming in my life.

When the CIEE hired me to go to London, it was with the understanding that I would remain for two years to establish the exchange programs, and then return to Paris and my old job. Part of the deal was that I would be able to live in a charming apartment on the Île Saint-Louis where the director of the Paris office had lived for many years. He had recently remarried, and his new wife wanted to live in more bourgeois comfort. The apartment was in an historic eighteenth-century building on the Quai de Bethune, from the windows of which I probably could have seen tourists dining on pressed duck at *La Tour d'Argent* on the opposite side of the Seine. It would have been the perfect place for a bachelor to live in Paris.

However, as the time for me to leave London approached, I came to realize that I was very tired of leading a double life, of hiding from all my colleagues and some friends the person I really was. This was brought home to me when one of the members of the board that had been formed to oversee the exchange programs arrived late for a meeting. He apologized, saying that he had been interviewing candidates for headmaster of a school where he also served on the board, and that it had run overtime. "It was so difficult to decide on just one because there were so many highly qualified candidates. Of course, we knew that none of them were criminals or homosexuals." I smiled and nodded and remembered that when I first began to work at CIEE in Paris, my boss had taken me around to meet my new colleagues. The last was a middle-aged American man, originally from Arkansas, who worked in the mail room. As soon as we were out of earshot of him, my boss said to me: "Reggie is very smart, but we could never give him a responsible position because he is a homosexual."

I had spent almost all of my adult life hiding from an antagonistic world behind a lie. Most starkly during the years I served in the US Navy, when I was just beginning to explore my life as a gay man, and when I was most at danger from discovery. I was well aware that a dishonorable discharge for simply being who I was would destroy my prospects for a good life and haunt me for the rest of my days. There was some respite from the pressure when I lived in Florence because, even though homosexuality was frowned upon, the Italians were more tolerant. They also expected foreigners to be different and didn't really care with whom we slept.

I knew that if ever it were discovered that I was gay, it would have meant the immediate end of my career in educational exchange. That was a given in those days. I enjoyed my job very much, and there was evidence that I was good at it. But I felt I could no longer pretend for much of the time to be someone who I was not. It was time for me to find something else to do with my life and the beginning of a period of searching and false starts.

After I moved away, I kept up with many of the people I had met at 9 Lower Mall. Peter, to whom I was closest, had first made a name for himself a few years before we met with critically acclaimed productions at the Royal Court of three neglected plays by D. H. Lawrence. The Court also put on two of his early plays: *The Sleepers' Den* and *Over Gardens Out*. He had been an associate director of the Royal Court since 1964, and was named first director of the new Riverside Studios in Hammersmith in 1976. He turned it into one of the most significant theatrical venues in London. His first production, Chekov's *The Cherry Orchard*, opened to rave reviews. Bernard Levin, the leading theater critic of the *London Sunday Times* wrote: "Peter Gill has directed *The Cherry Orchard* with a cast so astonishingly suitable that I began, hallucinatorily, to believe that they had been assembled first, and that Chekhov had then written the play round them.... *The Cherry Orchard* has almost never, in my experience, been at once so harrowing and so glittering; nor its fragile rhythms so finely, surely spun, its development so natural, human and real."

In 1980, Peter became an associate director of the National Theatre and directed the Studio Theatre of the National, The Cottesloe, where I had the pleasure of seeing his much-praised production of Sam Shepherd's *A Fool for Love* in 1984.

Peter, a bit younger than I, is still busy writing and directing plays. His latest play was to have been done "at a tiny theatre in Jeremyn Street," but was canceled because of the pandemic.

A few years ago, he moved out of 9 Lower Mall, where he had lived most of his many years in London, and into another flat on the river, not far away.

In a letter Peter wrote me a few months ago, he mentioned the happy times we had all had together in the early 1970s. "There was indeed, of course, a suspicion, or rather a hope, that you worked for the CIA. Tall, white, charming, good-looking, intelligent, well-educated, and from the South. How could we not think that?"

I saw Martha frequently in the years to come. Often on my trips to Manhattan, we met for lunch and talked over old times. Once she told me about a visit she had made to the cabin that Donald and George owned as retreat from London in a wild part of Wales. She was spending a weekend there alone with Donald, and one night while they were having dinner, they heard a terrible crash. They ran outside into a very dark night to see what had happened and found a man who had been thrown out of his car into a ditch and knocked unconscious. He woke up while they were standing over him to see tiny Martha holding a lighted candle, and tall, skinny, gothic-looking Donald with a lantern. The man opened his eyes and began screaming. He must have thought that he was either dead or had woken up in an Ingmar Bergman movie. Martha, alas, was the first of that circle of friends to pass away, early in the new century.

Nicholas Wright has also had a distinguished career as a playwright and director. One of his notable successes was *Vincent in Brixton*, a play he wrote about the sojourn in south London of Vincent van Gogh. It opened at the National Theatre and eventually transferred to Broadway.

George Goetschius, who had become increasingly horizontal while I was living in the house in Hammersmith, eventually became totally bedridden. His physical deterioration had its origin in the time he spent in India, where he was sent by the Ford Foundation in 1958 to work on the master plan for Delhi that had been commissioned by Prime Minister Nehru. While there, he contracted a very serious form of hepatitis from which he never fully recovered.

George spent most of the 1980s at Tyn y Pant, the cottage in Wales, where he was lovingly looked after by Donald. In the 1990s, George had recovered sufficiently to begin spending some time again in London, seeing old friends, resuming in a limited way his former life. In 2004, he went to live in Galsworthy House, a very posh nursing home in Kingston Upon Thames. It is on a hill overlooking Richmond Park, the largest of London's Royal Parks, and is the former home of Sir John Galsworthy, novelist and playwright who is best remembered as the author of *The Forsyte Saga*.

And after more than fifty years, sometimes apart, but mostly together, in 2004 he and Donald legalized their relationship with a Civil Partnership, which had just become law in England. It was a joyful celebration at which Galsworthy House provided the champagne.

George died two years later, and Donald buried him at their cottage in Wales. He sent me a DVD that he had made of the entire event, starting with Donald being put into a wicker casket in London and transported to Wales. He filmed his friends digging the grave, and when it was dug, the feast that followed, with champagne, pumpkin pie, and a bonfire. And he filmed George being put into the earth the next morning under a gray sky dripping with rain.

Since Donald was away for the entire time that I was living at 9 Lower Mall, I did not really get to know him while I was living in Hammersmith. However, we developed an epistolary friendship while he was in South Africa. He wrote that he was living in a room with a window through which he could see a Jacaranda tree that reminded him of the Catalpa tree that grew outside the house on Lower Mall, and he described the difficulties he was encountering in getting his play produced. "So far, I've had no luck, rejections from both Black and White companies.... They wouldn't do serious theatre if they were allowed to ... nothing remotely difficult or different. But I'll win in the end. They'll bloody well have to do my things—even if amateurs do them."

Donald finally did manage to put on his version of Shakespeare's play: *Othello Slegs Blankes* (*Othello for Whites Only*) at the recently founded Space Theatre in Cape Town, and directed three more of his plays at the same venue. He decided that it was more effective to fight against apartheid from inside the country than by international boycott and became an active participant in South African protest theater. He ended up staying in South Africa for almost four years. When he did return to London, he concentrated on introducing Black South African actors and playwrights to the London stage.

While I was writing down these memories of my time in Hammersmith, the sad news arrived that Donald had died. Described as "the last of the angry young men," his obituary in the *Daily Telegraph* said that he was "one of a group at the Royal Court in London who helped to transform modern British theatre."

He was also one of a group who helped me transform my life and made me realize that I could no longer live in the cramped confines of the closet. The life I was briefly part of for those two years in London, surrounded by creative, energetic friends, showed me how exhilarating and life-affirming a life lived openly could be. They inspired me to live my life entirely as the person I was meant to be, to stop pretending and hiding. It was time to admit that to myself.

38

EIN WANDERJAHR

In the summer of 1973, I decided I could no longer continue living a lie to protect my professional life, to conceal an important part of who I truly was, and I resigned my position with the Council on International Educational Exchange. It was a sensible and liberating decision, even though what I did next turned out to be neither rational nor wise. Following my heart turned out to be a very bad idea.

On a Saturday in April 1970, I was in Frankfurt, one of the stops on a trip through Germany to visit American academic programs for the council. I had finished with the last of my appointments that morning and was free for the weekend. I had bought a single ticket for the Frankfurt Opera that night, a production of Richard Strauss's *Die Frau Ohne Schatten* (*The Woman without a Shadow*), and on Monday I was flying to Berlin.

It was a warm and sunny afternoon. I had a solitary lunch and then, while strolling around the city, found a seat at a table on the terrace of a coffee house. I had been drawn to a particular table by a handsome man reading a newspaper, but after a while the handsome man, having shown no reciprocal interest, folded his paper and left. It was then that I noticed another man at the table staring at me, not exactly handsome, but attractive with a dark shock of hair. I smiled at him, and he smiled back. We began an inconsequential conversation while never taking our eyes off each other. His name was Dieter, he told me. We spent the afternoon together, and when I came out of the opera that evening, he was waiting for me, and we spent the night together.

The next morning, we took the train to Wiesbaden, near Frankfurt, where Dieter wanted to show me the gardens. But it was a cold, gray day, dripping with rain, so instead we spent several hours in the café of the train station, talking and drinking beer. Dieter told me a great deal about himself. He had grown up in the small town of Schramberg in the Black Forest, graduated from the university in Tübingen, and was working for the American company Battelle in Frankfurt.

He was very active in the Social Democratic Party, then in power under Willy Brandt, whom he idolized and for whom he did volunteer work. His father, also a Social Democrat, during the War had been the foreman of the most important local industry, the Junghans clock factory, and had several times been put in a concentration camp because of his political beliefs, but always released because he was so important to the smooth running of the factory. Dieter said his first memory was of the headlights of the cars of Nazis surrounding their house when they came to arrest his father. At the end of the war, his father was elected mayor of Schramberg, but was in such poor physical condition because of his time as a prisoner, that he soon died. His mother raised him by herself. Her principal source of income was from making little costumed dolls to be sold as souvenirs. Dieter himself had worked hard to pay for his education. And, while a teenager, he discovered that his parents were not his real parents but had adopted him when he was newly born. He said that once he had gone to find his real mother, but was so disgusted by what she was, that he did not try to see her again. He did not elaborate, and I did not ask.

Even though I was moved by Dieter's story and enjoyed the time we spent together, when I left for Berlin the next morning, I had no thought that we would ever see each other again. But when I was back in Paris, he telephoned and asked if he could come for the weekend. "Of course," I said. It was the first of many weekends spent together in Paris, and later, after I moved there, in London. Once we met in Amsterdam and felt the freedom of being in what was then the most liberal city in Europe, not fearing to be seen in public as a couple. We both took two weeks of vacation and flew to Tenerife in the Canary Islands, much beloved by German tourists. One Christmas, we went together to Schramberg and stayed in the modest house where his mother lived, and I endured hours of boredom in a beer hall listening to his conversation with his friends, understanding nothing and drinking too much beer. But deep down, I was very happy to be considered part of his family. I became very fond of his shy, tiny *Mutter*. On Christmas Day we took her to the best restaurant in Schramberg for a festive meal, and her eyes, which had seen so much suffering, grew wide with delight.

When we were separated, there were almost daily telephone calls, even when we had little to tell each other except what the weather was like and how much we loved each other and missed each other. With a German/English dictionary in hand, he composed and sent me frequent letters. In the first he wrote: "Meeting you was the nicest hazard in my life," not exactly what he meant, I am sure.

Music brought us together, especially Mahler, Beethoven, and Mozart, and we spent many hours quietly together, listening to favorite LPs. One Christmas we surprised each other with the same new recording of Mahler's Fifth.

During one of Dieter's visits to London, I bought orchestra seats at Covent Garden for *Don Giovanni*, an opera we both loved. In the second act, Donna Anna lost her voice halfway through an aria, and Dieter did what Germans do when singers lose their voice in Germany. He booed loudly. A shock went through the rows around us, and many of the polite and well-bred Englishmen turned and glared at us. This was during the great debate about whether or not England should join the Common Market, and a few days later, a letter to the editor appeared in the *London Times*, with the heading: "Concerning the recent booing at Covent Garden." The outraged correspondent wrote: "Should Great Britain continue to forge ahead with the folly of joining the European Union, much more of such boorish public behaviour can be expected."

As my time with the council neared its end, Dieter and I began to discuss what should come next. He was eager that I come live with him in Frankfurt and proposed that I join him and one of his friends from university days in investing in and opening a wine bar, something they had been talking about for years. I was not excited by the idea, but saw it as a way of staying with the man I had decided I wanted to spend the rest of my days with. I had adapted to life in Italy, then to life in France, so why not begin again in Germany?

While I was working for the council, I had written a student guidebook to Paris that was given to all the students taking their charter flights, an aspect of their activity that, since the demise of student ships, was greatly expanding. After I left their employ, I had a contract with them to write student guides to Italy and to Greece and, on my own, I had secured an agreement to write one to Hamburg by that city's tourist bureau. It would give me a source of income and an interesting way to spend a year while Dieter and his friend were getting ready to leave their jobs and start working on opening the wine bar. They hoped it would be the first of many.

In August of 1973, I put many of my possessions in storage, told my friends in London goodbye, and took a train to Frankfurt. It arrived a little before midnight on a sultry, oppressive evening. Just before the train entered the station, I looked out the window and saw flames and dark clouds of smoke spiraling skyward from a burning skyscraper. When the conductor opened the door and let down the steps, hot, acrid air hit me in the face and made my eyes burn. Blaring sirens assaulted my ears, and the platform was crowded with tired and harried disembarking travelers, burdened with luggage, pushing and shoving. It seemed like I was descending into Hell.

Dieter was waiting for me, and as soon as I looked into his eyes, I knew that I had made an enormous mistake. There was none of the love I had grown used to seeing there, only a cold, unwelcoming stare.

I spent a week with Dieter in Frankfurt before leaving for Italy to begin writing the first guidebook. By the time I left, there was no doubt. For him, it was over. I was puzzled and profoundly hurt.

It was the beginning of a difficult time that had come without warning. I felt lost and unmoored. I had cut loose from everything my previous life had been, and suddenly all the plans I had been working toward turned to ashes.

I was grateful for my writing project and for Italy. It was a diversion and a balm. I was soon back with good friends in the noisy, familiar streets of Florence and busy researching and writing. There were trips to Venice and to Rome, and then when I was ready to put it all together, I rented a farmhouse from my dearest Italian friend.

When I had first met her ten years before, Simonetta was not quite twenty, extraordinarily beautiful, and the heiress of a real estate fortune put together by her grandmother who had a passion and a gift for acquiring buildings and land that were *occasioni* (bargains). Simonetta's grandfather was not nearly as astute in business as his wife. Shortly after the war, Simonetta told me, her grandparents had an option to buy one of the grand palaces overlooking the Arno. But without telling his wife, her grandfather lent the money they were going to use as a down payment to one of his friends, who then bought the *palazzo* out from under them. She never really forgave her husband. Simonetta told me that she still had to be careful when driving her grandmother into town not to get anywhere near the lost *palazzo* because even many years later, when her grandmother was reminded of the treachery, she would get furious all over again and her blood pressure would soar. The family fortune was assured when the grandfather died young and *la nonna* was free to follow unfettered her own instincts.

One of her family's many properties was a large vineyard near Volterra with a handsome villa and several small stone houses for the farm workers. The villa, only one story tall, had once had a second story that was no more. When bombs began to fall on Florence, Simonetta's grandparents fled, planning to take refuge in the country. But when they arrived at their vineyard, a fierce battle was being waged over it between the Germans and the Americans, and they hurried back to the relative safety of Florence. When they were finally able to return, they saw that the top floor of the villa had been destroyed. They never built it back. Even without the second floor, it was spacious and comfortable.

For a nominal rent, Simonetta rented me the second floor of Casa San'Alessandro, a stone dwelling about half a mile from the main villa, that she had fixed up to rent to friends as a weekend getaway. It had electricity and running water and was simply but adequately furnished. I bought a Grundig short wave radio for company, a cheap used Fiat sedan, and after I had finished my research and was ready to put it all together, settled in at the vineyard. It was September, the beginning of a golden Tuscan autumn. The *vendemmia*, the annual grape harvest, was approaching, and Simonetta, her husband, Eugenio, their infant daughter Anna, together with Simonetta's grandmother and aunt, were often at the villa to help prepare for this important event. When they were in residence, I often took my evening meal with them at the villa. But usually I would fix a simple meal for myself. I drove into the nearby village of Pomarance every morning to buy provisions and a copy of *La Nazione*, the daily paper of Florence, which I would peruse while drinking a couple of tiny, strong cups of espresso made on a hotplate in my little aluminum espresso pot.

At the beginning of mushroom season every year, *La Nazione* always published a long feature article about an unfortunate family returning from a mushroom-picking expedition and dying from eating poisoned mushrooms, having mistaken them for the edible kind. The article was filled with pathetic details. Usually, there was one survivor, who for some reason had abstained, often a small child. There were always heartbreaking photographs of the soon-to-be deceased, already looking doomed, of the piteous orphan, and a close-up of one of the homicidal mushrooms. One morning I had just finished reading the gruesome, annual article describing the mushroom massacre, when there was a knock at the door. It was Eugenio bringing me a pail of freshly picked mushrooms. I thanked him profusely for the generous gift and as soon as he had gone, I chopped them up and flushed them down the toilet.

That year, Simonetta had invited a few friends down for the *vendemmia*, including Terry Hughes, an Australian who lived in New York and worked as a commentator on the American news desk of the Canadian Broadcasting Corporation. Terry had brought for his fellow guests Mickey Mouse T-shirts to wear during the harvest, why, I am not sure. The *contadini*, for whom the vendemmia was serious business, were not exactly welcoming to us amateurs, and the image of Mickey on our chests did nothing to win them over. They looked at us with undisguised scorn.

On the day the harvesting began, everyone took part, including Simonetta, Eugenio, and Aunt Marisa. Only the grandmother, who was too old, and the new daughter, who was too young, remained in the villa while the rest of us lugged plastic bins through the rows of grape vines, grasping the bunches in one hand and snipping them off with a pair of shears in the other. I soon realized that it was hard work, not the romantic outing I had imagined it would be. Finally, when the sun was about to set, we put down our shears and, exhausted, hiked back to the villa. Family, friends, and *contadini* gathered at a long table that had been set up in the central hall, and large platters of steaming lasagna and bottles of Chianti made from the previous year's harvest appeared, ample reward for our hard labor, and a magical end to the day.

On the morning of October 10, as usual I was up early, listening to world news on my Grundig while making a pot of coffee. One of the first items was the resignation of Vice President Spiro Agnew for tax evasion and other alleged felonies. I knew it would be of interest to those in the villa and opened my door to see if my main mode of nonurgent communication was available. "Brie," a scrawny, friendly mongrel, spent her days ambling between the villa and Casa San'Alessandro and I used to send Simonetta messages tied to her collar. Sometimes they arrived within minutes; sometimes they took hours. That morning Brie was indeed napping on the landing outside my door, so I wrote the news bulletin on a scrap of paper and tied it securely to her collar, gave her a little shove in the right direction, and told her "Vai all villa!"

Almost an hour later, Terry Hughes, the CBC commentator, was sitting on the front steps of the villa enjoying a cup of coffee when Brie finally wandered up. He saw the piece of paper marked "important" on her collar and removed it. Terry, who was used to being at the center of breaking news in the CBC newsroom, said this was certainly the first time he had received an important news bulletin from a dog.

At the end of October, I left Tuscany for Hamburg, a German city I had never visited. I spent two pleasant weeks ferreting out affordable places for students to eat and stay, exploring its parks and museums, especially the Kunstehalle, one of the largest museums in Germany where much of the large collection of nineteenth-century German romantic painting exuded a melancholy that matched my own. A self-portrait by Philip Otto Runge moved me almost to tears.

I was given free tickets to the Hamburg State Opera every evening and saw some splendid performances, the most memorable being a brilliant production of Strauss's *Ariadne auf Naxos*. Some months later I was to see the same opera in Athens, not far from the actual Naxos, with the two sopranos singing in German, the tenor singing in French, and the chorus in Greek, an almost total mess.

On the way back to Italy, I stopped in Frankfurt, thinking that I might telephone Dieter. It was a balmy late autumn day, and I spent the afternoon in the botanical garden, grieving and trying to decide whether or not to make the phone call. In the end, I didn't, and I was not to see him again until thirteen years later, when he finally explained why what had happened had happened, and I forgave him.

On a business trip to Ohio for Battelle, for whom he was still working, Dieter managed to spend a few days with me in a small town on the coast of North Carolina where I was then living. He told me that he knew how much he had hurt me, but he had not been ready psychologically to take the step of living openly with a male lover. It was true that our times together had mostly been in Paris, London, and elsewhere, not in Frankfurt. "But I never really forgot you," he said. "And I never forgot you," I replied.

He had, he told me, eventually begun a relationship with a man, an architect, who had left his wife and children to live with him. They had been together for some years and had recently bought a house on the Greek island of Skopelos where they spent their holidays and hoped someday to live. "I would like it very much if you would come with us to Greece, that we should all be friends, and that you would be part of my life again." "I would like that, too," I told him. When Dieter returned to Germany, we began again to speak on the phone, and he wrote me letters that, as he used to, he signed: "Love, Dieter."

One day when Dieter called, I could tell immediately from his voice that something was very wrong. "I have received a terrible diagnosis," he said. He did not need to tell me more. He was in and out of the hospital for the next few weeks, and each time we spoke, he sounded weaker. I hoped to fly to Frankfurt to see him, but it was several months before I would have the time to do so. I was making my plans for the trip when his lover telephoned to tell me that Dieter had died of AIDS.

Returning from Germany to Italy, I was happy to spend the Christmas season in Florence, relaxing, seeing friends, and spending much time wandering through its museums that were almost empty of tourists. On Christmas Eve I went to midnight mass at the beautiful Romanesque basilica of San Miniato al Monte on a high hill overlooking Florence. According to legend, Miniato was an Armenian prince who served in the Roman army of the Emperor Decius. While the army was camped outside the gates of Florence, Prince Miniato converted to Christianity and became a hermit. He was brought before the emperor who ordered him thrown to the beasts in the amphitheater. This was done, but the beasts refused to harm him. Then the Emperor had him beheaded. Miniato is said to have calmly picked up his head, crossed the Arno, and walked up the hill to the spot where his Basilica stands today. I had often gone with friends to Christmas mass at San Miniato because the ecclesiastical music was said to be the best in Florence, but this year it seemed especially appropriate for one who had lost his head, not to mention his heart, and yet was still walking.

In late February, I flew to Athens to gather information for my third guidebook. It was still wintery in Rome when I left, but Greece was already on the verge of spring. I spent a couple of weeks exploring Athens and sites around it under clear blue skies. I was almost alone the morning I hiked up to the Acropolis and looked over the modern city bathed in light. In the evenings, I enjoyed dining by myself in some taverna, watching the crowd and drinking just enough *Retsina* to get a slight buzz and the blissful feeling of detachment that came with it.

I had made plans, after my work was done in Greece, to meet my brilliant, learned, and witty friend, Timothy Verdon, in Istanbul. I first met Tim in the early 1960s when he was a precocious undergraduate from Weehawken, New Jersey. He served as my assistant on a student ship on which I was directing the orientation program and kept the crossing lively with his surreal sense of humor and a series of practical jokes. We had stayed in touch through the years and Tim, who was either finishing or had just finished his PhD in art history at Yale, was an excellent traveling companion. He wore his learning very lightly and joyfully shared it. We visited all the important monuments of the city: Santa Sophia, the Blue Mosque, Topkapi Palace, the Archeological Museum, and a number of obscure ones.

We stayed in a modern and nondescript hotel near the bazaar. The window in my room opened onto a brick wall on which had been stenciled a black and white portrait of Ataturk, founding father of the secular Turkish Republic, who stared fiercely back at me each time I looked out the window.

One day we decided to take a bus across the newly opened bridge over the Bosporus, connecting Europe to Asia, and spend a day exploring the eastern part of the city. We planned to wander around for a while, have lunch somewhere, and then, later in the afternoon, take a ferry back to the west. We thought it a good idea to make inquires first at the Istanbul Tourist Office located in the Hilton Hotel. "Could you recommend," I asked the woman behind the desk, "a good place to have lunch on the other side of the bridge?" "Oh, no," she gravely told me, "there are no suitable places for lunch in Asia."

I was somewhat taken aback by her sweeping statement, but we did not find a place for lunch in that little bit of Asia. We did have an interesting day poking around and looking at the architecture and as the sun was setting, we took a crowded ferry back to Europe.

We were tired and dirty when we got back to our hotel, and I noticed in the lobby a flier extolling the merits of a Turkish bath that claimed to be the oldest in Istanbul. The list of past customers was impressive and included Lady Mary Wortley Montagu, writer and wife of the English ambassador at Constantinople in the eighteenth century and Lord Byron in the nineteenth. There were other famous bathers as well, but somehow those are the two who have remained in my memory.

The Cagaloglu Hammam was only a few blocks away, so we decided to give it a try. We paid the modest fee and were given huge towels and bars of soap and escorted into the vapors. We each had an attendant who scrubbed us so clean I thought my skin was coming off. And then we had vigorous massages. Mine was given by a pot-bellied Turk with a moustache who pummeled and pressed and rubbed vigorously until I was completely limp. As I was lying there almost comatose, suddenly a young man with long hair, wearing a leather jacket and jeans, arrived and enthusiastically introduced himself. He had, he said, recently inherited the hammam and when he heard that there were two Americans in the bath, he was eager to meet us. His enthusiasm for Americans, it turned out, was the result of a year spent in Vermont on an exchange program sponsored by the Experiment in International Living. It had been, he told us, the best thing that had ever happened to him. And then, revealing the dark side of educational exchange, he announced that his time in America had inspired a plan to convert the ancient and venerable Cagaloglu into "a unisex sauna and kebab house." I recently did an internet search for the Cagaloglu Hammam and was reassured to find that it is still very much the traditional Turkish bath that Lady Montague and Lord Byron would recognize.

Tim and I tried a number of different restaurants in Istanbul, from elegant to simple, and had some tasty meals with a variety of side dishes, but somehow, we always ended up with a kebab of some sort. It seemed inevitable, inescapable, so much so that after a week Tim remarked, "The infamous fleshpots of the East seem to be filled mostly with shish kebab." As a memento of our trip, Tim gave me a small cookbook entitled *Turkish Cooking*, which with a pen he had subtitled "or—'The Pocket Fleshpot.'"

Shortly after I returned to Florence from Istanbul, season tickets for the Maggio Musicale, the "May Musical," the annual spring music festival that begins at the end of April and runs to the end of June, went on sale. The Maggio always offers a rich program of operas, ballets, concerts, and recitals, most of them in the main theater in Florence, *il Teatro Comunale*, but there are always a few productions al fresco in the amphitheater of the Boboli Gardens. When I first arrived in Florence in 1962, the Maggio was in full swing, and I was able to get tickets to a few of the productions. In the years I lived there, I always looked forward to the festival and usually bought a season ticket.

I was in the lobby of the Teatro Comunale almost an hour before the ticket office was to open, and there was already a sizeable crowd waiting to buy season tickets. There was nothing that could be described as an orderly line . . . Italians are not keen on standing in line . . . but a Swiss music lover arrived and began to organize us all, giving us slips of paper with numbers on them and marshaling us into a queue. I had noticed an attractive man with typical Florentine coloring—pale skin and dark eyes—who seemed to be noticing me, and we contrived to be next to each other in the line. We had almost an hour to converse before the *biglietteria* began to sell tickets. When it finally did, I was delighted to score what was arguably the best seat in the house: a single right in the middle of the first balcony, with a perfect view of the stage. My new acquaintance was buying tickets for himself and a friend and ended up with a pair of seats on one of the back rows of the far right of the second balcony, much less desirable, if not quite the worse seats in the Comunale. We continued our conversation at a nearby café and discovered that we had a lot to talk about. Giuliano was his name and he told me that he had a frame shop and art gallery near Santa Croce. To make a longer story shorter, we were soon living together in his apartment on Piazza Peruzzi, across from his tiny shop on via dei Benci. Reluctantly, I exchanged my terrific first balcony seat for the second balcony seat he had bought for another friend and watched the Maggio craning my neck and unable to see about a third of the stage.

What Giuliano and I had in common was an interest in art. I had begun collecting and studying seventeenth-century Italian etchings when I first moved to Florence a decade before. I had started with Alinari reproductions of the Old Masters, then, when I discovered that original prints were fairly easy to find and not very expensive, I began to buy impressions of works by Jacques Callot, a French artist who often worked in Italy, and by the Florentine Stefano della Bella whose elegance took my breath away. When I lived in Paris, I would visit the venerable gallery of Paul Prouté to browse and carefully add to my collection. Dieter had a friend in Frankfurt who was an assistant in the gallery of the dealer in old master prints and drawings, Helmut Rumbler, and from him I was able to buy crisp impressions of Jacques Callot's etching of the Ponte Vecchio in Florence and Stefano della Bella's etching of the Place des Vosges in Paris. They are hanging, side by side, above my desk, as I write this, archivally framed with all acid-free materials, Museum Glass™, and out of direct light, protected as works on paper always should be.

I had one more writing assignment after Istanbul: a student guide to Lisbon for the Portuguese Student Travel Association. I had not yet set a date for my departure for Lisbon when one day I received from the Association a request for a detailed outline of what I planned to write. I realized that they probably wanted the information because they had decided to have someone on their staff write it, but I complied with their request anyway. I had begun to see the possibilities of turning what had been a hobby into a career that was much more interesting and challenging than writing guidebooks.

A number of my friends in Florence were art historians and it was not difficult to obtain a card that allowed me to visit Il Gabinetto dei Disegni e delle Stampe (The Drawing and Print Cabinet) of the Uffizi Gallery where I was able to spend hours studying prints and drawings from their vast and priceless collection.

I was always struck by how casual the staff, most of them young women, were in handling their riches. The first time I requested a folder of della Bella drawings, I was startled when it was just dropped unceremoniously on the table at which I was sitting. Someone told me about an American graduate student who was writing a dissertation on the Florentine Mannerist Baccio Bandinelli. One day when he was in the *gabinetto* going through their holdings of Bandinelli drawings, he noticed that one had become detached from its mount. Holding it carefully, he brought it to the woman at the front desk. She took it without looking at it and, evidently mistaking it for scrap paper, wadded it up and tossed into a wastepaper basket. The astonished graduate student let out a yelp of pain and told her what she had just done. Unfazed, she replied: "Non importa. Ne abbiamo tanti." (It doesn't matter. We have lots of them.)

For the next two years, our usual Sunday routine was to spend an hour or so in one of Florence's many museums, often carefully and quietly examining the contents of just one room, and then go for a meal at some trattoria to discuss what we had seen.

My career as an art dealer thus began in Florence, starting with an immersion in the wonders of Renaissance and Mannerist art, preparation that gave me the foundation for appreciating the art of later centuries that became more meaningful and gradually led me to focus on the art of the twentieth century, and a new career in which there was no longer any need to pretend that I was someone I was not.

39

THE RETURN OF THE PRODIGAL SON

My father died in April 1972 while I was living in London. Not long after that, a friend who perhaps knew me better than I thought he did, told me: "You'll probably be going back to live in the States now." I was surprised. "Of course not," I protested. "I've lived in Europe for years and I've built my life here. All my friends are here. I'm not interested in returning to the States."

But it was true that my difficult relationship with my father was one of the main reasons that I had gone to live in Europe. I loved my father very much but felt more comfortable with an ocean between us. I know that he also loved me very much and always acted in what he was convinced was my best interest, and for a long time I was not strong enough to resist his dominant presence in my life. He set a path for me toward what he wanted me to become, and until I went to Europe in the summer of 1962 and unexpectedly remained, I always stayed upon it, even though it was never where I really wished to be.

During my senior year in high school, he urged me to take the test for an NROTC scholarship, and I unenthusiastically did. He then insisted that I put down as my first choice, should I win it, Tulane, though, under the spell of a childhood visit to Chapel Hill and my intoxication with the novels of Thomas Wolfe, I had long dreamed of going to the University of North Carolina.

New Orleans was, of course, much closer to home, a place where my father thought he could more easily keep an eye on me. And his close friend, Dr. Rufus Harris, was Tulane's president, another pair of eyes to keep me in check.

I won the scholarship, went to Tulane, and majored in English with the idea that one day I would become a professor and, if my father got his way, return to teach at Southwestern, marry a nice local girl, join the Rotary Club, and remain in my father's orbit for the rest of his life. That was his dream.

It was not mine, but at times it felt as if it were inevitable.

One problem with my father's plan for me was, of course, that it became harder and harder for me to imagine myself married to any female, no matter how hard I tried. And I had tried, along the way hurting several girlfriends who were perplexed by my behavior.

During my years in the navy, I began tentatively to leave the closet, even though I realized that I faced serious peril if my sexual orientation were discovered. I immediately would have been kicked out of the service in disgrace.

Over time, my parents must have begun to suspect that I was gay, but it was never discussed. Once when I was returning home from Italy for a summer visit, I made an earlier connection in Atlanta than I had planned and arrived at Lafayette airport several hours before I was expected. There was no one to meet me, so I took a taxi to my parents' house. When I went through my father's study to put my bags in my room, I noticed a book open on his desk: *Homosexuality: Its Causes and Cure* by Havelock Ellis. My father must have been reading up on the subject in anticipation of his prodigal son's visit. After I deposited my bags and returned to the study, I saw that the book had been put back on a shelf.

The next day, chatting with my parents in the study, I rose from my chair and made my way to the shelf where I had spotted the red spine of the Ellis book. I did not go directly to it, but started a few books away, pulling a book off the shelf, examining it, then putting it back, slowly making my way toward *Homosexuality: Its Causes and Cure*. I was just a book away when my father could stand it no longer, stood up, and said: "Come, Joel. I want to show you something in the garden." He did not want to discuss the topic, and I really did not either.

A turning point in my relationship with my father occurred in the summer of 1964, when my parents visited me in Europe, their first trip abroad. Our tour together began in Italy. I had lived there for more than a year and was becoming proficient in Italian. For the first time in his life, my father was totally dependent on me. He was lost in a foreign culture, which must have been unsettling for someone who was very much used to being the boss. He could not even order a cup of coffee unless I did it for him. For the very first time in my life, I was in charge, and it changed our connection forever.

And three years after his death, I found myself returning to live in Louisiana, which I would not have done had he still been alive.

I came with an Italian lover, which ultimately did not turn out well. But I had spent too many of my forty years leading a secret life and decided that I could not do that anymore. On my frequent visits home, I had discovered a gay community in Lafayette, many of whom were openly leading quietly productive lives and seemed to be respected and well-integrated into local society.

My mother was delighted when I came back to live and welcomed us both. Giuliano and I lived in a little cottage, given me by my parents, on the edge of the property, across the driveway from the larger house.

We arrived in Lafayette on a perfect October day, one of those rare days in southern Louisiana when the temperature is pleasant and the humidity is low. Le Bocage Vert (The Green Grove) the name given to the property by a visiting Frenchman soon after my parents purchased it in the 1940s, was part of an ancient pecan grove that tapered down to a "coulee" (Cajun for creek). My father had loved breeding camellias and irises, and there were many beautiful examples of both, as well as magnolias, cypresses, oaks, and other trees. That October night, under an almost full moon, it seemed a magical place indeed.

Although we never discussed it, my mother accepted my relationship without question, as I expected she would. She became fond of Giuliano, and he was always very good to her, as Italians are famous for doing with mamas. When she would introduce us to someone, what she would say evolved from: "This is my son, Joel, and my adopted son, Giuliano" to "This is my son, Joel, and my son-in-law, Giuliano." Indeed, even as our relationship painfully unraveled, Giuliano remained kind and attentive to my mother.

Mother was overjoyed to have us next door, and she became a welcome and integral part of our social life, presiding over the lunches and dinners we had for friends and clients who were always charmed by her wit. As noted photographer Philip Gould, who was often at our table, told me recently, "She was first class, old school and fun." She had suffered from the isolation after my father died and as her contemporaries dwindled. Now she had something to look forward to almost every day.

1976 was the Bicentennial year, and the event that introduced me and Giuliano to Lafayette was an exhibition of European prints and maps of American subjects from the sixteenth to the twentieth century that we had put together over a few years. *America Through European Eyes: The Graphic Image* opened in January 1976 at the university art museum. I wrote the catalogue; Giuliano, a gifted craftsman, built the frames for the fifty-five pieces. The earliest piece in the exhibition was an engraving of American Indians by Theodore de Bry from the second edition of his *Grands Voyages* published in 1592. The last piece was a postcard published in Paris during the First World War of a woman with her head swathed in an American flag.

The exhibition, also shown at a museum in Shreveport and a gallery in Houston, was a success, and, most importantly, it introduced us to potential clients in southwestern Louisiana at a time when the oil boom was at its height and launched us as art dealers.

We were able to buy part of a nearby nineteenth-century farmhouse that was about to be demolished, have it moved across the road, and added it to the little cottage as a proper gallery. It turned out to be a great time to open a business such as ours. One oil man who became a loyal customer would come into the gallery every time one of his wells came in and buy a roomful of pictures.

What I had not anticipated, and what caused me much grief over the coming years, was the toxic jealousy and homophobia of my oldest sister who lived in nearby Baton Rouge. I had not given her much thought in many years, but my difficult relationship with her began before I was born.

My mother was almost forty when she became pregnant with me. My sister was fourteen and horrified and embarrassed. My parents, also, were not thrilled by the idea of having another child so late in life to add to their three daughters, the youngest of whom had been born eight years earlier. The idea was floated of having me aborted, and Ellen was no doubt in favor of it. I suspect she lobbied for it. I was told by my sister Lorraine that once the pregnancy began to be visible, Ellen refused to appear in public with my mother.

It was the middle of the Great Depression, and while my father was gainfully employed, albeit with a modest salary, another child meant more expenses and another mouth to feed. So, my parents came to the decision to have me aborted. My mother had developed a rash in the early days of her pregnancy and that was the official reason they gave to Dr. Hamilton, the family doctor, who signed the abortion order. My parents made an appointment at a clinic in New Orleans where such procedures were done.

On the morning that they were packing the Plymouth for the trip to have me out, just like the Angel of God who appeared to Abraham and prevented him from sacrificing his son, Isaac, my uncle Claude unexpectedly arrived and saved my life.

Uncle Claude was a crusty, outspoken, devoutly Catholic Cajun medical doctor in the town of Welsh, about fifty miles west of Lafayette. He had been the most decorated soldier from Louisiana in the First World War, served in France and rose from first lieutenant to major. He fought in the battles of Château-Thierry, Soissons, St. Mihiel, Meuse-Argonne, Champagne-Marne, and Aisne-Marne. He was awarded the Distinguished Service Cross, Croix de Guerre with two silver stars, the Purple Heart, and five battle citations, three given by General John J. Pershing.

After the war, he married my mother's sister, Ruth. Like my mother, my aunt Ruth came from a strict Presbyterian upbringing in Protestant north Louisiana and was a card-carrying member of the Woman's Christian Temperance Union when she moved to Welsh to be a schoolteacher and met her future husband. Shortly after their marriage, Uncle Claude was paying the household bills and came across one for her annual dues for the WCTU. He wrote the check, adding the notation: "She has a cellar full of liquor." This was true because Uncle Claude was fond of wine with his meals and had a sizeable collection of good vintages. They had no further communication from the WCTU.

Fortunately for me, Uncle Claude had bank business in Lafayette the morning my parents were getting ready for their drive to New Orleans, and he decided to stop by unannounced for a visit. When Uncle Claude learned of the scheduled abortion, he became furious. I was told that he shouted at my mother: "Fannie, if you have a rash, get in bed and take nothing but tea and toast, but you let that child be!" Such were his powers of persuasion that my parents called the clinic and cancelled the appointment. And later that year, to my oldest sister's perpetual chagrin, I was born on my parents' fifteenth wedding anniversary. When I was growing up, my father often joked that I was born on his wedding day.

I have no doubt that my mother and father realized that they had made the right decision and were grateful to my uncle Claude for his intervention. They were devoted, loving, and generous parents.

The only Bible story that I recall my father reading to me was the story of Abraham and Isaac, and I was always a little nervous that the Angel of God just might not arrive in time. Years later, I wondered if perhaps I had only imagined that he had often read me this passage from Genesis. But thirty-seven years after I was born, when I was back in Lafayette for my father's funeral, I picked up his Bible and it opened to that very page.

My first memory of my sister Ellen, when I was about three or four years old, is of her kicking me down the stairs. As I was following close behind her as she mounted them, one of her high heels caught me very near my left eye, and I went tumbling down. Her heel left a visible scar that disappeared only when the wrinkles of old age finally obscured it. Whenever I mentioned the incident, Ellen always protested angrily, "It was an accident!!" After I was nearly grown and beginning to gain a veneer of education and sophistication, I would reply, "Freud says there are no accidents," which made her even more furious.

Ellen seemed always to consider herself a victim and was envious of her siblings. She had been the first, a beautiful, golden-haired child, made over by everyone until the rest of us began to arrive and she had to share the spotlight. First, Lorraine who turned out to be much smarter. Then Flo, who was much more beautiful, and then, when she was in her teens, I arrived. The little prince, the only boy, who from birth was being groomed to take my place in the southern white male patriarchy. I must have been the last straw!

Ellen was born on the cusp of the Great Depression. My father was earning very little money as an instructor at the state college and there were few luxuries available for her growing up. But by the time I came along, our lot had vastly improved. Shortly after I was born, my father was made dean of the School of Agriculture and we moved to Whittington Hall, a beautiful, white-columned house on the school farm. We had a cook to prepare the abundant food that was produced on the farm. I had Wilbert Sam, a companion to look after me. I had a Shetland pony named Betsy. And even though my father was still making a small salary, the job provided him with enough perks for us to live very well. And then, when I was five, as a result of the Long scandals, my father became president of the college and we moved into the imposing new mansion that my father's predecessor had finagled for himself. We not only had a cook to prepare our meals, but a maid to do the cleaning, and a male servant who came early in the morning to perform all other tasks. We were not rich, but we lived almost as if we were. As the youngest, I was given all kinds of advantages that Ellen never had. All the things that Ellen had to do without in her early years, I was handed on a silver platter. I can understand why she developed a lifelong envy of me that, because of strict southern decorum, she was unable to openly express. It must have long festered in her heart.

I remember Ellen as a mostly unsmiling presence who worried a lot and seemed to lack the joie de vivre and sense of humor that I shared with my other sisters. Ellen was often angry and complaining about something or other. Lorraine once remarked that Ellen had "an inferiority complex," a term she had probably learned in a college psychology class, and afterwards, whenever I heard the term, I always thought of Ellen.

When the war years brought V-6 and V-12 officer training corps to Southwestern, my two younger sisters, Lorraine and Flo, enjoyed flirtations with some of the cadets, something Ellen disapproved of. She was always the prude, disapproving of many things, and was always ready to snitch to our parents when Lorraine and Flo engaged in behavior she thought inappropriate, as when Flo told Mother and Daddy that she was going to spend the night at a girl friend's house, and actually went dancing at the louche Cajun dance hall, the Wild Cherry, in nearby Breaux Bridge.

By the time I entered the first grade, Ellen had graduated from Southwestern and found a job with Louisiana Power & Light in Algiers, across the river from New Orleans. She went to live in a yellow stucco apartment building in the Garden District and took the ferry over the Mississippi to work every day.

I visited Ellen in New Orleans once when I must have been about eleven or twelve years old. The visit was not a success. One morning she took me to Algiers on the ferry across the Mississippi River and was horrified when I began a conversation with a tipsy young sailor. When the sailor lifted his jersey to show me his appendicitis scar, something I had no objection to inspecting, my sister grabbed my arm, jerked me away, and told me that the sailor was disgusting and so was I.

On that same visit, Ellen had some friends over to dinner in her immaculate apartment. At one point, she asked me to move a dining room chair. I lifted it over my head, ignoring the rotating ceiling fan above. A blade of the fan hit a leg of the chair, and the fan came crashing down, smashing a coffee table and spewing black oil on the white rug beneath it. I was never invited back for another visit.

I remember being surprised when Ellen, at the age of thirty, became engaged. I had somehow assumed, without giving it too much thought, that she was going to be an old maid like my father's sisters in north Louisiana. I don't remember her dating anyone when she lived at home. She was certainly not "boy crazy" like my youngest sister, Flo, who always had a string of suitors.

Ozro (Ozzie) was an accountant from Mississippi. He was tall, blond, and, though on the plump side, considered good-looking. He projected an image of joviality, and loved cooking, eating, and drinking.

They had a rather grand wedding in the First Presbyterian Church of Lafayette. It was in the middle of winter, and my other sisters, dressed in green velvet, were the bridesmaids. I was an usher and charged with lighting the candles, nestled in greenery, in the windows of the church.

The newlyweds got off to a poor start. As they were driving away from Lafayette on their honeymoon, they struck a cow that was crossing the road. The only damage was to the cow and the car, but the honeymoon had to be postponed until the car was repaired. The accident was perhaps a foreshadowing of what lay ahead for them.

Ozro was an accountant, and, probably with my father's help, he managed to get a job in the accounting department of LSU. He took the CPA exam a number of times but never passed it, which meant his career prospects were not brilliant. It was another thing for Ellen to worry about.

She was a chronic worrier. Her philosophy of life seemed to be that if she always expected the worst, it might not happen. She never seemed to realize that living with the constant anticipation that something bad was about to happen poisoned her life as much as if it actually had occurred.

The couple's firstborn was a son. Ellen endlessly fretted over the baby. Once when she was heating, then cooling, then heating, then cooling the baby bottle so that it would be exactly the right temperature, our youngest sister, Flo, watched with disdain. Flo, even though she was much younger, was already on her second husband and by then had two children whom she was raising with a much more laissez-faire attitude. "I don't know why you're taking all that trouble," she told Ellen. "It's so easy. You stick the bottle in his mouth. If he turns blue, the bottle is too cold. If he turns red, it's too hot."

Their son was a bright and handsome child but grew to be a taciturn and moody teenager. Once when he spent a summer in California visiting Lorraine, who was always a fond and generous aunt to her nephews and nieces, she complained that he had gone the entire visit hardly saying a word. While he was in high school, he developed severe ulcerative colitis and was in and out of the hospital, yet another addition to Ellen's worries.

Their son was a good student and early on decided he wanted to be a medical doctor, not surprising since he had spent so much of his young life being surrounded and cared for by doctors. Eventually, he had to have a proctocolectomy. In spite of this impediment, he finished medical school, married twice, and has had a successful career as a doctor.

Four years after their son was born, Ellen and Ozro had their second and final child, a girl they named after our mother. By that time, I was away in the

US Navy and did not really spend any time with my new niece until I was back in Lafayette for a year in 1961 and found her to be a smart and beautiful child with very pale skin and red hair. She was studying piano, and I have a vivid memory of her in a starched pink dress, her red hair in a ponytail, sitting at our piano playing Mozart and playing it quite well. I thought, mistakenly as it turned out, that I had found a new family member with whom I would have a special bond.

After that year at home, I went to Europe for the summer and, except for fairly frequent visits to the States, remained there for the next dozen years. On one of my trips back to Louisiana, I took the legendary train, the City of New Orleans, from Chicago where I had gone to see a friend. My parents asked Ellen, who was by then living in Baton Rouge, to meet my train in nearby Hammond. Reluctantly, she did and was there, the usual frown on her face, when I stepped onto the platform. The very first thing she said to me was: "I'll bet that you're not voting for Goldwater." She was right, of course. On the short drive back to Baton Rouge, where our parents were to meet us and take me home to Lafayette, we had very little to say to each other.

And not long after I returned to live in Lafayette in 1975, something happened that was a warning bell for the problems I was going to have with my oldest sister in the future.

Margaret MacMillan, a retired physical education teacher at Southwestern, had gone out of her way to be kind and helpful to my youngest sister after her husband was killed in a plane crash in 1958, and she had moved back to Lafayette with four young children. While Flo was going through this very bad time, Margaret often volunteered to entertain the children, give them swimming lessons, and generally was supportive of Flo in any way she could be. Margaret was also one of the old family friends who from time to time stopped by to visit with Mother at Bocage. During one of her visits, Margaret admired her small collection of miniature Royal Doulton Toby Jars, the kind that sell on eBay for about ten dollars, certainly not priceless family heirlooms. "Margaret, why don't you choose one of them," said Mother. "I would love for you to have something of mine to remember me by." So, Margaret, very pleased, did choose one and thanked Mother for this little memento.

A few days later Ellen came for a visit and Mother mentioned to her that Margaret had come by and that she had given her a Toby Jug. Ellen said nothing, but inside she was furious, and when she got back to Baton Rouge, she telephoned my other two sisters and told them that Margaret had conned Mother out of part of their inheritance and that one of them should call Margaret and insist that she give it back. Fortunately, they both discouraged the idea.

There were other signs. Once before an announced visit from Ellen, I heard Mother tell Mary Helen, her maid, "Hide the blue bowl in the living room before

Ellen gets here. I know she will want to take it home and I'm just not ready to give it to her yet."

Whenever Ellen arrived to visit Mother, the mood of the household darkened.

Some years after I had moved back to Lafayette, the son of my father's lawyer who had taken on his late father's practice, told me: "I've been looking through your father's papers and have found something a little strange. It seems that your father's will was not executed the way it was intended, and you were not put into possession of all the property you were willed." By the time of my father's death, his lawyer, who was entrusted with settling the estate, was elderly and not quite on top of things. He had let my brother-in-law, the executor of my father's will, do all of the work and signed off on whatever Ozzie gave him.

Ozzie had put me in possession of only a small part of a large lot that was left me in the will. We asked my mother about it, and she said, "Of course, we intended to give you the entire lot." She asked Welton to quietly fix it, which he did, without telling Ellen and Ozzie, because Mother wished to avoid a confrontation. "When the time comes," Mother said optimistically, "your other sisters will back you up." This turned out to be a major mistake. Ellen did find out about it and went ballistic. It happened while Giuliano and I were on a trip to New York.

When I phoned from Virginia on the way home to find out how things were going, Mary Helen, Mother's housekeeper and companion, answered the phone. "Ellen and Ozzie are here and they sure are mad about something." It was not until I got home that I discovered the problem. I tried to explain calmly to Ellen what had happened and why, but she was not interested. She was convinced that I had conned Mother and would not even listen to what Mother and I told her.

And she and Ozzie were outraged that I would even suggest that Ozzie had done such a thing as fiddle with our father's will. A few years later, however, Ozzie, who was keeping the books for Theta Xi fraternity at LSU, my father's fraternity when he had been a student there, was found to be embezzling money from the fraternity funds, lost his job at the university, and narrowly escaped prosecution.

It was after this incident that Ellen and her daughter began to wage open warfare against me. They weaponized the fact that I was gay and began using it to try to poison the minds of our sisters, our aunts in north Louisiana with whom I had always had a warm relationship, and anyone else who would listen to them. I was able to cope with their attacks and largely ignore them until Mother had a stroke about the same time as my relationship with Giuliano began to unravel.

Giuliano, born during the Second World War, had a very hard time growing up in a poor family, and any success he had in life was entirely of his own making. I found this very admirable, and it had not been a problem when we lived in Florence, but when we came to live in the States, I realized that, just like Ellen, he came to resent deeply the fact that I had been given so much, while he had had to struggle for everything. And because he came speaking very little English, he became totally dependent on me for all that he wanted and needed, another reason for his growing resentment. It was not a healthy situation.

He could at times be very sweet and thoughtful, but he was also given to unpredictable rages and long-lasting pouts over small slights, many of them imaginary, and these increased with time. Mine became a life of walking on eggshells. Or, as I described it to someone, "It's like being trapped in the Second Act of *Tosca* where I am always Scarpia while Giuliano runs around screaming *Vissi d'Arte*."

When Mother became ill and I had the primary responsibility of looking after her, the behavior of Ellen and of Giuliano, by then both at war with me, made life during the next four years very stressful. Ellen could have been supportive and helped to make Mother's remaining years happier for her, but she had no interest in doing so, and seemed to be completely obsessed instead with her eventual inheritance, which in any case was not going to be very significant.

Ellen and her daughter did not succeed in their attempts to turn my sister Lorraine and my maiden aunts against me. They were too smart and too loving. Flo, however, whom I had always considered an ally, was swayed both by Ellen and her own homophobic husband and cut me out of her life. Fortunately, her first-born son, Paul, kind and intelligent, has remained my last close link with that part of the family. As the oldest, he suffered the most from his father's tragic death in a plane crash. I was sixteen when he was born, about the same age as Ellen was when I was born, and he has become more like a brother to me, who never had one, than a nephew.

One of his siblings let me know that she loved me in spite of who I was, but by then I had realized that was not enough. I only wanted people in my life who loved me because of who I was.

After Mother passed away, I learned from Lorraine that Ellen was convinced that because I was a homosexual, she could have me declared mentally incompetent and have herself appointed my legal guardian. She tried to persuade my other sisters to join her in the effort, but, more in touch with reality, they did not.

A few years after I had moved to Virginia, I received a letter from Ellen on her blue, monogrammed stationary in her neat, carefully formed handwriting. The first sentence was: "I have decided to forgive you." I did not read the second sentence. I threw the letter in the trash and seldom thought about Ellen again. It was as if a curtain had come down on all the misery she had caused me; it was now part of a past that I had moved far beyond.

Ellen died in April of 2005. She was by then a widow and living in a retirement home. I was given the news in a telephone call from Abu Dhabi by one of my great nephews who was working abroad for Shell Oil. It was 9 a.m., and I had to wait until it was a decent hour on the West Coast to call Lorraine. We both struggled very hard to find something nice to say about Ellen, but with limited success.

A few days later, I had a phone call from Lorraine. She had talked to someone in Baton Rouge who had been to Ellen's funeral at the Trinity Episcopal Church the day before. She said that the minister, who was new to the pulpit and had never met Ellen, asked at the end of the service if anyone wanted to stand up and say something about her. No one stood up.

The reception after the funeral was held at her son's home in Baton Rouge. "And," Lorraine told me, "all they had for refreshments were a couple of Winn-Dixie party platters!" Anyone born in the South knows just how damning that is.

It has been difficult to recall these ugly memories and to write about them. I am truly sorry that my oldest sister had such a toxic and unhappy life. I was fortunate to have other family members and friends who helped me through a difficult time.

In the late 1980s, after the Lafayette economy crashed and my relationship with Giuliano was unsalvageable, I left Lafayette and moved to the charming town of Edenton, North Carolina, where I began to restore a brick firehouse that had been built around 1900. I chose Edenton because a dear friend, an antiques dealer, lived there part time and part time on Manhattan's East Side. Edenton, pretty as it is, is a tiny, isolated town, and I knew no one else there. Barbara was away a lot, which meant I spent a lot of time alone. As it turned out, it was just what I needed to heal. It was a joy to inhabit a quiet space where I could relax and think and plan and not worry that a frothing Italian or a scowling sister might intrude unexpectedly to destroy my peace of mind.

I began to exhibit in antiques shows, gradually getting into the better ones, developing an East Coast clientele for the art I was selling.

But after several years in Edenton, I was ready to move on. My friend Barbara was spending less and less time in North Carolina, and I was finding my solitary life more lonely than comforting. And the restoration of the firehouse was not going well. The address was 111 West Water Street, and there was lots of water. The land it was built on had been reclaimed from Albemarle Sound, and the sound was trying very hard to get it back. After the third flood, I telephoned friends in Fredericksburg and asked if they knew of any apartments that were available that day. I had visited them several times and realized that Fredericksburg would be a much more suitable location for the business I was developing. It was close to Washington and not that far from New York. Via I-95, the entire East Coast was more accessible. It was a good move.

By this point in my life, after a number of romantic relationships that had ended badly, I decided that I was more cut out for friendship than for love, and along the way I had made some wonderful friends with whom I diligently stayed in touch, realizing how much they enriched my life. I was more-or-less reconciled to my situation, but I was aware that there was a hole in my solitary life that friends and art and books and music, as important as they were, could not completely fill.

In early spring of 1993, I was invited to give a talk to an American art study group at the Virginia Museum of Fine Arts in Richmond. The topic was "The History of American Watercolors," and there were about forty people in the auditorium of the museum. The lecture seemed to hold their interest, and when it was done, I asked if anyone had questions. A handsome, broad-shouldered, blue-eyed man in front raised his hand. I nodded at him, and he asked his question: "Do you have plans for lunch?" Unfortunately, I had, but a short time later John Alden Copenhaver came to dinner and, essentially, never left.

John, born on a farm in southwestern Virginia, is an accomplished artist with two degrees in art. He also studied at the Art Students' League in New York and for eighteen years had a career in art education in the public schools of Virginia.

For almost thirty years now, watched over by our guardian angels, with good fortune perhaps from hawks, we have loved one another, have lived and worked together, created a happy life and successful business, traveled, made friends, and have had many adventures. My years with John have given me much to write about. But that will be for another book.

EPILOGUE

In March of 2013, John and Joel, in front of a group of close friends, were married in the Baltimore home of Robert and Jackie Smelkinson by Judge Charles Moylan. His wife Marcia recited Shakespeare's "Sonnet 116": "Let me not to the marriage of true minds / Admit impediments." When Judge Moylan pronounced them legally wed, there was not a dry eye in the room. The ceremony was followed by a sumptuous and joyous lunch accompanied by an abundance of Veuve Clicquot champagne.

ABOUT THE AUTHOR

Photo by Jackie Brenner

Joel Lafayette Fletcher III was born in Lafayette, Louisiana, and graduated from Tulane University. He served as a commissioned officer in the US Navy and lived for a dozen years in Europe. In Florence, Italy, he co-owned and ran a private language school. He worked in Paris for the Council on International Educational Exchange and with the Study Abroad Programs of the City University of New York. He also lived in London for several years while setting up educational exchanges between the United States and Great Britain. He returned to the United States in 1975 and began another career as an art dealer. In 1993, Fletcher and John Alden Copenhaver established Fletcher/Copenhaver Fine Art, dealing in nineteenth- through twenty-first-century American and European fine art, with an emphasis on modern figural art of the twentieth and twenty-first centuries. They dealt privately and exhibited at charity antiques and fine art shows throughout the country. They curated two museum exhibitions of the work of noted American figurative artist Moses Soyer (1899–1974) and helped organize the first American museum retrospective of French artist Alix Aymé (1894–1988), curated by James Archer Abbott, at the Evergreen Museum and Library at Johns Hopkins University in Baltimore, for the catalogue of which Fletcher wrote the principal essay. He is now retired and living in Fredericksburg, Virginia.